JEFF GORDON

HIS DREAM, DRIVE & DESTINY

JEFF GORDON

HIS DREAM, DRIVE & DESTINY

JOE GARNER
FOREWORD BY TOM CRUISE

JEFF GORDON INC.

CONTENTS

OPPOSITE: The No. 24 Axalta Chevrolet SS on the track during Jeff's final Cup race. Homestead-Miami Speedway, Florida, November 22, 2015.

FOREWORD

BY TOM CRUISE

I HAVE ALWAYS LOVED RACING. Growing up in the South, it's just what we did. I can remember taking my mother's car—I only told her about it years later—and racing with my friends down the dirt roads of Kentucky. We worked on engines. We built our own motorcycles. And when NASCAR was on television, I always watched. I loved the sport, and I dreamed of being able to go do something like that.

When I met Paul Newman in the mid-1980s, I raced for his team at an amateur level and even ran a couple of pro races sanctioned by the Sports Car Club of America, but what I really always wanted was to make a film about racing. So after I finished *Top Gun* with director Tony Scott and producers Jerry Bruckheimer and Don Simpson, I pitched them the idea of doing a movie about NASCAR. Tony was a true visionary, and I knew that the way he would direct it, in terms of camera angles and colors and making it more cinematic, would help people see racing in a new way, make them feel like they were in the driver's seat. That was part of my goal in making *Days of Thunder*—to really contribute something to a sport I loved.

During filming, I met Rick Hendrick, and he and I became friends. Back then, Rick was really building his team, and it was fun having some of these incredible racers teach me how to drive. I got to take a car around Daytona at 200 mph. Rusty Wallace let me drive his car at Charlotte. I hung out with Darrell Waltrip and Richard Petty. I got to meet Dale Earnhardt

TOP: Tom Cruise and his daughter Suri with Jeff and his daughter Ella at Infineon Raceway in Sonoma, California.

out on his farm. In the film, the character of Rowdy Burns, who's notorious for his aggressive banging and bumping, says, "Rubbin' is racing." That line came straight from Dale. I had the privilege of meeting all these guys, all of them legends in their field. It was an extraordinary experience.

Days of Thunder came out in 1990, and to be able to introduce NASCAR to a worldwide audience and share something that meant so much to me growing up is something I am still very proud of.

The film's release also coincided with a new era of growth for NASCAR, and that's when a kid named Jeff Gordon came on the scene. Rick Hendrick told me early on he had seen this driver who was a different kind of guy. Jeff was unusual in that he had started racing at five years old, and he just crushed it. He had this blazing, brilliant young career. He was a born competitor, a born winner.

Jeff was an outsider, an open-wheel racer from California—in his case, by way of Indiana—and now here he was in NASCAR, still very much a Southern sport, competing against this legend in Dale Earnhardt. And you saw that he wasn't going to back down from Dale. It was very, very exciting. Every race, you'd wonder what was going to happen with these two guys who were just going at it. It was wonderful. It was a great story, and I became a fan. I'd watch all the races. I really wanted to see Jeff do well. He brought a real sense of drama and excitement to it all.

At the same time, the sport was evolving. It was starting to look better on television and to attract more fans. And the racers really began to change how they trained. They became athletes at a high level and just kept pushing the bar higher and higher. There's a lot of endurance that comes into play and a tremendous amount of work that goes into preparing. I don't think many people truly understand the level of discipline and athleticism it takes to be a NASCAR driver, to be in that car for so many hours, week after week.

But it takes much more than fitness to succeed in the long term. It takes real dedication, a true passion and love for what you do. You have to gear your whole life around it. From the time I was four years old, it was my dream to make movies, and for me, it's a privilege that I get to do something I love. When you look at Jeff Gordon, when you look at how he competed at such a high level for so long, when you see the dedication it took day in and day out, you begin to understand the deep passion and love he has for the sport. No matter what you're doing or what's coming your way, you have to know: "I love doing this." You saw that with Jeff. It was there the whole time.

It's what motivated him to perpetually strive for perfection, to be constantly learning. I remember watching Jeff in his post-race interviews, and each time, he was very clear about what had happened. When he didn't know, he admitted he'd have to figure it out. Every race, he was learning something. You're forever facing that challenge, whether it's making the car better or understanding what you can do better as a driver. In my profession, that same kind of self-evaluation, that willingness to be a student of the game and to learn and improve, is very important. In racing, it's what separates the champions from the also-rans.

Equally important is the understanding that no one goes about it alone—you need to have people around who support you in your dream. I was always amazed by the crews and crew chiefs, all the guys dedicating seven days a week around the clock to getting those cars ready. Jeff recognized that. With him, it was never just *me*—it was *us*. Always us. He never failed to thank his crew and the people he'd been able to work with. I always respected that about him. He's incredibly gracious, and you see that in how he treats people. Jeff may have been a very tough competitor, but he was a great sportsman. The man always had class.

I was disappointed, as we all were, when he retired. I had hoped he would race for a few more years, but it was his decision. I had the opportunity to speak at the year-end banquet when he was honored by NASCAR and his fellow racers, and it really meant a lot to me to be a part of that. I'd been pulling for him all those years, and as I said then, when you're treated to excellence every week for twenty-three years, that's not something you let go of easily. But there's comfort in the fact that he brought something exceptional to racing and that he leaves behind such a tremendous legacy of passion and professionalism to a sport I, and all of us, love so much.

BEHIND THE VISOR

BY JEFF GORDON

FOR MOST PROFESSIONAL ATHLETES I know, game day begins in solitude. It's all about getting in the zone. For me, race day started the night before. Sometimes I would have difficulty going to sleep. It depended on how the day went in practice. Did it go okay? Did I qualify well? Is the car really good? If it wasn't running well, I'd get concerned and hope we could make it better. I'd be anxious about the opportunity we had to win.

When I woke up, typically the only things on my mind were the race car and what I might experience in the race that day. Will I be starting tenth on the outside? What's that first turn going to be like? While it's good to think about some of those things, I could really get myself worked up. I'd have to stop and shift my thinking. I'd tell myself, "Don't worry about that now, deal with it later." I could get so worked up trying to anticipate every little scenario that I'd exhaust myself before I even got on the track.

I've had moments when I'd wake up and think, "Okay, today's the day we're going to wear out the competition." Then the green flag would drop, and it couldn't have gone worse. There were days where we had the absolute worst practice and I thought we were going to finish twenty-fifth, but we'd blister them and win.

I didn't try to set my expectations too high because I didn't want to be disappointed. So I'd go into it hoping for the best but with zero expectations.

I've never believed in luck. If you perform well, execute, have a good race car and a good race team, you're going to increase your chances dramatically of having better results.

WHILE MY MAIN FOCUS WAS ALWAYS on the race, there were many obligations to be met before I'd ever get on the track. My PR man, Jon Edwards, would lay out a detailed schedule with everything geared toward getting me to the driver's meeting.

Mornings typically started with media interviews, then it was on to sponsor events. Pre-race meet-and-greets and appearances at sponsor hospitality suites are part of the deal. You can choose to see them as a huge distraction or have fun with them like I did, understanding that sponsors are what make the world go around for us. It's the part of the business that enables us to do what we love doing, and I was fortunate to have awesome sponsors throughout my career. So you take some pictures, sign some autographs, and move on to the next step of the day.

OPPOSITE: Jeff mentally prepares for another battle. He's buckled up tight and in the zone.

After the drivers' meeting, I'd do my stretching and workout routine and then I'd head to the hauler to meet with the team to get ready for the race.

Seeing the fans was always a big part of the race day excitement. There's no other sport that gives fans more access. Periodically, over the years I've seen drivers fight against it. Some guys had the mindset of, "I'm here to race. They pay me to race, they don't pay me to do these other things." They're wrong. Nobody's going to pay you to race if there are no fans in the grandstands or watching at home. When you get to the big leagues, you've got to be professional and understand all the things that come along with it. I accepted the fact that fans, sponsors, and the media are all a part of the process. If you accept that fact, then you're more comfortable and you have more enjoyment in life at the racetrack.

Even if I was running to the drivers' meeting or to the track or just trying to get to the bathroom, and I spotted an enthusiastic fan, they've got all my gear on, they're screaming, I felt guilty if I didn't stop to sign an autograph. I'm not saying I stopped for every person, but I tried to always make some sort of effort. Sometimes it's taking a selfie. Sometimes it's just a fist-bump, a high five, or a handshake. But I've always believed the fans deserve my attention. They deserve an experience.

When I see a kid waiting for an autograph, I think back to my own experience getting Rick Mears's autograph. It was a big moment for me. So I always think to myself, "Okay, I need to stop for that kid because this could become that same big moment for them."

WHEN I'D STAND NEXT TO THE CAR ON the grid, I guess you could say I was zoned out. My mind was split. Half of it thinking about the race, and the other half just going through the motions. You could've had a conversation with me. I'd smile. I'd wave. I'd take pictures. I'm pretty good at appearing calm and cool. But if I was asked something complicated or something that really required focus, I'd avoid it at all costs.

It took me several years to learn how to balance race day obligations while focusing on the race. I had to work at it. Another adjustment came when Ingrid and the kids joined me

TOP: A fan favorite nearly his entire Cup career, Jeff always made sure the fans knew how much he appreciated them.

at the car before the race. Kids being kids, they'd tug on me and want to get in the car and play. It was a distraction at first. But then I realized that a little interaction at that time was important for us as a family. I was getting ready to risk my life, and they just wanted to give me that last good-luck hug and kiss.

WHEN I FINALLY TOOK THAT STEP INTO the car, that's when I truly got in the zone. I loved that moment.

I had a routine for how I buckled in, how I put on my helmet. I'd always do it in a certain order so I didn't forget anything. First, my lap belt. Then crotch belt. Left shoulder belt. Right shoulder belt. Then the head and neck support, earpieces, nose strip to help me breathe a little better, and eye drops for moisture in my eyes. Helmet. Gloves. Then steering wheel. There's a mark that lines it up to the steering column preset from the day before. I'd give it a good tug to make sure it was on nice and tight.

I'd have a quick conversation with my crew chief while getting settled in the car. Even with him, I was only half paying attention. I can remember several times when I'd have to ask him to repeat what he'd said because I was getting into the zone.

He didn't tell me what I should be doing on the track. He left that completely up to me. His job was to look me in the eyes, give me his thoughts, and remind me of certain details like a setup change or how to get in and out of the pit stall, or remind me how bad the wheel spin for restarts was at that particular track. Then I'd give him a fist-pump and a look of confidence that I was ready to go get the win. Once the window net went up and the engine fired, I was truly thinking about nothing else but the race.

I'd tighten the belts as much as I could, turn on the team communication radio, and head out. Once I was on the track, it was just me at peace, in a place where I was very comfortable.

When the green flag dropped, I was all business. I'd think of it as a battle because I'm constantly fighting all kinds of adversity and challenges.

The start. The first couple corners. That's when I'd get the feel of the car. That's when I was anxious, because I didn't know exactly how the car was going to react. You have to be prepared for all sorts of things. Is the grip level going to be higher or lower than I anticipated? I had to think about the drivers around me. Some were super-aggressive, and might want to take the third lane as I'd get through Turns 1 and 2 on a restart. So I had to be prepared to block. I might also have to be concerned and extra cautious about the level of talent of the driver in front of me. There were just so many factors to process all at once.

It was never easy. It was always tough. You could have the best car out there and you're still going to have moments that are tougher than others. Some days, I didn't have a good car, and I'd have even more of an uphill battle. Sometimes I'd be expecting the car to be loose and not very good, and all of a sudden I'd drive by five cars in the first lap. I'd be like, "Man, this is awesome!" I'd be thinking these guys are either really bad, or we're really good. But to

TOP RIGHT: Once he stepped into the car, Jeff would focus all thoughts on the race. TOP LEFT: Jeff following his routine for adjusting and tightening the seat straps before getting on the track.

be clear, that wasn't me as much as it was the car. It meant I was getting out of the car what I should get out of it. That was the crew doing a really good job setting it up.

From 1995 to 1998, we had a pretty distinct advantage over the competition with our cars. While the top three to five drivers were fierce challengers, the depth of competition wasn't what it is today, so we just dominated. I'd be out there with a five-, six-, eight-second lead, just on cruise control, and I'd be thinking, "Hmm, what am I going to have for dinner?" And then I'd go, "Okay, stop that. Pay attention."

Nowadays with the "free pass," "double-wide restarts," and the level of competition in general, there's no relaxing anymore. The cars have much more grip and reliability, and you're able to push them harder every single lap. You have to push track position. You're not conserving tires, brakes— nothing. It used to be a marathon, and you had to figure out where you could conserve. It was all about who could survive, who could hang in there and be around at the end.

FANS STILL TAKE PICTURES AND VIDEOS, but you don't see multiple flashes going off anymore. Now, during night races, you just see one constant light from the camera phones. But when Earnhardt and I were battling for the championship in '95, or I was chasing Rusty during the night race at Bristol—those significant moments when passes really mattered—I would make the move to get inside, and all of a sudden I'd look up and see flash bulbs firing off. POP! POP! POP! You're like, "Whoa, what was that?" I can remember the first time it got my attention; it caught me off guard, and I probably didn't complete the pass. But it would get me excited. I'd pass that car and those light bulbs would go off. Fans don't do that unless they like what they see. It's a way of linking up and connecting with them. I knew they were enjoying that moment.

IF I WAS IN AN INTENSE BATTLE with somebody, my heart rate went up. I didn't blink. My grip on the steering wheel was tighter, and everything was tense. I'd be fighting and fighting, motivated by anger or the speed of the car or the fight I was having with the car. There are all kinds of things motivating you.

When I was in the car, all I was thinking about was driving it, racing it. *I've got to go faster. I'm sixth, I need to be fifth. Don't screw up the pit stop. Don't make a mistake on the restart. I've*

TOP: From 1995 through 1998, the No. 24 DuPont Chrevolet rainbow car was dominant and consistently out front.

got to pass that car. I have to win. It's tons of pressure, and there are a lot of expectations. That process is not enjoyable to me. It's not fun. It's the results that are fun. It's getting yourself in that mindset, going through it and getting the results. That's the fun part. Not the practice, not making a qualifying lap. It's not fun until you cross under the checkered flag. Right up to that point, it's just stressful.

If the race wasn't going my way, there'd come a time where I'd have to start accepting what had happened, and believe me, it's easier to accept a top five than it is a fifteenth or twentieth. If we were the dominant car leading the race and we finished third, then I was upset, because we should have won the race. If we ran tenth all day and we finished fifth, then I was happy. That's like a victory, because we got more out of the car. It's always about getting the most out of the car. If I made a mistake, I was mad at myself. If I felt like someone else contributed to that mistake, even though we were a team, I wasn't going to beat them up for their mistake. I'm pretty good at letting things go.

But if it was a mistake that cost us a championship, it stuck with me for a while. Like Texas in 2014. We had it won so many times, and then the caution kept coming out. We'd have to rerack and do another restart. I just didn't do as good as I possibly could. In the clutch, I didn't get it done and allowed Brad Keselowski to take advantage and give me a cheap shot. Yeah, I was mad at him, but I was just as mad at myself. I feel like it was my job to prevent that from happening. At that time, I knew 2015 was going to be my final year, so I knew how crucial it was, and that probably contributed to what happened between us later on pit road. I held on to that one for a couple weeks.

A VICTORY IS A HUGE ADRENALINE RUSH; it's extremely exciting. You're just really proud of yourself and your team. I can remember back in the mid-nineties winning quite a few races and I just couldn't wait to get home. In recent years if I won a race, I was like, "Man, give me another hat to put on. Let's take another picture!" You couldn't get me out of Victory Lane. I'd take my sweet time because I'd want to take it all in. It's such a great moment. There aren't many things that can compare to that feeling, and you want to be around the people who contributed to it and the people you care about. The most gratifying aspect of being in that race car is seeing all the effort that went into it and getting the reward at the end of the day.

I was truly ready to do something different. My body was telling me. My mind was telling me. My family was telling me. Since I made the decision, it really added pressure in the final season. But it was also a huge relief.

I KNOW HOW FORTUNATE I WAS to get to do something that I loved, was good at, got paid a lot of money to do, and was successful doing it. I got the chance to drive great cars, be a part of great teams, and have the most amazing experiences I couldn't even have imagined. "Dream" is in the subtitle of this book for a reason. Since I was five-years-old, my dream was to become a racecar driver, and it came true. To this day, when I think about all the things that have happened for me as a result of realizing my dream, I still pinch myself sometimes to know it's all real. But it is. It all happened. As I look back over the journey of my life, I think it's one of the coolest stories ever.

TOP: Jeff in his final Victory Lane celebration, Martinsville 2015. "There aren't many things that can compare to that feeling," says Jeff.

1

THE KID FROM CALIFORNIA

AMERICAN STOCK CAR RACING HAD a long, proud provenance as the sport of the Southeast. It sprung from the illicit tradition of moonshining, the birthright of the sons of the Piedmont plateau and Appalachian hills, who carried loads of mountain dew to market in souped-up sedans, outfoxing and outdriving federal agents. These were the good ole boys, and this was their sport. If you told those folks in 1970 that in a mere twenty years or so a boy from California's Bay Area would become the public face of their pastime, they probably would have spit tobacco juice in your eye. But the boy was Jeff Gordon. And the place he was from? Well, hardly anybody outside the state had heard of it.

Twenty-five miles northeast of San Francisco, Vallejo was a blue-collar burg, a military town whose naval yards built the nation's first West Coast warships. The USS *Ward*, which fired the first shots in defense of Pearl Harbor, had been assembled there in a record-setting seventeen days. The war brought prosperity to the town, tripling its population.

When the war ended, most of the newcomers returned to their hometowns, but many stayed on, adding a rich mix of German, Irish, Polish, Italian, Mexican, and black, to the ethnic pot. The postwar town grew into something of a Main Street USA, albeit one where sailors' saloons and tattoo parlors dotted that street. It was into this Vallejo that Jeff's parents, Billy Gordon and Carol Houston, were born—delivered by the same doctor, in fact, who would also deliver Jeff's sister Kimberly. It was a world of mom-and-pop stores and roller rinks and soda fountains.

It was at the local Foster's Freeze that Billy Gordon first laid eyes on Carol and was smitten. "I was in eleventh grade, she was in tenth," he recalls. "She was with a guy I knew, and I thought, man, if this guy can be with her, I've got a great shot." It was an unlikely pairing. Carol was a reserved and respectful girl, the daughter of a delivery truck driver and a seamstress who stitched clothes for local department stores. She was what most people would call "well raised," and even as a girl, she understood the importance of family and the value of hard work.

On the other hand, Billy was a balled-up fist, ready to spring in whatever direction adventure blew. His mother and his father begged him to buckle down in school, go to college, and get a well-paying job. "My older brother, Howard, didn't care about school. Cars, girls,

OPPOSITE: Jeff at seven years old posing in his uniform purchased from Simpson Race Products, Torrance, California. Jeff's stepfather, John Bickford, had to special order the uniform directly from owner Bill Simpson because the company didn't routinely make a uniform that small.

JEFFERY GORDON

A baby boy weighing 7 pounds 13 ounces was born Aug. 4 in Kaiser Hospital to Mrs. Carol Gordon, wife of William G. Gordon II.

The father is a joiner. He is the son of Mr. and Mrs. William G. Gordon, Davis. Mrs. Gordon is the daughter of Mr. and Mrs. Patrick A. Houston, 209 Fairmont Ave.

The baby, named Jeffrey Michael, has a sister, Kimberly, 4. The family lives at 208 Westwood St.

TOP: Jeff's mother Carol in 1965. MIDDLE: A newspaper clipping announcing Jeff's birth, August 4, 1971, with his first name misspelled in the article. BOTTOM: Four-month-old Jeff and his four-year-old sister Kimberly with their father, Billy Gordon.

guns—that was his thing, that whole young, go-get-'em thing," Billy says. "I wanted to be like him." And he did a respectable job drag racing, drinking, and fighting.

In 1966, a year after Carol's graduation, an unplanned pregnancy beckoned them to the altar. "I didn't want to be married. I was twenty. She was nineteen. I was in full bloom. I had money, I had a car. I was having fun." Billy lived it up, racing, carousing, and cozying up to other women.

Coming from a close-knit clan, Carol hoped for a family with household unity. "Everything we did when I was young, we did as a family," she says. "That's how I grew up. That's what I wanted." After some cajoling from Carol, Billy promised to settle down and do better, taking an apprenticeship at the naval yard, which his father helped him land. But you can't bottle a whirlwind. They split up and then made up; split up and got back together. "We were really living separate lives together," he recalls. The couple made a decision many troubled couples make. They chose to have another child.

On August 4, 1971, Jeffery Michael Gordon made his grand entrance. Two days later, Bobby Allison edged out Richard Petty to take NASCAR's Myers Brothers 250 in Winston-Salem, earning $1,000. At the time, no one knew this little bundle would grow up to make his Cup debut in Petty's final race and go on to become the winningest driver in NASCAR's modern era.

But before Jeff had seen his first Christmas, Billy had taken up with another lady in the neighborhood, a recently separated but still married woman whom he confessed to have fallen "crazy in love with." Carol knew she should leave, but leaving wasn't something that just happened. There were logistics, there were kids, there were house payments—but every one of those considerations fell away when she received a phone call from Billy's flame. "She said that the police had just been at her house," Carol remembers. She told Carol to hide the drugs. "There were a lot of things going on that I wasn't comfortable with, but that one pushed me over the edge. That's when I knew I needed to leave."

"I didn't have anywhere to go," she recalls. "I couldn't afford the house, I didn't have a job." A girlfriend down the street offered to let them bunk with her until they got back on their feet. So Carol, four-year-old Kimberly, and three-month-old Jeff moved in.

As for Billy, he wasn't caught. He married his new sweetheart and eventually moved to Fort Ross, a secluded area about eighty miles north. "Carol is a fantastic woman, and she put up with way more than any person should. Jeffery says I have an excuse for everything, and he's right. Me and my daughter Kimberly were tight, but I made the decision to be with this new woman mostly based on the fact that it was better to go before Jeffery knew me. . . . I'm thankful every day that he even talks to me or has anything to do with me. And Jeffery doesn't know this, but when all this was going on, I used to go out in the backyard and cry and pray. I prayed that Carol would end up with a guy that would be great for her, and I prayed that she would find a man that would be a great stepfather to my kids. I prayed for that. And so my prayers came true."

★　　★　　★

When you ask people about John Bickford, the same words keep popping up: determined, competitive, detail oriented, independent, savvy, visionary. No problem couldn't be solved, no hurdle couldn't be overcome with the right amount of fortitude, observation, and common sense. It's a philosophy that led him to cobble together a working go-kart out of random

two-by-fours and a lawn mower engine at the age of nine, and to go on to build the first quadriplegic-operated vehicle by the age of twenty-four. "I didn't have a mentor," he says. "I feel like I'm an intelligent person, I'm a good observer, and I don't quit easily."

Racing had always been his passion. John graduated in the class of 1965 from Napa High School, about fifteen miles from Vallejo, and was married within a year. The problem, as far as his wife was concerned, was that he couldn't seem to keep his hands off cars. He and a group of friends pooled their resources to purchase and fix up a broken-down sedan to run at Vallejo Speedway. Later, he traded a decrepit military jeep for another hardtop and recruited his friend's brother to drive it, while he served as engineer, builder, head wrench, crew chief, and everything else under the mechanical sun. "I was absolutely the worst teenage husband that was ever created," he remembers. Although he and his wife, Rosie, had a son in 1967, they divorced two years later.

By that time, John had found a niche for himself at a Vallejo medical supply company called Robin-Aids. He'd started at the bottom, scraping caked food off veterans' wheelchairs, but it wasn't long before the higher-ups discovered his mechanical ingenuity. "They just kept bringing me problems and I'd solve them, and then they'd bring me another problem." Soon he was busy designing and building vehicles for disabled people.

With all that work, John spent a fair amount of time in the company's billing department. And when a good-looking clerk named Carol Gordon was hired in January 1972, he started logging perhaps a little extra time. "We had a lot of interaction," John says. "I was always talking to her, getting her life story. She's single, got two kids." He helped her out at the laundromat, holding six-month-old Jeff and talking to Kimberly while Carol washed diapers, even though he was due to be married again in a few months. John's second union lasted just four months before it was annulled. "I don't even know why I got married, really," John says. "But it was over like it didn't even exist, and so I asked Carol, 'Well, you want to go to the races?'"

TOP LEFT: Four-year-old Jeff playing at Blue Rock Springs Park, Vallejo, California. TOP RIGHT: John Bickford at Capitol Quarter Midgets, Rio Linda, California, 1978.

It was Labor Day weekend, the sun was bright, and John and Carol and the kids were together, surrounded by loud, fast cars. Never mind that Jeff, who had just turned one, slept his way through most of the event. It was a perfect snapshot of their future. John and Carol were already living together in a modest three-bedroom house in Vallejo when they wed in May 1973. "It was kind of like night and day," says Kimberly. "My mom and John are day, and my father, Billy, is nighttime. John is just so good with my mom, and he always treated her like an equal partner. And John loved us and treated us like his own."

*   *   *

As early as anyone can remember, Jeff had a well of energy that seemed to run to the center of the earth. He was like a creature unleashed, and Vallejo offered plenty of opportunity to rollick.

In the mid-1970s, the town had its share of vacant lots. On their way to and from school, Jeff and his kindergarten cronies would romp through those rubble-filled landscapes like soldiers at war, chucking dirt grenades and spear fighting with stalks of wild fennel. There were days he'd spend hours blasting video-game aliens on the family's new Atari or play with *Star Wars* figures and army men in his room.

He was just a typical kid blessed with an extra dose of energy. But he did have one chink in his boyhood armor: he was extremely wary of grown-ups. "There was definitely a period of time, up until my teenage years, when I was shy," Jeff admits. "I had no problem with other kids and friends—I was a chatterbox when it came to that. But if I didn't know them very well, I didn't say much."

"He didn't talk to anybody," John says. "Most people thought he had a speech impediment because he wouldn't say anything." Carol remembers it being like a steel door slamming shut each time a human over five feet tall opened their mouth.

"I had a neighbor I used to like hanging out with, and we'd play G.I. Joe together," Jeff recalls. "I'd tell my parents, 'I'm going over to Steven's.'" "If Steve didn't happen to be outside," Carol remembers, "Jeff would simply open the neighbors' front door without knocking and walk to Steven's bedroom. Sometimes he might not even find Steven, but no matter. He would just play in the bedroom. And then when he was done, he'd walk back out. He never spoke to the parents."

As reticent as he was with adults, he could be bold and brash with kids his age. "As far as playing with other kids in my neighborhood, yeah, I was pretty competitive with it," he remembers. Whether it was a neighborhood game of hide-and-seek or four square on the school playground, Jeff had a need to win that could at times seem pathological. He would play until he won. To this day, his friends recall that he could not stand to lose, or even to be second. He still reminds some of them how he used to dominate them in something as simple as a video game. "You could say that he was cocky, all right," says his boyhood buddy Rod Sherry. "He was a cocky, little kid and he was confident, and I'm sure that came from his natural ability—he was coordinated and he was smart."

That natural ability and drive were traits John was determined to nurture in his unique Bickfordian way. "From the time he was little," John remembers, "he wanted to be better. You inherit a lot of stuff, but you have to want to succeed." One day, Billy dropped off a secondhand bicycle for Jeff, and he was eager to learn to ride it. As John recalls, the bike was well worn, with small-diameter wheels and hard rubber tires. He wasn't even sure it was street worthy.

But instead of upsetting Jeff by pitching it outright, John set before his four-year-old stepson a challenge. "Bottom line," John told him, "no training wheels. When I come back from the shop, you're either riding it without training wheels, or I'm putting it in the car and it's going to the dump. So you choose."

Most kids that age would have collapsed in a pool of tears. Jeff didn't complain. With a little help from Carol, he figured out how to mount the bike from the curb. "He was so short, and his legs wouldn't touch the ground," she recalls. "The next thing I knew, he came in and he said he could do it." Within a day, he'd managed to face-plant on the curb and bust his lip, but he was undeterred and quickly developed a new obsession. "We lived on a hill, and it didn't take long before I was going up the hill and down it," Jeff says. "That was really my first introduction to speed, going down that hill, pushing the limits of how fast I could go." Weeks later, he asked to be taken to the BMX racing track in the neighborhood.

"He didn't even know what racing was," John remembers. "He just wanted to do it." The first order of business was to get Jeff a new bike. John went out and purchased a top-of-the-line frame, which he customized in his machine shop to accommodate Jeff's tiny body—modifications that by his own admission might have strayed just a hair's breadth from the BMX rule book. He and Carol gave it to Jeff as a birthday present.

"And then we started practicing," John recalls. "I'd take him every day. We'd go to the BMX track, just by ourselves, and we'd practice and we'd practice and we'd practice and we'd practice." Jeff learned the best way to start, how to take the first corner, how to pedal through turns. When it finally came time for a sanctioned race, Jeff, who had just turned five and was competing against bigger, stronger kids, placed third. He brought his trophy home, his first ever, and placed it in the front window of the house.

"I may have won a couple races, but I was usually finishing second or third," Jeff says. "I was too slow, and I was too little. But it was an influence that's still there today—just tapping into that competitiveness, going and competing against others." He may not have overshadowed the field, but he made it to the 1976 state championships. "When you're a miniature five-year-old and you're competing against some long-legged seven-year-old, that's pretty tough, but he was fast and focused," John remembers. "He rode the hell out of the bike."

LEFT: Jeff racing at the BMX bike track in Vallejo, California, in the summer of 1976—the year he placed fourth in the state championship. Jeff still has the helmet. RIGHT: (left to right) Patrick Gerard, Jeff, and Tim Clauson proudly displaying their quarter-midget award plaques.

By then, however, Carol had seen enough. He'd only been racing for a few months, but there were too many broken arms and collarbones and concussions in the sport. "It made me very uneasy, and I personally was going to have a hard time watching that," she says. "So John and I had a long talk about it."

"If she says it's too dangerous for him, all right, we won't do it," John recalls. "But we both agreed that Jeff was going to be a lot of trouble if we didn't keep him busy. He just had tons of energy."

Within days of that final BMX race, John made some phone calls and gathered up $450 and left the house. A few hours later, he returned towing a little flatbed trailer. When Jeff poked his head out the front door, his eyes lit up. On it were two quarter-midget race cars, one for him and one for his sister, Kimberly.

*　　　*　　　*

By the time Jeff won his first big race in July 1977, he'd logged thousands of practice laps, first on a small, weed-strewn patch of concrete his folks had cleared at the nearby Solano County Fairgrounds, and later at a proper quarter-midget track near Sacramento, in Rio Linda. Three days a week, John picked Jeff up from kindergarten, and the two of them would make the hour-and-a-half drive up north, where they'd run lap after lap, racing against the stopwatch, looking to take better lines, and figuring the best way to corner. "I'd get so mad at him, but I couldn't be mad," John says. "Really, you wanted it to be fun, but I wanted to win. But I couldn't tell him that."

John, who was then running a fledgling business with Carol manufacturing and selling custom vehicle parts for the disabled, logged extra hours in the shop to get every advantage he could out of Jeff's car. "If I have any faults, Jeff would tell you, I'm not a regular dad," he says. "I don't know how to do anything in the middle. I'm way over here, or I'm way over there, but I'm never in the middle. And 'over here' is usually extreme."

As a stepdad, he may not have been one for throwing a football or giving hugs or having a good-natured wrestle on the living room floor, but Carol was convinced he would always do what he thought best for the children, for her, and for the family. If John said quarter-midget racing was safer than BMX bikes, if he thought pushing Jeff was going to have a benefit, then so be it.

TOP LEFT: Jeff at Capitol Quarter Midget Track, Rio Linda, California, April 1977. BOTTOM LEFT: Jeff in his white Simpson race uniform at Baylands Quarter Midget Track, Sunnyvale, California, July 1978. RIGHT: Jeff proudly standing next to his car on the front lawn of the Bickfords' home with his first real trophy, a fourth-place finish, May 1977.

CAPITOL QUARTER & HALF MIDGET ASSOCIATION

SECOND PLACE

QUARTER MIDGETS OF AMERICA QmofA

Official Driver's Log Book

Quarter Midgets of America

JEFF GORDON

PROBATIONARY PERIOD (5 RACES MIN.)

Date	Track	Event (M-SM-C)	Qual. Time	Start Position	Finish Position	Cars Passed	Remarks
4/30/75	CAP	1st Heat MONZA	N/A	3	4	0	WELCOME TO 1/4 MIDGET RACING GOOD RACE
		2ND HEAT					did not complete -
5/7/77	CAP	TD	8.63³	2	3	0	
		HEAT	↑	3	3	0	
		MAIN	8.22⁰	5	4ᵒᵗ	0	Good race
...ton	M	795	5				

CLOCKWISE FROM TOP: Jeff grabbing the checkered flag to win a race at Baylands Quarter Midget Track, Sunnyvale, California, April 1978; The cover and a page from Jeff's Quarter Midgets of America Official Driver's Log Book; Jeff racing at Capitol Quarter Midgets, Rio Linda, California, 1977; Jeff's Quarter Midgets of America patch; Capitol Quarter & Half Midget second-place ribbon awarded to Jeff for a novice event in April 1977, before he became an official quarter-midget racer.

TOP: Jeff in his car just before his race at Capitol Quarter Midgets, Rio Linda, California, 1978. BOTTOM: John shaking hands with Jeff after crossing the finish line. "It was sort of our standard procedure after every race," John says.

"The greatest genius of John is that he was not my real dad," Jeff says. "I think he had just enough of a disconnect between being my real father and being an influence on me." That slim line, he speculates, is what allowed John to lean on him a little harder and, perhaps, bypass a parent's natural misgivings about strapping an undersized five-year-old into a car that could reach speeds of 50 mph.

At one point, the family got John's biological son, John Jr., a quarter midget, but his son's mother "hated racing" and was unsupportive of the practice regimen. "We'd go to pick up John Jr. at the agreed-upon time and location and he wouldn't be there," John says. "She just wasn't going to cooperate." John Jr.'s visits were more about fun, like the time he and Jeff raced a neighbor's go-kart down a hill, a thrill ride that took a painful turn. "I felt a tug at the right seat of my pants, then some serious pain," John Jr. recalls. "My pants were shredded. Apparently, I had gotten too close to the sprocket on the axle and it cut into me. I remember a trip to the ER, and I have the scar to this day." With all the stepbrotherly horsing around, there wasn't much room for reflection in Jeff's young mind, but he did sometimes wonder about the attention and instruction John lavished on him rather than his real son. "I remember feeling a bit of, 'Does he feel left out?' but that wasn't really my place." John Jr. enjoyed his visits, even wished sometimes he could've stayed, but he also admits he felt left out. "I had a lot of animosity internally. Didn't show it to anybody. Didn't ever say it. It was all just something inside that I dealt with because, as a kid, you don't understand what's going on. They didn't mean to make me feel that way. But that's how I felt as a kid."

Jeff, too, had to navigate a relationship with his own biological father. At first Billy had supervised visits at Carol and John's, but eventually Kimberly and Jeff spent time with Billy at his house. It wasn't always easy, Jeff remembers. Billy's wife, Jeannie, had two daughters of her own, and when it came to their upbringing, Jeannie was strict as a whip. "There were times when I felt she was not kind to me," says Jeff. "She wanted more discipline. John and my mom were definitely more open-minded, probably a little more spoiling to us as kids. Jeannie was more disciplined in general than, say, my mom was on certain manners, certain behavior."

Things may have been a bit looser at John and Carol's home, but it wasn't all ice cream and merry-go-rounds. "I don't believe in screaming and yelling," John says. "That accomplishes nothing. And I never believed in spanking kids." When Jeff crossed the line, John would send him to his room, telling him, "I feel bad for you because I had you at a higher bar. I thought you were a little smarter than that. Once again, I was wrong." It drove Jeff batty. He'd feel so bad that he'd scream at John to just give him a whipping like other parents, and be done with it. "John was great at that," Jeff says. "And it worked."

Jeff himself was a bit more physically aggressive by nature than his stepdad, which often came out in schoolyard confrontations. "I wasn't some big tough guy," he says. "I was left alone for the most part, and I left others alone." But there was no way he'd take a backward step if he was charged. Carol remembers having to retrieve him from school from time to time after a scrap. "It was his size," she reflects. "He was small, and small boys get harassed." His friend Rod Sherry remembers things a little differently. "He could talk smack with the best of them," he says. Sometimes it was Jeff's mouth that got him in trouble.

But as the racing heated up, Jeff spent less and less time in the neighborhood and more and more time at the track. "Once I got introduced to racing," he says, "most of my thought process revolved around racing." It was a steep learning curve, but he and John were ramping up fast. By the end of 1978, Jeff was like lightning on the track, smoking the competition and leaving the other fathers hollering about illegal parts and gathering up officials to take that engine apart piece by piece to find the infraction. John and Carol told Jeff it was just the way things were done—when you won, they tore your car apart. "I knew what was going on," says Jeff. "It was a little frustrating to be accused of things we weren't doing . . . but mostly for my parents because it caused friction with the other parents."

Between 1977 and 1978, he won thirty-five main events and set five track records. While winning was great, it was more important to win right. "I had a rule," John says. "Don't be banging on the other cars. Set them up; pass them. You can't just drive in there and ram into people." At a race in the spring of 1979, Jeff had gotten a bit too aggressive in passing another driver and ran over his wheel—whether intentionally or unintentionally, he and John disagree to this day—on his way to the checkered flag. While Jeff was busy celebrating, John coolly walked up and told him to give his trophy to the other kid. Jeff pleaded his case, but John was adamant. Jeff broke down and cried, but he did what John asked. "He had to be professional in everything he did," John says. "You don't have Mommy and Daddy zip up your jacket and put your helmet on. You put it on and adjust it yourself. . . . You get in that car and strap your belts. You're a professional. Act like one all the time."

At their peak, they would hit three tracks on a weekend, leaving home Friday for Rio Linda, practicing Friday night, running a race there Saturday night, then taking off for a Sunday morning contest in Hayward and an afternoon event in Sunnyvale. They'd run main events in two classes at each track to boot, before straggling home Sunday night dirty and tired. "I remember one time Jeff hadn't done his homework," Rod Sherry recalls, "and his excuse to the teacher was, 'Well, I was at the racetrack all weekend and didn't get a chance to do it.'" Jeff's age and success were a novelty that began attracting national media attention. ABC's television series, *Kids Are People Too*, and the nationally syndicated *PM Magazine* both featured segments on Jeff. *Super Kids*, another popular series at the time, focused an entire episode on Jeff's young racing exploits. Suddenly Jeff's celebrity was on the rise. John recognized the impact of television and the importance of developing a media-friendly image, which ultimately became a differentiator for Jeff as he progressed in his racing career.

John and Carol tried to stay on Jeff about his grades, but Carol never had an objection to the racing or the hectic schedule. "I loved it," she says. "And you know why I loved it? Because we were doing it as a family." At Rio Linda, Carol was the head scorekeeper and did some announcing, and boy-crazy Kimberly was the trophy girl, which meant she'd get a peck each time she handed brass to a winner. John was the regional director for the sport, and had his network of fathers and other enthusiasts with whom he exchanged information and sold tires and his custom-made parts.

Veteran sprint car driver Greg DeCaires, a childhood friend of Jeff's, also competed at Rio Linda. Although the two aspiring racers didn't compete against each other—Greg was a few years older than Jeff—the two would race during the day and pal around between races. DeCaires remembers Jeff as a smooth, smart driver. "He very rarely was involved in any kind of contact with any other car on the track. He knew how to keep a consistency out there. A lot of kids lose their focus or are just sporadic. Lap after lap, Jeff was always the one to watch on the track for sure."

DeCaires remembers John and Carol's motor home being a popular hangout for the parents. "They had a really cool margarita machine on their countertop. A couple of times a band showed up in the evening, set up and played music. . . . I remember once all the adults

TOP: John helping out the other racers with their cars at the Baylands Quarter Midget Track, 1978. BOTTOM: Jeff racing at Capitol Quarter Midgets, Rio Linda, California, 1979.

ended up dancing the conga around the track. Us kids would go find someone's camper and just hang out."

It became such a family project that at one point in 1978, they purchased a quarter midget for Carol so she could serve as a challenger for Jeff when he practiced passing and restarts. "He hated to practice," Carol recalls.

"I did practice," Jeff says, "because I was pushed to practice. But I definitely saw and understood the benefits. I didn't see that—I didn't have the self-discipline—with anything else." Billy had gotten him a set of drums. It didn't take. The saxophone? Lessons were too boring—he didn't want to learn scales. "With racing, that's just the influence of John, my mom, the competition—whatever it was, practicing racing was the one thing I was OK with."

It paid off: 1979 was a huge year for him. They dominated the Northern California tracks and for the first time left to compete in other states. Jeff took the Grand Nationals in Colorado—the sport's biggest prize—and ended up winning fifty-two races and setting eight track records. The following year, he won forty-six, posting the fast time in every one of the fifty races he entered. "I had a lot of confidence," Jeff says about his growing feeling of invincibility. "When we went to the track, I felt like we were there to win." In 1981, he took second place in the Grand National championship, this time in Oklahoma, in addition to dominating the go-kart races he competed in, which he and John had taken up as something of a sideline hobby.

"When you look at the statistical information, from April 1979 until 1981, we almost never lost a race," John says with only the slightest exaggeration. With all that winning, Jeff's first BMX trophy had some pretty prodigious company. "In my parent's shop, there was a loft where we kept the trophies. And every once in a while, I'd get a ladder and I'd go up there. And I'd go through each one of them, and remember where I got them," Jeff says. "I remember, I used to love to do that." Not many ten-year-olds can take a trip down memory lane.

"By 1982, we accomplished all we set out to," Jeff says, "and we weren't as challenged as you need to be to stay motivated." But they kept racing—and winning—anyway. "We did honestly think he was burned out," Carol recalls. "He kind of got stale, or bored. We cut back to twenty-five or so weekends of quarter-midget racing," says John. They bought a boat for

RIGHT: Jeff and Greg DeCaires hoisting Jeff's car off the scales at Capitol Quarter Midgets, Rio Linda, California, 1981.

Jeff to practice waterskiing. He went to windsurfing school. They moved to a new house. In junior high, he discovered break dancing and fell in love with it. There was still bike riding, skateboarding, and playing pickup basketball at the park. He kept busy, but the absence of racing left a time vacuum, especially during the period after school and before Carol and John returned from work. "When you kept Jeff occupied, you were good," Kimberly says. "But when he had downtime, he didn't always make the best choices. He'd tend to pick the mischievous kids and hang out with them."

"My influences changed a lot when I went to junior high," Jeff says. "I started break dancing and listening to different music and had other friends in my new neighborhood"—a number of whom were at least a couple years older and a bit more delinquently inclined.

"We started hanging out with different crowds," Rod Sherry remembers. "He was with some guys who were getting in a lot of trouble—at that age I guess it was kind of the cool thing. I didn't get along with them that well because I thought they were kind of punks."

One of those new acquaintances was a fifteen-year-old named Chris, whose single mother worked nights and who had been cruising in his own car for several years. "There were a lot of very good reasons why we didn't like him," says Carol. Lack of parental supervision. Petty vandalism. Girls. Beer drinking. Pot smoking. And what she didn't know, she suspected. "I'd probably be very naïve to think Jeff wasn't doing that, too." Jeff had his own assessment: "He was fun to hang out with. It was never boring."

The two youngsters had a common ruse: Chris would knock on Jeff's front door for Jeff to come outside and play. Carol would watch them set off on foot, but they'd quickly turn the corner and hop in Chris's ride. Soon those daytime excursions turned into nighttime. "When my parents went to bed, I would sneak out of my bedroom window," Jeff recalls. "I'd taken the screen off and had a ladder so I could climb down. One night we drove to San Francisco—it's like an hour drive—because Chris said, 'There's this parking garage that's awesome to ride skateboards in.' That was pretty big for a fifteen-year-old kid who had other kids that were fourteen, thirteen, and twelve in the car with him at midnight."

The adolescent crew arrived in the city pre-dawn and broke into the locked carport. "It was a spiral garage," Jeff remembers, "and we went up to the top, and we would get on our stomachs on the skateboards and race all the way to the bottom. It was one of the greatest nights of my life. Then we got in the car and drove back. I remember it being like three o'clock in the morning. I got back in the window and went to sleep and went to school the next day." But the amateur sneak had forgotten to put back the screen, as his mother discovered the next day. "She knew something was up," Jeff says. "I was a terrible liar."

One night, at one o'clock, she went to check on her son. His bed was empty. "I don't remember where we went that night," Jeff says. "But I remember coming home and the lights were on and the front door was cracked open, and I thought, 'Uh-oh, I'm in big trouble.'"

"I was like, 'Get your ass in here right now!'" Carol says. "Yeah, that was not a good night for Jeff in our house." Jeff recalls that his parents told him to pack his bags, he was on his way to military school. Carol remembers him sitting on the front porch in the early morning with his belongings, crying his eyes out. "In total, I snuck out of the house maybe a handful of times. It wasn't a regular occurrence," Jeff recalls. "There's obviously a theme. I've never been afraid of trying new things, even when risk was involved."

While he never went off to become Sgt. Gordon, Carol and John knew they needed a new plan to harness their son's energy.

TOP: Jeff relaxing after a race at Baylands Quarter Midget Track, San Jose, California, 1980. BOTTOM: A Pennycook School sixth grade class photo of Jeff at eleven years old.

2

YOU LIED TO ME!

FROM THE TIME HE WAS A TEEN, Jeff Gordon wanted to be a racecar driver. Racing filled his day-dreams, even if it no longer filled his weekends. "I wasn't being challenged," he recalls. "In 1983 and 1984, we didn't do a lot of racing because there was no place to transition to."

He waterskied, skateboarded, and competed in the odd quarter-midget race from time to time, just to knock the cobwebs off. He watched Indy car racing, thumbed through his copies of *Open Wheel* magazine, and marveled at the exploits of A.J. Foyt, Johnny Rutherford, and Rick Mears. He went to local sprint races and became a huge fan of Steve Kinser, reading everything he could get his hands on about his new idol. It was then he came across a story about another sprint racer, Sport Allen, who was just fifteen years old—older than Jeff, but it got him thinking.

In October of 1984, Jeff raced an event in Indianapolis, where he handily won both races. Following the victories, John and Jeff drove to see Lee Osborne, a former modified-racer and sprint car champion who had opened a business building sprint chassis. John told him he was in the market. "Aren't you a little bit old to be starting sprint car racing?" Osborne asked. It's not for me, John told him. It's for Jeff. "Picture it," John chuckles. "Jeff's standing there, and even soaking wet with a hundred dollars' worth of quarters in his pockets, he didn't weigh a hundred pounds."

"There's no way," John remembers Osborne saying. "He's too little." Jeff stood quietly the whole time. Finally, Osborne addressed the thirteen-year-old directly. "You think you can drive a race car?" "Yes, sir." "What makes you think that?"

Jeff gave a humble rundown of his quarter-midget and go-kart successes and mentioned the article he'd read on Sport Allen. "[Osborne] just shook his head as if to say, 'Please leave, you're both crazy and I don't deal with crazy people,'" John remembers. John continued to butter up Osborne by phone after they flew back to California. After several weeks, Osborne relented.

At the end of November, a crate arrived in Vallejo. Inside was their new Osborne sprint chassis. It took a frenetic few months of bartering and building; locating a used motor, wheels, a rear end, a front axle, and other parts; designing a custom undersized seat for Jeff; and cobbling the whole thing together. Most nights, Jeff would finish his homework and come down to the shop to help out. "I saw this car being built and I saw the engine," he says. "And I was nervous."

OPPOSITE: Fourteen-year-old Jeff does a pre-race check of his sprint car at Freemont Speedway in Freemont, Ohio, 1985.

TOP: Jeff in his red driving suit, 1985.

Jeff's friend Rod Sherry remembers coming down to John's machine shop to take a look. "He had this sprint car with the big wing on top. I don't even think he'd driven it at that point, but next to Jeff, it was just a massive, massive car. And I remember saying, 'Dude, you're crazy if you're going to drive that thing. You're going to kill yourself.' It just looked really intimidating."

When it was ready, Jeff, John, Carol, and friends Vern Kornburst and George Brown loaded the newly built car into a trailer and drove out to rural Dixon, California—twenty-five miles southeast of Sacramento. They rolled the car out of the trailer and strapped Jeff in. While the truck got in position to push start the car, John gave him the instructions: Put the car in gear, turn the fuel lever to 'open.' The wheels will lock up for a split second as the truck starts to push the car. As the tires turn over watch the oil pressure. As the pressure rises above twenty to thirty pounds, flip the starter switch on, and *boom* the engine will fire immediately. Then pop it out of gear and keep it running to let the engine warm up.

"So he hits the switch," John recalls, "and suddenly he has six hundred fifty horsepower coming off that alcohol-powered motor with no flywheel. Just vrrrooooom! The exhausts coming out and making all these fumes, and he's just sitting there, rocking back and forth, and his eyes are as big as saucers. So were his mother's."

"It scared the crap out of me," Jeff recalls. "I was petrified. I thought, 'I don't know if I'm going to be able to do this.'" Moving up from quarter midgets to sprints was like giving up roller skates for a rocket. Jeff may have been competing against older, bigger kids most of his life, but this was a man's sport. These cars went from zero to sixty in three seconds and topped out at 150 mph. Wrecks were serious. People lost their lives. For all his competitiveness and zeal, this was something beyond. "We had this trip planned to Florida, and at that point John was fully committed," he recalls. "There was no backing out."

Jeff may have bitten down hard, realizing how much his stepfather had poured into the looming pilgrimage to Speedweek—a series of professional sprint events that would mark Jeff's first chance to pilot the machine—but Carol was having a tough time. "When they went off to Florida," she says, "Jeff was scared to death. Literally. He was thirteen years old and he was scared to death."

"She goes, 'Is he going to be all right?'" John says, smiling. "'Oh, he's going to be fine, dear,' I told her. 'Don't worry about it. He'll be good.' And she said okay."

"It's not because there was a lack of trust for what John was doing," Carol says. "I have all the trust in the world in him, and he's just amazing when it comes to looking down the road. It's just that I react to what Jeff reacts to because he's my son."

Carol stayed behind, which she admits was a good thing. During that first week of February 1985—just after Jeff, John, and Brian Bell, one of John's eighteen-year-old employees, set out from Vallejo for Jacksonville, Florida—a freak storm hit the Southwest, dropping snow, sleet, and ice from the California border clear across Texas. In the midst of a storm, John was maneuvering the Ford pickup and a thirty-eight-foot trailer containing the sprint car while mollifying his two teenage passengers, who had the fear of God stamped across their faces. "There were so many accidents and spinouts," he remembers. "We had people crash in front of us. We had a car flip by us." At one point, John nearly lost control of the rig but managed to lock up the breaks and slide to safety down an ice-covered off-ramp. "The whole trailer jackknifed," Jeff recalls, "and John panicked a little bit because it caught him off guard. But he straightened it out. We may have even gone into the intersection a bit. That was pretty scary."

"Jeff and Brian were patting me on the back and telling me it was the greatest piece of driving they'd ever seen," John laughs.

With temperatures dipping to thirty below, motels were either filled up or closed. The only place to stay was in the pickup. The three of them hunkered down in the cab and kept the motor running all night, a piece of cardboard wedged in front of the radiator to redirect the engine heat inside. "We froze our asses off," John remembers.

It took two days to get to Houston, but by then the storm had dissipated, and they decided to make a quick afternoon detour to Gilley's, the legendary honky-tonk from the 1980 film *Urban Cowboy*. Jeff quickly found something that piqued his interest. "He just kept hitting me up for quarters," says John, who figured Jeff was probably in the back playing video games. He was half right. "I did play video games," Jeff confesses, "but one of the games was like five card draw poker, and there was this image of a girl. Every time you won a hand, her top would come off, and you know, I was just mesmerized. It was the coolest thing I'd seen. 'Can I have more quarters?'"

After John managed to tear Jeff away from the strip poker machine, they sailed through the South. A day later, they rolled into Florida, ready for what would be the biggest challenge of Jeff's young life. The All Star Circuit of Champions Speedweek, which featured five nights of racing on two tracks—Jax Raceways in Jacksonville and East Bay Raceway in Tampa. And most importantly, unlike in California, there was no official age limit. John had used his powers of persuasion to convince the track owners and officials that a kid who looked even younger than his actual years should be given a shot. Younger drivers existed—Sport Allen, who was almost sixteen at the time, showed up to race in Tampa—but no one was quite prepared for just how tiny Jeff was.

"I mean, he wasn't just thirteen years old—he was a runt, you know? He was a small little dude," recalls legendary open-wheel racer Jack Hewitt, who had come to stake his claim in Florida along with other top-flight drivers like Doug Wolfgang, Dave Blaney, Rick Ferkel, and Brad Doty. None of the guys wanted some scrawny, untested waif wrecking them and robbing their payday. "I didn't agree with it," Hewitt says bluntly. "Nobody agreed with it."

TOP: Jeff proudly standing next to his sprint car in the Red Roof Inn parking lot in Tampa, Florida, just before heading to East Bay Raceway for his very first track race, February 1985.

Bill Holder, who wrote for *Open Wheel* magazine at the time, concurred. "You've got a kid that weighs about ninety pounds, with no upper-body strength, in a powerful, six-hundred-horsepower race car, and I just didn't think it was safe."

Even the fans were shocked. Dave Heitmeyer, who later became close friends with John, Jeff, and Carol, remembers sitting in the stands. "First, I couldn't believe that a thirteen-year-old was racing one of these cars. But then I was in awe when I saw him. I thought, 'Wow, this kid's good. But boy, is he little.'"

When the concerned track owner came over, John turned a deaf ear. "They came in," Jeff recalls, "and they were like, 'I'm sorry, but that boy is not getting in that car.' And John just said, 'Try and stop me.' He'd done his homework, and there was nothing they could do." After all, they'd driven three thousand miles to get Jeff some experience, and that's what was going to happen.

John's philosophy was simple—or crazy, considering Jeff had still never driven a sprint: Learn by being around the best. Watch them, talk with them, race with them, absorb what they do. "When you're there with the best in the world," John says, "something's got to rub off, right? So he's going to get the right stuff."

As for Jeff, the doubts and insecurities flooded back the moment he settled behind the wheel. The very fast, half-mile track was made even more slick and muddy after a rain. They were going to "hot-lap"—run the track with other drivers to test the cars out before the competition. "Obviously, John believed in me more than I believed in myself," Jeff recalls. "I was seriously nervous." And then the green flag dropped.

Jeff started off slowly, tentatively. "Vroom, vroom, vroom, vroom! Cars were going by me," he recalls. "And I was trying, but I really wasn't doing it. And then I stood on the gas." The car shot off, and as Jeff came out of a turn, the powerful sprint's back end slid around on the rain slicked track and scraped the retaining wall. It wasn't a bad impact, but it was enough. Jeff stopped. The caution flag came out. It began raining harder, which ended the race for the night. No matter. Jeff was done. Done with Florida, done with sprints.

"I was crying," he remembers. "It scared the daylights out of me. I was really upset. I went up to John and said, 'You lied to me! There is no way I can do this.'"

"He said, 'You don't understand, I'm scared to death. I cannot do this. We need to go home,'" John recalls. "He was pretty upset with me."

Still, John was convinced that if Jeff could just get over his fear, he had more than enough skill to make this work. Rain ended the racing for the night. They went back to the hotel and had a heart-to-heart. "I just needed some time to build his confidence up," John says. Somehow, John's calm demeanor and a night's rest brought Jeff back into the fold. "I remember John saying, 'Nobody said it was going to be easy. Every one of these guys had to

TOP: Jeff at top speed in his No. 16 sprint car at Kings Speedway, Hanford, California, March 1985.

learn how to do it, and I believe in you. You can do it.' I was so petrified prior to that. The fact that I got back in that car two days later is, to me, the miracle of all miracles," Jeff says.

Despite Jeff's rekindled confidence, he and John were met by even stronger opposition when they pulled in to East Bay Raceway. This time it wasn't only the track owner that had issues. Bert Emick, president of the All Star Circuit of Champions, was adamant Jeff wasn't going to compete.

"Bert, you let us race at Jax Raceway," John said.

"Well, that wasn't an official All-Star Race. This is," declared Emick.

"But you've already promoted that Jeff Gordon's coming from California to race," John reasoned. "What are you going to tell the folks in the grandstands?"

Emick wasn't having it.

"Bert, we didn't have any issues at Jax. We'll start at the back," John pleaded. Emick, a man Jack Hewitt describes as "too nice a guy for the job," stopped and thought for a moment. Looking at John, Emick grinned and said, "All right, you can race."

So there he was, on a cold Wednesday night in his microscopic race suit, still scared but sliding around Tampa's East Bay Raceway with sprint car racing's cream of the crop. "We were pretty excited that he was as good as he was," John says. "He had just run with some of the best in the world." John was clear about their mission: They were not there to try to win. No matter how high Jeff qualified, he was to start in the back of every race, and he wasn't allowed to pass anyone unless they dropped off. "We were there for the experience, for the laps," he says. "I didn't want him out there mixing it up with professional guys who were earning a living, who were making house payments and paying for their kids to go to school. He was there to learn. And you're going to learn a whole lot more following cars and understanding how they use the track than you are trying to drive past a guy because you think you're faster."

The next night, Jeff was back at the track, and his qualifying time was even better. He was quickly becoming a fan darling, the track announcer regularly drawing attention to "Jeff Gordon, a thirteen-year-old racer from Valley-Joe, California." "It was a steep learning process," Jeff says, "but I excelled quickly. By the third night, I wasn't petrified anymore, didn't embarrass myself. I wasn't winning, but I was out there running very competitive laps."

TOP: Jeff kneeling beside his No. 16 sprint car, 1984. LEFT: Jeff blistering the competition in his yellow No. 16 sprint car at Warsaw Speedway, Warsaw, Indiana, 1987.

ATTORNEY OR PARTY WITHOUT ATTORNEY (NAME AND ADDRESS): — TELEPHONE NO — FOR COURT USE ONLY

WILLIAM C. SPAIN
1440 Broadway, Suite 302
Oakland, CA 94612

415-839-9890

ATTORNEY FOR (NAME): Petitioner

SUPERIOR COURT OF CALIFORNIA, COUNTY OF SOLANO
STREET ADDRESS 321 Tuolumne Street
MAILING ADDRESS
CITY AND ZIP CODE Vallejo, CA 94590
BRANCH NAME Vallejo

FILED
MAR 18 1985
NEIL CRAWFORD, County Clerk
By
DEPUTY CLERK

GUARDIANSHIP OF THE ☐ PERSON ☒ ESTATE OF (NAME):
JEFFREY MICHAEL GORDON,
Minor

CASE NUMBER
27737

ORDER APPOINTING GUARDIAN OF ☒ MINOR ☐ MINORS

1. The petition for appointment of guardian came on for hearing as follows (check boxes c, d, and e to indicate personal presence):
a. Judge (name): DWIGHT C. ELY
b. Hearing date: March 18, 1985 Time: 8:30 a.m. ☒ Dept. V ☐ Div. ☐ Room:
c. ☒ Petitioner (name): Carol A. Bickford
d. ☒ Attorney for petitioner (name): William C. Spain
e. ☐ Attorney for minor (name, address, and telephone):

This instrument is a correct copy of the original on file in this office
ATTEST: SEP - 9 1987
NEIL CRAWFORD, County Clerk and ex-officio Clerk of the Superior Court of the State of California in and for the County of Solano
By
DEPUTY CLERK

2. THE COURT FINDS
a. ☒ All notices required by law have been given.
☐ Notice of hearing to the following persons ☐ has been ☐ should be dispensed with (name):

b. Appointment of a guardian of the ☐ person ☒ estate of the minor is necessary and convenient.

c. ☒ Granting the guardian powers to be exercised independently under section 2590 of the Probate Code is to the advantage and benefit and in the best interest of the guardianship estate.

d. ☐ Attorney (name): _____ has been appointed by the court as legal counsel to represent the minor in these proceedings. The cost for representation is $ _____

e. ☐ The appointed court investigator, probation officer, or domestic relations investigator is (name, title, address, and telephone):

3. THE COURT ORDERS
a. (name)
(address) (telephone)
is appointed guardian of the person of (name)
and Letters shall issue upon qualification.

(Continued on reverse)

34

GUARDIANSHIP OF (NAME):
JEFFREY MICHAEL GORDON Minor

CASE NUMBER
27737

ORDER APPOINTING GUARDIAN OF MINOR Page 2

3. THE COURT ORDERS (continued)
b. (name): JOHN S. BICKFORD
(address) 132 Primrose Court (telephone): (707) 642-8967
Vallejo, CA

is appointed guardian of the estate of (name): JEFFREY MICHAEL GORDON
and Letters shall issue upon qualification.

c. ☐ Notice of hearing to the persons named in item 2a is dispensed with.

d. ☐ Bond is not required. ☒ Bond is fixed at $ 5,000 to be furnished by an authorized surety company or as otherwise provided by law.
☐ Deposits shall be made at (specify institution): _____ in the amount of $ _____ and receipts filed.

e. ☐ For legal services rendered on behalf of the minor, ☐ parents of the minor ☐ minor's estate shall pay to (name): _____ the sum of $ _____
☐ forthwith ☐ as follows (specify terms, including any combination of payors):

f. ☒ The guardian of the estate is granted authorization under section 2590 of the Probate Code to exercise independently the powers specified in attachment 3f ☐ subject to the conditions provided.

g. ☐ Orders are granted relating to the powers and duties of the guardian of the person under sections 2351-2358 of the Probate Code as specified in attachment 3g.

h. ☐ Orders are granted relating to the conditions imposed under section 2402 of the Probate Code upon the guardian of the estate as specified in attachment 3h.

i. ☐ Other orders are granted as specified in attachment 3i.

j. ☐ The inheritance tax referee appointed is (name and address):

4. Number of boxes checked in item 3 2
5. ☒ Number of pages attached: 1

Dated: 3/18/85
Judge of the Superior Court
☐ Signature follows last attachment

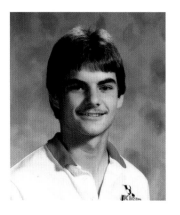

TOP: Pages of the filed emancipation document granting Jeff partial independence from his parents and the right to sign the track legal waivers. BOTTOM: Jeff in his school photo, 1986.

On the final night of the event, John removed the reins. In his heat race, Jeff qualified for the third-tier main event. This time, he started in sixth position out of twelve cars, but with a green light to pass other racers, he nearly won, finishing a close second. The performance bumped him into the second-tier 'B' main event, with a chance to qualify for the top-tier 'A' main event. Starting sixteenth out of twenty-two cars, he quickly worked his way up and was running among the top ten when a chunk of dirt kicked up by another car nailed him in the helmet obscuring his vision. He pulled up the track to get his bearings, but he hung tough, kept control, and finished seventeenth. "He pulled in after the race, and we're all excited," John recalls. "The grandstand is going nuts. TV cameras, they're interviewing him. He was on the Speedweek show on ESPN. He did excellent."

Bob Kinser, the father of Jeff's racing idol Steve Kinser and a racer himself, came down to the infield to get a closer look at the young phenom. "Kid, this your car?" John remembers him asking. "Yes, sir," Jeff replied. Kinser then put a hand on the young man's shoulder and said, "Kid, my balls wouldn't fit in that seat."

Even Jack Hewitt, who had been so adamant about the dangers Jeff posed on the track, seemed to be singing a different tune. "John didn't let it get out of hand. Jeff went in there tippy-toeing. He just had to stay out of the way and learn the skills, and that's what he did. And it made him a smart little racer right off the bat."

He was, to everyone's knowledge, the youngest person to ever race a sprint car. His name was now on the professional motorsports radar, and most observers expected they'd be seeing a lot more of him. But it was impossible not to hear the critics, the charges of irresponsible parenting, recklessness, even abuse. These were accusations that would dog John and Carol throughout Jeff's early teens. A journalist in Arizona, after witnessing Jeff's performance in Florida, demanded that John be prosecuted for child endangerment.

"It's not something I would recommend a lot of parents do," John says today, half-jokingly. "Why did I? I'm eccentric, I guess."

"Looking back," Jeff admits, "when you see how young and raw I was, I'm surprised John didn't get taken to jail. I'm not saying he was putting me at death's door, but there's no way I could ever do that as a father. To actually say, 'Yeah, let's go put our thirteen-year-old son in a sprint car.' . . . But I say that laughingly, too, because I couldn't be more thankful that he did."

Back home in Vallejo, Jeff settled into day-to-day life as a normal eighth-grade kid. Few of his friends knew anything about his experiences in Florida. "Racing was just something he did on the weekends," Rod Sherry remembers, "not something he talked about all that much."

"No matter how successful he was or how much he was winning, I never saw Jeff get arrogant," Carol recalls. "He was very grounded, and he never got a big head about it. He just doesn't have that in his nature." John agrees: "Jeff always downplayed how good he was in anything that he did."

He may not have been especially vocal about his racing, but in his head he was already entertaining dreams of a future. Yet finding opportunities to race sprints in California was proving next to impossible. Nobody wanted to let him compete. Most sanctioning bodies insisted he be at least sixteen—some said eighteen—and have a driver's license. There was the negative public opinion, plus legal barriers and insurance issues. Finally, a track in Hanford, about five hours south of Vallejo, agreed to let them come down—not to race but to hot-lap. It was opening day of the season, and a number of California's better-known sprint racers would be there. When it was announced over the loudspeaker that there was a thirteen-year-old who was going to run practice, there was a general sense of bemusement.

Jeff ran one lap at a decent speed, and then he turned it on. "He just slammed it to the floor," John recalls, "and he never lifted off the throttle." Jeff kept it in control and finally brought it into the infield. The other racers stood gape jawed. "I look at my stopwatch, and he's running as fast as the veterans," John says.

"I couldn't afford to crash or do anything dumb, or they would have said it was because I was too young," Jeff says. "And luckily I didn't. I still have people come up to me saying they were at Hanford that day, and they tell me how they couldn't believe it."

By the end of the afternoon, the older drivers were coming up to Jeff to talk shop about track conditions and car adjustments. "Big West Coast guys like Brent Kaeding and Jimmy Sills," John says. "They didn't down-talk to him. . . . I was pretty proud of him."

The raceway asked John and Jeff to come back to hot-lap again in a few weeks. In the absence of other opportunities, they agreed, but they both wondered how long it would go on. Three to five years of just running laps was flushing away Jeff's talent.

It was a legal issue. All tracks had racers sign a waiver ensuring they wouldn't sue in the case of death or injury. In California, any contract signed by a minor could be legally voided. So Jeff couldn't sign. And John couldn't sign for Jeff.

Cary Agajanian, an attorney and well-known Los Angeles–based track promoter, had refused to let Jeff race at Southern California's Ascot Park for precisely that reason, and when

TOP: A newspaper ad for an autograph signing with Jeff at Dave Heitmeyer's car dealership, H&M Motors, July 23, 1985.

33

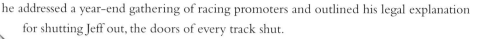

he addressed a year-end gathering of racing promoters and outlined his legal explanation for shutting Jeff out, the doors of every track shut.

Ironically, it was Agajanian who decided to help. "I knew Jeff Gordon knew how to race," Agajanian recalls. "He was a prodigy. It wasn't like you were putting a kid in a car who had never driven before." So he set to work drafting a document that would offer Jeff partial emancipation—a status that would allow him to legally sign track liability waivers while maintaining his standing as a minor in most other areas. They took the document to court, along with affidavits attesting to Jeff's driving ability, and sent the thirteen-year-old before the judge. In the end, the judge approved the emancipation. Today it is known as "approval of a minor's contract," and has been used by countless underage athletes since.

"We had this paper, so now we can legally sign," John says. "But nobody gave a shit." The approval to let Jeff race remained at the descretion of the tracks. As the school year wound to a close, it became clear that if they had any hope of finding some real, honest competition, they'd need to set their sights elsewhere. And the one place that seemed promising—with the fewest age restrictions—was the Midwest. Basing themselves out of Ohio, they crisscrossed the region, running more than twenty races over the next three months.

Dave Heitmeyer, a used-car dealer who'd seen Jeff run in Florida, offered Jeff and John a couple rooms in his Findlay, Ohio, home for the summer. Being a devoted racing fan, he often traveled with them from track to track, helping out. The first time Jeff ran at Findlay's Millstream Speedway, Heitmeyer recalls, "he started at the tail and passed three or four cars, and by the end of the back straight he was in the lead. And the people just cheered. That was probably the first time they'd heard of him, but immediately he had a big following."

With John's knack for promotion and the support of Findlay-based print shop owner 'Big' Jim Streicher and his son Mike, they started capitalizing on Jeff's growing popularity. A onetime Indy car mechanic, Jim also provided a building for John and Jeff to work from. They had a background sheet they handed out so everyone knew their story, and provided T-shirts featuring Jeff and his yellow No. 16 sprint that local track announcers gave away. There were "California Kid" bumper stickers and other paraphernalia. Jim had the idea to run off three-by-five sticky pads with Jeff's image that he could use for autographs. "Isn't this what other drivers do?" John asked. It wasn't, but it worked.

"As he started getting more popular, the girls swarmed him," Heitmeyer says. "We'd get to the racetrack and the girls were falling all over for him. And he was just thirteen." They all wanted a signature or a T-shirt or just a moment with the eighth-grade cutey. "Oh, hell yeah," John remembers. "Every girl from ten to nineteen."

Jack Hewitt, the Ohio-based open-wheel racer who had competed against Jeff in Florida, took the young novice under his wing. He gave Jeff some simple advice: sign his name so that people could read it, and always be there for the fans. "But you didn't have to tell him that. He knew it already, the little creep," Hewitt recalls with a chuckle.

As much as Jeff's post race sessions resembled a teenybopper stampede, he had come to race. He qualified for the top-tier "A" race roughly a dozen times and finished second in several races. He also managed to flip his car at K-C Raceway in Chillicothe, Ohio, as well as slide off the track sideways into the fans' parking lot at Millstream. He was learning—quickly. "Obviously, he was special because of his age and the fact that he wasn't intimidated by the other cars," Heitmeyer says. "You knew there was no doubt he was going to climb the ladder."

TOP: A "California Kid" souvenir button featuring Jeff and his yellow No. 16 sprint car.

"All the steps John took were the right steps. But believe it or not, Jeff had a little bit to do with it, with his driving ability," Hewitt says. Add to the fact that he always conducted himself like a professional, the team was building a solid foundation for success. "He was just a kid, but gosh, he had manners you wouldn't believe," Hewitt says.

Still, it was going to be a long year back in California. From September until the following June, John and Carol scrimped and saved, whittling down their nest egg to get Jeff to the races across the country. "We had invested in a sprint car, a trailer, the rig—everything—to go racing," Carol says. "And we were just sitting there in California with all of this stuff. To keep Jeff racing, we needed to make some kind of drastic move."

For John, it was a no-brainer. He laid out his "relocation" checklist for Carol: Jeff could grow up in the Midwest, where he wouldn't get into trouble. They'd be close to where sprint cars were manufactured. They could race three nights a week without having to schlep two thousand miles, and they might even find a car owner to race for. The cost of living was lower. John could set up a shop to make some extra cash building sprint parts. Kimberly was leaving for college in the fall, so she'd be fine. They could put someone in charge of their medical supply business and just go. He even had the location: Pittsboro, Indiana.

John was never one to get sentimental, but Carol needed time to think. "That was scary," she remembers. "It was hard for me because of my family and friends. In the beginning, I didn't want to do it. But there were a lot of things about it that would be good for Jeff." Truth was, she'd never felt Vallejo was a great place for him socially, and Kimberley had warned her more than once to pull him out of the school he was in. Even Jeff agreed. "We didn't live in a rough neighborhood, but Vallejo is a rough town, and it definitely has certain rough areas."

Jeff had few qualms about moving halfway across the country. "It didn't bother me at all," he says. Sure, he'd miss some of his buddies, and there was one girl he'd have to kiss good-bye for the last time, but a single factor seemed to override everything. "I knew I was going to get to race."

Just before summer, Carol set out alone for Pittsboro, Indiana, to find a place for the family to live. She still laughs when she remembers John and Jeff, towing the sprint trailer and all their belongings, arriving in Indiana. John phoned her for the address of the five-acre property she'd purchased. "I said, 'I don't know. I don't think it has an address. It's a rural route or something.' I mean, there were only four or five houses on the whole road." The real estate agent didn't even have a key for the house. Everyone just left their doors unlocked. One thing was clear: they weren't in Vallejo anymore. "I think Jeff would tell you it was one of the best moves we did for him," Carol says. "Absolutely."

TOP LEFT: Jeff holding the checkered flag and first-place trophy following another Friday night feature race victory at Bloomington Speedway, Bloomington, Indiana, 1987.
TOP RIGHT: Jeff at the track in 1987.
BOTTOM RIGHT: Jeff's childhood home in Pittsboro, Indiana.

3

BRING ON THE THUNDER

"I REMEMBER THE DAY HE GOT HERE," says Chris Cooper, who became one of Jeff's close friends in Pittsboro. "Todd Osborne brought him to a little party, fresh off the boat, and said, 'This is my buddy Jeff Gordon and he's an up-and-coming sprint car racer.' And you got this little, scrawny wet-bag. The kid didn't weigh 110 pounds. He looked like he was six-years old with hair on his lip. We thought there was no way a guy can drive a race car and look like *that*."

For the next few months, they put the newbie through the wringer. *You big enough to see over a steering wheel, Jeff? You sure you can reach them pedals, Jeff? Hey, Jeff, I think you got a little dirt there under your nose.* Jeff took it all on the chin. "I've never been somebody who shied away from making new friends," Jeff says. "And I wanted to fit in."

"We gave him a hard time, but he actually loved it," Cooper says. "He was just one of those funny guys—he'd feed it right back to you. Next thing you know, he was just one of us."

At Tri-West High School, the urban transplant was shocked to find there wasn't a single male with long hair or an earring. No gangs, no drugs, no one trying to lay some devious plan on you. "These were country people," Carol recalls. "The kids, when they left school, they went and worked on their parents' farms or their grandparents' farms." It wasn't a place where skate-boarding or break dancing held sway. Rather it was rustic pursuits like barn basketball in haylofts.

"It was the weirdest combination I've ever seen in a guy," recalls Jim Bear, another of Jeff's high school friends. "So laid-back and humble and nice until it comes to being competitive."

At fifteen, he *was* a driver, and there was no place he was more cutthroat than on the racetrack. They'd come to the Midwest to race, and that's what they did. "I can't even dream how many thousands of hours we ended up driving," John laughs. "We'd leave Pittsboro, drive ten hours to Kansas City and race, get in the truck and drive twelve hours to Haubstadt, Indiana, and race, drive six hours back to the house." "It was crazy, that's about the only way I can describe it," Carol remembers. "But I enjoyed every bit of it."

That first year, Jeff racked up a number of good finishes, was written up in *Open Wheel* magazine, and managed to notch his first main-event win at K-C Raceway in Chillicothe, Ohio.

"When I first moved to Indiana, it was just racing cars, going to school, hanging out with friends, and girls. There was no pressure. I was happy. I didn't feel any real sense of responsibility. . . . Only John knows if we were paying the bills."

OPPOSITE: Jeff prior to the "Night Before the 500" race at Indianapolis Raceway Park, 1989, where he set a new track record and won the race.

37

They were, but barely. John and Carol were drawing a small sum from their business in California, which they'd sold part of to finance the move. John was manufacturing and selling sprint racing parts out of his shop behind the house. For the time, Jeff's racetrack earnings, meager as they might have been, were the family's primary source of income.

As the first race season drew to a close, some drivers were heading to sprint-crazy Australia. It seemed a perfect way to keep Jeff's skills sharp and, with a little self-promotion, begin building a fan base overseas. But they might as well have been sending the boy to the moon, for the overhead it required. So John and Carol sent a letter printed on letterhead featuring a Jeff Gordon Motorsports logo and an image of his winged No. 16 sprint car to dozens of friends and associates to request donations—an approach they used several times over the years. It worked. In February 1987, John and Jeff touched down in Perth.

The Australian track promoters played up the "baby face" angle. They christened him the "Teenager Rager" and photographed him, mulleted and micro-mustachioed, holding a baby kangaroo. But he also showed them why he'd come, setting a track heat record, winning one main event, and finishing second in another while racing against Australia's best, and American stalwarts like Jimmy Sills and Randy Smith.

That year, Jeff, who had been racing competitively since he was five, finally became street legal. His Indiana driver's license opened doors to the more prestigious races sanctioned by the United States Auto Club (USAC) and the World of Outlaws. He soon found himself regularly pitted against the likes of Steve Kinser, Doug Wolfgang, and Brad Doty—titans of short track who weren't going to take a back seat to Jeff.

"There were two things in my racing career I didn't want to beat me—a girl or this kid," recalls Jack Hewitt. "I'd probably crash before I let that punk beat me." But for all the bluster, Hewitt and a number of other older drivers took a shine to Jeff. "It was always nice being around him, because you *did* like him, you know?" Hewitt says. "We'd tease him about girls and stuff like that. And when John wasn't around, he'd try to get back and say little things that were cute. He wanted to be one of the boys so bad."

"I looked up to all those guys," Jeff says. "And I wanted to race with them. . . . It was weird. I guess because I was young and looked up to them. I wanted to be their friend."

Hewitt remembers one of Jeff's first big victories, an All-Star race at Sandusky Speedway. "He won the feature, and we were so tickled and so pumped. This little shit went out and did it, you know?" But for Jeff, the highlight came at Eldora Speedway in New Weston, Ohio, where he bested Steve Kinser, his childhood hero. "Granted, it was just a heat race, not a main event," Jeff says, "but talk about me beating my idols. And Steve came up to me after the race, and I'll never forget what he said. He's like, 'Boy, you going to be a good 'un.' Not 'a good one' but 'a good 'un.' I was like, wow, Steve Kinser just spoke to me and told me I was going to be good. That was huge, huge, huge for me."

While Jeff and John posted a handful of wins in local non-sanctioned features, they weren't dominating in the upper level of sprints. With the added pressure of USAC races, World of Outlaws events, and the extra travel, it was getting tougher to keep Jeff in a top-of-the-line sprint car and still make ends meet. "We were just a mom-and-pop organization," Carol recalls. "We weren't going to pour every last nickel and dime into it, plus we still had a daughter that was going to college."

John kept reaching out to contacts, looking for any opportunity to land a sponsor or lock Jeff in a good ride with financial backing. "I'm sure there was pressure on John to pay

TOP: Jeff playing with a kangaroo in Perth, Australia, February 1987.

JEFF GORDON MOTORSPORTS

NOVEMBER 10, 1986

DEAR FRIEND:

JEFF GORDON'S METEORIC RISE IN THE EXCITING WORLD OF SPRINT CAR RACING HAS CAPTURED THE IMAGINATION OF COUNTLESS FANS ACROSS THE UNITED STATES. AS YOU HAVE FOLLOWED JEFF'S CAREER IN MOTORSPORTS, YOU HAVE NO DOUBT MARVELLED AT HIS GRIT, HIS DETERMINATION AND HIS PASSION FOR EXCELLENCE.

NOW, AS THE YOUNGEST SPRINT CAR DRIVER IN THIS COUNTRY, JEFF ASPIRES TO PIT HIS SKILLS AGAINST THE SEASONED DRIVERS ON THE INTERNATIONAL CIRCUIT WITH A TRIP TO AUSTRALIA FOR THE FIRST EVER WORLD SPRINT CAR CHAMPIONSHIPS EARLY NEXT YEAR.

THE UNDERTAKING WILL BE A TREMENDOUSLY EXCITING ONE, AUSTRALIA'S CLAREMONT SPEEDWAY IS THE OLDEST CONTINUOUSLY OPERATING SPEEDWAY TRACK IN THE WORLD, AND IT HAS PLAYED HOST TO TOP DRIVERS FROM AROUND THE GLOBE.

THE WORLD SPRINT CAR CHAMPIONSHIPS WILL BE ONE OF THE MAJOR OFFICIAL EVENTS OF THE **"AMERICA'S CUP FESTIVAL OF SPORT,"** AN INTERNATIONAL SPORTING SPECTACULAR EAGERLY AWAITED BY SPORTS FANS AROUND THE WORLD.

SPRINT CAR RACING IN AUSTRALIA HAS BECOME THE BIGGEST CROWD PLEASER ON THE DIRT TRACK CIRCUIT, WITH HIGH PERFORMANCE AUSSIE MACHINES FIGHTING IT OUT WITH VISITING **USA STARS** EACH SEASON.

THE **WORLD SPRINT CAR CHAMPIONSHIPS** POSE AN ENORMOUS CHALLENGE FOR JEFF, BOTH PERSONALLY AND PROFESSIONALLY, AND HE NEEDS YOUR HELP TO GET THERE.

YOUR CONTRIBUTION OF $_____$ WILL HELP SEND JEFF TO AUSTRALIA TO MAKE HIS DREAM A REALITY. WE ASK THAT YOU SUPPORT JEFF GORDON IN THIS NEW AND EXCITING PHASE OF HIS CAREER BY SENDING YOUR CONTRIBUTION TODAY.

SINCERELY,   MAKE CONTRIBUTION PAYABLE TO:
                                        JEFF GORDON MOTORSPORTS
JOHN AND CAROL BICKFORD

Thinking behind the wheel

Jeff Gordon, speedway's first overseas driver to compete this season, is the youngest to appear at Western Springs for some time yet he has crammed a lot of racing experience into his 17 years.

The American teenager (pictured) is considered one of the fastest drivers on any of the USAC, World Of Outlaws and All Star Tracks in the US.

To make the trip to New Zealand Gordon had to have a meeting with his Tri-West High School Board and ask for five extra days off school to go with his Christmas holidays. The board kindly granted the time off as it realises this lad is an exception in his sport.

Gordon has lived with his stepfather John Bickford since the age of three. Bickford soon realised Gordon was something special in the way of a driver when he started competing in quarter-midgets and go-karts from the age of five. He was always up the front and a thinker at the wheel.

He has now been driving sprintcars since the age of 13.

Only time will tell if Gordon is

Speedway

another AJ Foyt, Al Unser or Mario Andretti, but the signs are all there.

Bickford is the owner of the MPD Company which manufactures parts for sprintcars and midgets and Gordon spends his spare time in the Indiana shop getting to know all about the pieces that make a race car go.

Gordon raced for Terry Winterbottom in the US.

But for his New Zealand visit Gordon is racing a car owned by John Rae of Taranaki. Rae met Bickford in America and has brought back enough equipment to build a car that the young Gordon will know.

The Taranaki contingent have some very competitive sprintcars which are swelling the ranks in Auckland more and more, making for some great racing.

Gordon is the first of the American drivers to come over for this season but plans are afoot to have more visitors racing soon at both Western Springs and Meremere.

CLOCKWISE FROM TOP: The letter from John and Carol on Jeff Gordon Motorsports letterhead soliciting contributions for Jeff's trip to Australia; A Jeff Gordon autographed hero card, 1986; Jeff (far left) out to dinner with the Rush family and friends during his return trip to Australia in 1989 (Garry Rush, in the striped shirt at far right, is ten-time Australian national sprint car champion); Jeff's first passport for his trip to Australia; A newspaper article about Jeff competing at Western Springs in New Zealand, 1987.

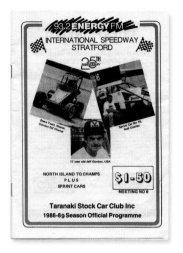

the bills on the race car, which he didn't really make me aware of," Jeff says. "But sometimes he would say, 'Hey, you need to call this guy, he's interested in sponsoring the car,' or, 'I got a call from this guy who'd like you to drive for him and I think you need to call him back and talk to him.'"

They ran a few races for two different owners that year, winning a feature for one, but nobody was ready to gamble on a sixteen-year-old high school student. That winter, Kiwi car owner John Rae, who ran in both New Zealand and Australia, invited Jeff to come race for him for a few weeks. He'd seen Jeff's potential in Perth the previous year and had followed his progress back in the States. Jeff's natural evolution as a racer kicked in. He demolished the competition, winning fourteen out of fifteen races. Nobody treated him like a novelty act any longer.

Back home in Pittsboro, John heard that well-known Ohio race-team owner Terry Winterbotham was down a driver and convinced him to give Jeff a shot. "Truthfully, I had a great driver in Kevin Huntly at that time," Winterbotham confesses. "But John told me what he could bring to the deal and I went for it." The two men did have one disagreement before finalizing their deal. "John didn't believe that I should pay Jeff if he ran worse than third. That was John trying to teach Jeff how to become a real racer," Winterbotham surmises. "In John's words, 'He's just practicing if he finishes worse than third.'" But Winterbotham refused to put that kind of pressure on Jeff. They agreed to split the prize money equally for a win. Jeff received thirty percent for anything other than first place.

Jeff was thrilled. He'd raced against the team's drivers and knew their equipment was top quality. He also realized he needed to make the most of the opportunity, for his career and for John and Carol. "Terry gave me a chance at a young age that nobody else was really willing to give me," he remembers. "I felt a lot of pressure to excel with that team because it was a big step for me."

He didn't disappoint. Jeff's first race out, he set a track record and won the main event. The rest of 1988 only got better. "It was amazing how he could adapt to a track," recalls Winterbotham. Jeff scored thirteen victories and captured track championships at three Ohio raceways.

TOP LEFT: Cover for the International Speedway Stratford program 1988–89 season, featuring Jeff. TOP RIGHT: Jeff standing next to Terry Winterbotham's black No. 6 sprint car after a feature win at Millstream Speedway, Findley, Ohio, 1988.

★ ★ ★

In his two years in Pittsboro, Jeff felt more at home than he ever had in Vallejo. "I loved being out in the country," Jeff recalls. "I've always been a person who likes that. And I loved how easygoing, how laid-back and just comfortable everything was." Jeff's success in 1988 was a minor windfall for the family. His earnings gave them some room to breathe, but they weren't about to start throwing money around. "I'll be the first to admit, I never felt like an overly spoiled kid," Jeff says. "My mom and John didn't shower me with a lot of things, and they made me appreciate what I had. . . . When I started making money in racing, they were really good about saving for my future . . . but they did allow me to spend some of that money."

Jeff settled on a cell phone and a new Chevrolet step-side pickup. "It was a model that just came out," he recalls, "and I put aluminum wheels on it, and that thing was, wow—that thing was awesome." His friends remember that it didn't take much to goad him into demonstrating what it could do. "You'd just kind of give him that, 'Come on, show me what you got, Mr. Racecar Driver,'" recalls Chris Cooper.

He'd turn donuts, run 110 mph down dark county roads, tailgate his buddies within millimeters, see how close he could get to bridge pylons before his passengers yelled uncle. "But when he drove, he wasn't, like, angry. He could just do it like it was nothing," says pal Bruce Pfeifer. "He's literally so laid-back that we'd be going through the neighborhood I live in, like nintey miles an hour everywhere, and he'd be asking, 'So, what've you guys been up to?' And we're like, 'Aaaahhh!'"

On one occasion, Cooper was driving Jeff to go play pickup basketball on an evening when the fog was so thick that the headlights reflected back into the car. "We're driving down the road and got the music going, and the next thing you know, we see this sign and bang! We go airborne. It seemed like *Dukes of Hazzard*. We hit a telephone pole, snapped it in two, and ricocheted into a line of trees.

"I bent the steering wheel over and hit the windshield, and I had a little cut on my head. And I look over, and I think, 'Oh my god.' Gordon's over there lying in the seat, this little itty-bitty fellow, and he's like, 'Ugh, ugh, ugh.' The windshield is just shattered, it's got a head imprint. His knees are cut, he's got blood running down his legs. There's smoke coming from everywhere. I'm thinking the car's going to blow up. So I go into panic mode, grab a hold of him, drag him across the car, and pull him out."

The local homeowners came running, followed by the cops, fire department, and paramedics. "We were both physically hurt—it was traumatic. So they're cleaning us up, and within three minutes, Jeff's like, 'Hey Coop, I'll see you later, man, I'm going to play basketball.' Brad Hawkins picked him up. I about kicked his ass. I told him later on, 'Man, you *must* be a racecar driver to get your ass out of the car and make a big show like that.'"

While Jeff participated in the usual high school pranks—painting abandoned barns with some less-than-savory slogans and helping to organize a twenty-five-car senior class automotive "parade," replete with a giant combine that backed up local traffic for miles—he avoided any serious trouble.

He was a typical high school student, albeit one who experienced an unusual number of absences on Fridays. He had a close-knit group of pals and a steady girlfriend. He played barn ball and basketball and was in the stands cheering at school football and basketball games. In

TOP: Jeff proudly displays some of his many trophies at home in Pittsboro, Indiana, 1988.

his senior year, he and his girlfriend were voted prom king and queen. Only his closest friends had any inkling how he spent his weekends.

"He never talked about it. Never wanted to talk about it," says high school friend Greg Waters, who frequently helped Jeff and John at the track. "He'd talk racing, but he'd never talk about how good he was. He was quiet. Laid-back. Real laid-back." At times, a teacher might make a comment about his racing in class, and on a few occasions, he spotted someone with Jeff Gordon Motorsports paraphernalia. "I remember him coming home one day," Carol says, "and he said he saw someone with one of his T-shirts at school. That pretty much blew him away, I think."

The line between his racing fame and his day-to-day life became thinner toward the end of his senior year. "That's when I won this race in Indiana, live on ESPN, and that's when it all kind of took off." Little in his life would be the same after that. "I have a great appreciation for friends who knew me before any of this really took off," he says. "I can just be myself and we can have regular conversations because we go back to those days . . . I think it's important to have friends in your life that think of you as just a regular person, because, really, that's all I am. That's all any of us are."

★　　★　　★

The win that changed the course of Jeff Gordon's young career did not come in Terry Winterbotham's No. 6 sprint car, nor did it come in the No. 16 sprint car with John. In fact, it didn't come in a sprint car at all. Rollie Helmling was a businessman who owned grocery stores and fielded a midget car race team. John, Jeff, and car builder Bob East attended the first race of the 1989 season at the Louisville Motor Speedway. Bob, who had recently set up Beast Chassis, near Indianapolis, wanted to talk with Helmling about selling him a car while John wanted to introduce Jeff to several of the team owners, including Helmling. "Rollie seemed pretty busy, so we just exchanged a quick handshake," Jeff recalls.

At that race, Helmling's driver was caught up in a wreck that destroyed their brand-new race car. With only three weeks before the ESPN-televised "Night Before the 500" race, held at what was then called Indianapolis Raceway Park, he was down a car and a driver. He told Bob he'd need a car from him and then asked if he had any thoughts about a driver. "Bob says, 'Well, what do you think about Jeff Gordon?'" Helmling recalls, forgetting he'd met Jeff briefly in Louisville. "I kind of took a breath and said, 'Isn't that that fourteen-year-old kid that's running sprint cars?'" East clarified that Jeff was now seventeen and urged Helmling to give the kid a shot. "So I called Jeff and we had a really good conversation," Helmling recalls. "The first thing I had to tell him was to quit calling me Mr. Helmling and call me Rollie. And when I talked to him, even at his young age, he was very good not to make any claims he couldn't back up and to convey a message that if he was given this opportunity, how much he'd appreciate it."

"Rollie was taking a huge risk," Jeff says. "I was a dirt sprint car driver who never raced on pavement, and this was, for him, the biggest event all year long. I was this unknown." They met a couple days later at Bob East's shop to see if they could hammer out a partnership. "Here's this little guy, very nice, very polite, and very much trying to look older than he was," Helmling recalls. "I was skeptical, and we weren't going to get any testing done, but I thought, 'Well, okay, let's give it a try.'"

TOP: Todd Osbourne, John Bickford, Jeff, and renowned sprint car builder Bob Trostle, Knoxville Raceway, Knoxville, Iowa, July 1987. BOTTOM: Jeff's No. 6 sprint car at Eldora Raceway, New Westin, Ohio, 1988.

Carol, who was visiting Kimberly at college, remembers Jeff calling her to give her the news. "I'll never forget getting that phone call from him. He was like 'Mom, I met this guy, he's got this car, he wants me to drive it, it's on asphalt, I've never been in a midget.' He's got all these emotions going on. And I said, 'Well what are you going to do?' He said, 'We're gonna do it. We don't know how it's going to turn out, but we're going to try.'"

When ESPN launched its *Thursday Night Thunder* racing series the previous year, it brought a whole new cache to short-track racing. John had seen the possibilities and had begun positioning Jeff toward an opportunity. "We were trying to race anything and everything, and that's how we found out about midget car races," Jeff remembers. "At the time, I was racing winged sprint cars on dirt, and none of that was on TV." USAC midgets, on the other hand, were the new television darling. So when Jeff wasn't behind the wheel, he and John would hit the midget races, glad-handing team owners, car builders, crew chiefs, anybody who might be able to help them and get their name into the mix. John knew at some point something would click. "You make your own luck," he says. "You create your own opportunities."

Getting a shot was one thing. Jeff still had to run the race, and do it in front of tens of thousands of television viewers. For a teenager who harbored dreams of a career in Indy car racing, the hunger to impress not only Rollie Helmling but scores of Indy fans was almost overwhelming.

"I'll never forget it," Helmling says of Jeff's reaction to the brand-new midget. "He was so impressed when I unloaded the car and he saw the side of it—it said 'Driver Jeff Gordon.' His eyes just lit up." Helmling got a few sidelong glances and snickers from associates at the track, but once his young driver got out and ran a few practice laps, he felt better. The car was fast, and Jeff seemed perfectly comfortable.

Sixty-one car-and-driver teams had shown up to qualify for the race. Stan Fox, Johnny Parsons—all the big-time teams were there. Jeff promptly went out and logged the fastest qualifying time, setting a track record. "I'm thinking things are looking pretty good," Helmling remembers. "But we've still got a race to run.

"Jeff was pretty nervous. . . . When he got in the car, I looked down, his knee is just bouncing up and down. And I told him, 'Just finish the race. When that checkered flag flies,

LEFT: Standing (left to right) Rollie Helmling, Terry Winterbotham, Jeff, John Bickford (Carol in the chair at the far left) preparing to race both the No. 4 midget car and the No. 6 sprint car. Lawrenceburg Speedway, Lawrenceburg, Indiana, 1989.

you drive under that checkered flag and finish the race. That's all I ask.'" Helmling says.

Because the race format inverted positioning of the twelve fastest cars, Jeff started out the fifty-lap race in twelfth position and quickly moved up to sixth, then fifth. "Then, pretty soon, he's third, then all of a sudden he's second, and he's coming and he just takes the lead and he just drives away," Helmling says. "I don't know who was the most surprised, Jeff, myself, or everybody that was there. But it was just amazing."

"Set a new track record, won the race, and just stomped them," Jeff recalls. "When I think back on that, it was like winning the Brickyard 400 for the first time. You just shake your head in amazement. This is Rollie Helmling and his car winning the biggest race—and who's this kid he hired? It was just, bam! Just unreal. And it was live on ESPN. All of a sudden, things started to change."

The win boosted Helmling's status and gave some visibility to Bob East's new chassis-building operation, but Jeff got more attention than he'd ever dreamed of. Racing folks were reaching out to congratulate him, talk about opportunities and his next TV race. People at the gas station recognized him and wished him luck. "It was so wild," Jeff says. "We weren't really aware *how much* TV could influence things. So we're like, we need to focus our attention on doing TV races." Helmling, who agreed to a longer-term partnership with Jeff and John on a handshake, was more than glad to oblige.

Two weeks before his big victory, Jeff graduated from high school, May 13, 1989, but he didn't hang around and party. "He just high-fived his buddies," John says, "jumped into the Suburban, and we hauled ass to Bloomington. He changed into his uniform at the track, and that was that." Racing was now his full-time job, and in addition to his midget deal with Helmling, Jeff was still trying to climb the ladder of sprint racing and put a little more cash in their pockets.

He continued performing well on the local level for the Winterbotham team, but in the summer of 1989, he got an offer from Stan Shoff, who ran one of the most respected operations in the Midwest, to pilot his No. 23 sprint in top-level USAC and World of Outlaws races. It was a deal he couldn't pass up. But as his pavement success blossomed, his fortunes in sprint dirt-track racing began to wilt. "We won some races, and I even qualified for the main event at Knoxville. Not an easy thing to do," Jeff recalls. "I was a good dirt sprint car driver, and on a local level I excelled. But when it came time to step up to the next level, especially at tracks I didn't know, I was mediocre. And I don't know if the pressure got to me, but I just started wrecking a lot of equipment."

Ultimately, Shoff would fire Jeff. It was the only time Jeff was fired by an owner, but it proved to be for the better. "Part of me was devastated," Jeff remembers, "but part of me was relieved because things were going so well for me on the pavement side of things—I was winning everything over there. The signs were on the wall, and by that happening, it really shifted more of my attention to the USAC pavement races on TV."

TOP LEFT: Jeff's graduation photo, 1989. TOP RIGHT: Jeff's Tri-West High School Diploma.

He finished up the season with Helmling on a high note, winning USAC's Midget Series Rookie of the Year award following a number of stellar performances on *Thursday Night Thunder.* "We just crushed it out of the park," Jeff says.

A future in Indy racing began to seem like a real possibility. He also realized that honing his image was as important as steering his car. John and Carol had been big on image since day one—you wear a polo shirt and khakis to the track, not some grease-stained rags. Speak intelligently. Act professionally. Sell yourself. But now, with TV cameras in his face, Jeff needed media skills.

John sat him down, and the two would examine televised races and the drivers' interviews. "We'd watch. 'What's that guy doing wrong? He's doing this, he's doing that.'" John remembers. "I was a relentless parent who was irritating the kid by making him pay attention."

Andy Graves, who now runs Toyota's NASCAR program, was then an eighteen-year-old car builder who moved in with the family to help John with the pavement sprint. "We were still teenagers," he remembers. "It would become frustrating at times for Jeff. He'd say, 'John is just on me all the time, he's dogging me about it.' But he always knew John was right. John's a very intelligent, very sharp man. He could see where the sport was headed."

It helped that the *Thursday Night Thunder* staff took to Jeff. "Jeff just had that quality, almost like a Sugar Ray Leonard or Ali, or even Isaiah Thomas, who had that shit-eating smile that just drives the other competitors crazy," *Thunder* producer Terry Lingner remembers. Commentator Dave Despain describes Jeff's look at race time: "The icy blue eyes, those cold blue eyes that were just totally focused and intense. He had that look in his eye that let you know he didn't care if the sun came up in a gunnysack."

Capitalizing on those qualities—the boyish charm coupled with that killer instinct—was the key to making entertainment. Jeff quickly became one of the show's featured stars, someone they'd go to for pre-race and post-race interviews, comments about track conditions, whatever else was needed. "ESPN host Larry Nuber, in particular, worked with Jeff early on to prime him for the spotlight. Along with Gary Lee," John says. "They'd help him understand what a storyboard is, understand the producer's job, the interviewer's job, the cameraman's job—then you're way better at being interviewed. And Jeff knows they're trying to create excitement."

TOP: Jeff racing Rollie Helmling's No. 4 midget car at the "Night Before the 500" at Indianapolis Raceway Park, Indianapolis, Indiana, 1989.

Naturally, he was creating excitement on the track as well. There was one driver, in particular, who was none too happy about it. At thirty-nine, Rich Vogler was a five-time USAC midget champion and two-time USAC sprint titlist who dominated the early stages of the *Thunder* series. "He wasn't very sophisticated," Lingner says. "He ruled with his right foot, and his right fist if he had to."

Throughout 1989 and early 1990, the two went at it on midget and sprint tracks. "The first year we competed against each other," Jeff recalls, "Rich and I kind of went back and forth on victories. But then I started getting the best of him, and you could tell it was affecting him," says Jeff. "Here's this kid coming in and giving Vogler all he could handle, but doing it in an 'aw shucks' way," Lingner says. "And man, creating that conflict and drama is what storytelling is all about. So we ran for all we were worth with that."

On the July 21, 1990, *Thunder* telecast, Vogler was leading Jeff going into the final lap of the sprint race at Salem Speedway. "He was driving so aggressive, like nothing was going to stop him from winning that race," Jeff recalls. Volger made contact with a lapped driver and lost control. His car sailed into the protective fencing and flipped back onto the track, losing its front axle and fuel tank and scattering debris everywhere. Vogler, whose helmet had popped off, was rushed to the hospital where he was pronounced dead of massive head injuries.

Jeff, John, and Carol were at a restaurant after the race when they got word. There had been a fatal accident in one of Jeff's quarter-midget races as a youngster, and John had seen more than his share of deathly wrecks in the sixties. Passing caskets never becomes easy, but they all knew that true racers learn to live with that fear buried deep in a corner of their mind. "There's danger in life," Carol says, "and if you just focus on all of that, you're not going to ever achieve anything. You can't just quit because a tragic accident happens."

"The week after Rich Vogler got killed," *Thunder*'s Lingner recalls, "we went and talked to the drivers, specifically Jeff. I thought it was going to spook this young kid . . . Heck, Jeff went out that next week and just smoked everybody. No problem."

A week after that, on the day he turned nineteen, he won the prestigious Midget Nationals in Belleville, Kansas, lapping all but the second-place car in what Helmling called the "most dynamic" race Jeff had ever run in a midget. "Jeff just had an innate, God-given ability to drive a race car," he says. It was also the richest race of the year. It paid $9,200 in cash—$2,200 for winning the preliminary race two nights earlier and $7,000 for the championship—and the team owner still recalls how uneasy he was walking around with that bounty.

"I've got ninety-two one-hundred-dollar bills in my pocket and I'm in the middle of this little fairground in a small town in Kansas," Helmling says, "I told Jeff, 'Get in the truck,' and he kind of looked at me funny. We get in, we lock the door, and I pull out this big wad of cash, and Jeff's eyes got pretty big. We always split the prize money, so we just started out—'one for me, one for you.'"

RIGHT: Jeff posing with his car after winning the 1990 Belleville Nationals.

BELLEVILLE MIDGET NATIONALS
1990 Belleville, Kansas 1990

That win, along with a repeat victory in the "Night Before the 500" and eight other checkers helped him earn that year's USAC Midget Series championship, making Jeff the youngest ever to capture the title. At the same time, he logged seven wins in the sprint car.

For years, a transition to Indy had been the natural pipeline, but the industry was changing. Big money was flooding in from well-funded foreign drivers, spawning a new buy-your-ride culture that left team owners far less eager to take chances on rookies with thin wallets. The earnings the family banked over the previous few seasons were light-years away from the going price—$2.5 to $5 million for a full season's ride.

There was the possibility of spending a couple seasons in a developmental series like Indy Lights, or there was Jackie Stewart's overture to run Formula 3 cars in Europe for a few years with the possibility of moving up to Formula 1. But neither option had any assurance. NASCAR was beginning to seem like a real option.

When Jeff visited the Grand Prix of Cleveland that summer, shopping himself to an Indy team, he trudged from hauler to hauler handing out his one-page bio and giving his pitch to anyone who would listen. He did manage a few fateful words with Al Unser Jr. and A.J. Foyt. Getting into Indy was going to be a long uphill battle, they told him, "You should go NASCAR racing."

John and Jeff didn't know a lot about stock cars. "I'm not so sure we didn't think 'Winston' was just some guy's name," John jokes. Nuber and Terry Lingner from *Thunder* covered the Winston Cup Series in addition to sprints and midgets. "When Jeff became the breakout guy," Lingner remembers, "the drivers would go to Larry and say, 'Don't let him get to Indy car.'" Humpy Wheeler, the NASCAR promoter and longtime president of Charlotte Motor Speedway, echoed that. "When I saw him drive that midget, I knew he had the ability," he recalls. "I said, this guy is going to make it big in NASCAR."

TOP LEFT: Jeff and his team celebrate his victory at the 1990 Belleville Nationals, one of the most spectacular races of his career. (left to right) John Bickford, Bert Dodd, George Tucker, Jeff Gordon, Trophy Girl, Rollie Helmling, and Lanny Gheridelli. TOP RIGHT: John embraces Jeff at the finish of the Belleville Midget Nationals, 1990.

TOP: A sticker commemorating the Hoosier Auto Racing Fans 1990 Driver of the Year Award for Jeff Gordon. BOTTOM: Jeff at Indianapolis Raceway Park, Indianapolis, Indiana, 1989. OPPOSITE TOP: A hero card commemorating highlights of Jeff's 1990 season, including the USAC National Midget Champion. OPPOSITE BOTTOM: Jeff (at far left) and the graduating class of Buck Baker's Driving School, 1990.

John knew he had to keep Jeff progressing and was willing to try anything. He and Nuber made a deal with Buck Baker, a former two-time NASCAR champion and the owner of a stock-car driving school in Rockingham, North Carolina. Jeff would come down and run their three-day program with an ESPN crew in tow, giving the school a bit of free publicity, in exchange for Baker waiving the $4,000 school fee.

Jeff flew down with Carol because he wasn't old enough to rent a car or hotel room. The only real worry he had, aside from the fact that the cars had manual transmissions, was that Baker wouldn't let him go as fast as he wanted. The first day on the track, he ran his first set of laps, and it was as if he was struck by a bolt of lightning. For Jeff, it had suddenly become clear what he was meant to do. Carol remembers him bursting into their hotel room that evening, breathless and wired. "This is what I'm going to do for the rest of my life," Jeff spit out.

It seemed everything had been leading to this. It didn't matter that a stock car was 3,400 pounds or that the thing took longer to accelerate or that it handled differently in the banked turns. "I felt like when I got in a stock car, this is what I've been training my whole life for," Jeff says. "It just suited me. It fit what I'd been doing. I liked the way it felt, and I liked what I felt I was capable of doing with that car."

Jeff drove the school's standard cars, which, from a power and performance standpoint, didn't quite measure up to the real deal. Hugh Connerty, a property developer and aspiring racer who kept his Busch-ready car at the school, was at the track and noticed the young hotshot driver. At Baker's urging, Connerty offered to let Jeff take his car out for a run. Connerty took the car out for some hard laps first to shake off the cobwebs. Then Jeff climbed in. On the mile-and-a-sixteenth track, he bested Connerty's time by almost a second-and-a-half. They were astonished. Then he climbed out and accurately diagnosed the car's shortcomings, pointing out everything they could do to make it faster. It was only his second day in a stock car.

Jeff arrived for his final day with all the self-assurance and satisfaction of someone who had found his calling. He wasn't sure how they were going to crack into the stock-car world, but he knew it was the place he had to be. Connerty invited Jeff to lunch. "He says, 'You know, I realize now that I don't need to be driving this car. You need to be driving this car. What do you think about that?'" Jeff beamed.

He hopped in his rental car and sped back to the hotel to give Carol the news. "I was just trying to slow him down," Carol remembers, "because, you know, people will tell you a lot of things, but whether they're ever able to come through, that's another story." It didn't matter to Jeff. He grabbed his mom, rushed her back to the track, and introduced her to everyone.

In Carol's eyes, Hugh Connerty, whose father-in-law happened to be Winston Cup team owner Leo Jackson, may have been promising them the moon, but he delivered it. "Hugh basically hired Jeff on the spot," John says. "Just said, 'Well, let's do a three-race deal and we're going to the Busch Grand National races. We'll put a team together and get some races in this year.' And that's exactly what he did."

Suddenly, after all the travel, money worries, time spent bent over cars, handshakes, hours at the track hunting down every potential opportunity, they were realizing a dream that had been born all those nights ago on a weed-strewn patch of fairground pavement in California. "All the right dominoes were falling at the right time," John recalls.

DIET PEPSI
ONE CALORIE

Diet Pepsi Racing Team
Jeff Gordon, Driver

1990 WINNER
* Night Before The 500
* Belleville Midget Nationals
* Hut Hundred

LINA MOTOR SPEEDWAY

4

MR. HENDRICK WANTS TO MEET YOU!

RAY EVERNHAM WAS AT HOME IN New Jersey in September 1990 when he got a call from his friend Andy Petree asking if he'd be willing to head south to be the crew chief of a NASCAR Busch Grand National race team. Petree, the crew chief for the No. 33 Winston Cup car driven by Harry Gant and owned by Leo Jackson, explained that Jackson's son-in-law had just hired a kid to run the last few races of the season. Petree was trying to do Jackson a favor by getting the Busch car ready and throwing together a crew. He'd already nabbed Phil and Steve Barkdoll to set the car up, and they mentioned Evernham might be available. Would he be interested?

"Who's the kid?" Evernham asked.

"Jeff Gordon," Petree told him.

Evernham smiled to himself. This was going to be good.

The thirty-three-year-old Evernham made something of a name for himself as a racer, running open-wheel modifieds around his native Northeast, but his reputation rested more on his mechanical know-how and technical ingenuity. To those who knew him, he was a mad scientist in the garage. "I was very interested, largely because Jeff was the guy everybody was talking about in the short track," Evernham says. "He was beating the veterans, and he was just fast, man. He jumped in several different cars and he was just fast."

Evernham was soon in Hendersonville, North Carolina. He arranged to sit down at a local hotel with Jeff and Carol, who had just arrived from Pittsboro, to introduce himself. When they met in the lobby, the lanky, six-foot Evernham was instantly struck by how small Jeff was. He also had to stifle a chuckle when he noticed the nineteen-year-old was carrying a briefcase, just like he was. "I had my notepads and my books and my notes for the Charlotte track, all those things," Evernham says. And in Jeff's briefcase? "I think he had some gum, a Game Boy, a stock-car magazine, he had peanuts. It was kind of funny." The two hit it off. "You want to

OPPOSITE: Jeff proudly standing next to his No. 1 Baby Ruth Ford, 1992.

51

work with people who are really excited to do things, and Jeff was," he says. "So I think we celebrated by taking his mom to Hooters."

The next day, they rolled Hugh Connerty's No. 67 Outback Steakhouse Pontiac onto the speedway at Charlotte. It was an open-practice day, and several other Busch competitors were running the track, including Davey Allison and Chuck Bown, who would go on to claim the series championship that year. It had taken some finagling to even get Jeff a practice spot, as raw and untested and potentially dangerous as he was. It would be his first time in a stock car since Buck Baker's school.

"I was doing okay, but I wasn't doing great," he says. "I was off the pace a little bit. And Ray went over to Chuck Bown and said, 'Jeff's having some issues in Turn 3. Can you help him out and get in the car and make some laps?' So Chuck agreed and got in and went three- or four-tenths of a second faster than I did. I didn't know the car was capable of going that fast. He came in and said, 'Nope, y'all, the car's really good.' So I got in and then I went three- or four-tenths faster than he did. As soon as I knew the car could go that fast and that I could push it that hard, I was like, 'All right, we're good.'"

Jeff continued to get faster all day, and by the time the practice was over, he was second in time only to Davey Allison. His speed was impressive, but what impressed Evernham even more was the way Jeff could break down what was happening with the car and the track and translate it to him with a clarity and precision that made it simple to see what adjustments were necessary. "At IROC, I'd worked with the greatest drivers," Evernham says, referring to the International Race of Champions. "And there's something those guys have when they communicate with you. . . . And that first day I worked with Jeff, I just realized he communicated at that level. When somebody is that young, it can't be experience, so it's just got to be natural ability and instinct. I knew he was a special kid."

For his part, Jeff was thrilled that Evernham was receptive to his feedback. "I mean, I didn't know anything about these cars, and he was willing to take input from me," he says. "It was similar to the way John and I worked together." In many ways, Evernham was a version of John. There was the same intensity, the same natural intelligence and wide-ranging technical expertise, and the same obsessive work ethic.

TOP: Jeff behind the wheel of the Hugh Connerty–owned No. 67 Outback Steakhouse Pontiac, 1990.

John himself wasn't there to meet Evernham—he'd stayed behind in Indiana to work on Jeff's sprint car for an upcoming race. "Jeff called me that night after the practice and he said, 'You're not going to believe this guy. He never stops working on the car, ever. He's even working on the car in his mind when he goes back to the hotel. He's constantly working to make the car better.' And he told me how organized Ray was, and I said, 'Really? He takes notes?' Jeff said, 'Yep, takes notes, writes everything down. He's just like you!' And I said, 'Well, I'm sorry to hear that,' and we laughed. So I pretty much knew Ray was the right guy before I ever actually shook his hand."

It certainly set John's mind at ease. The upcoming Busch races would be the first time in fifteen years Jeff would compete without any of John's input or hands-on help. He'd be just another guy standing in the infield and watching the cars whiz by. Which is exactly where he and Carol were on October 20 when Jeff climbed into the Outback Steakhouse No. 67 for the AC-Delco 200 at North Carolina Speedway (now Rockingham).

Jeff's first attempt at a Busch race, two weeks earlier in Charlotte, had been a bust. Rain washed out individual qualifying races, thus starting positions were allotted based on drivers' point standings. Jeff's goose egg meant he was forced into a short hooligan race in which the top finishers qualified for the main event. Running well after several laps, he collided with Randy Baker—ironically, his former instructor at the Buck Baker driving school—spun out, and hit the wall. And as quickly as that, their day was done.

It was a disappointment, but they still had two races. The team kept their spirits up and fingers crossed for Rockingham, and they got more than any of them bargained for. Jeff went out and logged the second-fastest qualifying time, beating thirty-eight other racers, including Winston Cup regulars like Dale Earnhardt, Davey Allison, Dale Jarrett, and Darrell Waltrip. In his first-ever NASCAR race, he would be starting on the outside of the front row. "That impressed a lot of people," Jeff remembers. "People who had never heard of me were now, all of sudden, going 'Oh, who's that kid?'"

His mom wasn't nearly as excited. "I was extremely worried," Carol recalls. "I wanted him to start in the back for all the reasons you can imagine. . . . The mother in me was, like, 'Maybe

LEFT: The No. 67 Outback Steakhouse Pontiac, Winston Classic promotional card, 1990.

they'll just be really nice and let him start in the back because he's new and it's his first race.' So that was very nerve-wracking for me."

In practice, Jeff told the crew he wanted his car loose so it would turn easier. Once the race started, he knew the adjustments backfired. His Pontiac needed to be tighter. He began the race in front, catty-corner to Earnhardt, and just in front of Bobby Labonte. He got too free, sliding into the outside wall on the thirty-third lap, giving him a thirty-ninth place finish. The team pocketed a paltry four hundred dollars, but they all saw the performance as a victory. Evernham, the Barkdolls, and the rest of the crew proved they could deliver a car that could run with the best of them, and Jeff showed he could compete.

The final race at Martinsville was a bookend to the first, with qualifying canceled due to rain and another hooligan race that ended with a busted crankshaft. Any hopes that Hugh Connerty would carry the program over into the 1991 season ended with the Iraq War. There wasn't a sponsor willing to part with a nickel in the face of an uncertain economic future. Without any great fanfare, the Outback Steakhouse team members shuffled back to their corners. Evernham returned to Jersey, and Jeff made the trip back to Indiana to finish out the last few events of his midget and sprint seasons.

★   ★   ★

It's tempting to ponder what might have been if certain shots had been missed or chance meetings had not occurred. So goes the story with Jeff Gordon's early career. Through a mixture of prodigious talent, hard work, timing, and luck, the right things seemed to happen.

Lee Morse, the manager of performance operations for Ford's racing division—the man responsible for scouting new talent—witnessed Jeff's startling qualifying run at Rockingham. Morse had heard Jeff's name from Larry Nuber, the former *Thursday Night Thunder* host. He heard it from others, too. *Watch this kid. He's going to be something.*

He agreed to meet with Jeff at the close of the Busch season. In late fall, Jeff, John, and Larry Nuber arrived at Morse's office in Dearborn, Michigan, armed with a videotape Nuber had helped produce chronicling Jeff's fifteen years in racing. "I took them to my director's office, Mike Kranefuss . . . We sat down and watched the video," Morse recalls. "It was a very, very well-done video, and I remember thinking at the time that it was very impressive. I had nothing at that time to offer them. But I had met Jeff and was impressed with what I saw. And it wasn't too much longer after that meeting that I learned that [driver] Mark Martin was wanting to move on and do his own program, so that left an opening in the Carolina Ford Dealers–sponsored Bill Davis Busch Grand National team."

The meeting in Michigan had sold Morse on Jeff Gordon, but convincing owner Bill Davis and the Carolina Ford Dealers organization to take a gamble on a teenage unknown with only thirty-three laps under his belt wasn't going to be easy.

Davis received a slew of calls from "countless people we'd never heard of, as well as people we were flattered to hear from," all looking to plant themselves in Martin's seat. Financially, he'd just rolled the dice by relocating his shop from his home in Batesville, Arkansas, to Thomasville, North Carolina, to be closer to the NASCAR campfire. He and his wife, Gail,

TOP: Jeff's first NASCAR competitor license.

were running their race program pretty bare bones. Ideally, what they needed in their car was a proven entity, but Morse was determined. He continued to talk up Jeff's potential, hinted at a bit more factory assistance, and offered to help by kicking in some extra cash to boost the Carolina Ford Dealers sponsorship.

"Ford came full bore. They wanted us to do it," Davis recalls. "They offered us what was probably a little bit better deal than we had. It wasn't any big money. . . . But hey, it was something. And it was a manufacturer at least." Ultimately, Davis told Morse they were keen but, naturally, couldn't invest in merchandise sight unseen; they set up a test in the No. 1 Ford at Rockingham that would include Jeff and two other drivers.

"I talked to Lee Morse," Jeff remembers, "and he said, 'We got an opportunity. We got this team that Mark Martin currently drives for and they're interested in you coming and testing for them.' And I was like, 'You better believe it. I'm there, man.' I didn't have anything else. That was it. I went to Rockingham and tested for Bill Davis in December or January—I remember it was cold as can be—and I was superfast, made great laps. They were impressed."

On that test performance, Davis decided to take the plunge, but it wasn't without some lingering trepidation. "Jeff really was a nobody," he recalls. "[Team owners] were pretty jaded—they weren't interested in some pretty boy from California that was driving open-wheel cars. . . . We took one of the very first big chances on a really, really young, totally unproven kid."

All that was left to do was sign on the dotted line. Bill and Gail Davis made the trek to Pittsboro to finalize the deal. The Davises were small-town Dixie through and through, used to dealing with Southerners in business and racing. Gail remembers a touch of apprehension about how the California couple might come across. Carol and John put them up in Jeff's bedroom and took them to dinner at Frank & Mary's Tavern, the legendary Pittsboro catfish joint and racer hangout. While Jeff periodically bowed his head to fiddle with his Game Boy, they hammered out a deal. Ultimately, they agreed to a year contract with a guarantee of at least fifteen races, the minimum needed to qualify for Rookie of the Year. Jeff wouldn't draw a salary—an unusual move in NASCAR racing—but he would earn half of whatever the car made.

Both sides came away from the meeting eager for the upcoming season. Those couple of days had also given the Davises an opportunity to get to know their future driver a bit better. Both Gail and Bill were smitten. "He was very, very cute," she says. "I mean, he was just darling."

Busch Grand Nationals meant Jeff was taking a step closer to his dream of someday competing at stock-car racing's highest level, but it also meant a move to North Carolina. At nineteen, he had never lived apart from Carol and John. "You bring up your kids to be self-sufficient, independent thinkers and doers, and that's what we did with Jeff," Carol says. "We did the education and we were sending him off. We were always going to be there to give advice and help out, but he needed to be doing stuff. Jeff needed to be an independent person."

LEFT: Nineteen-year-old Jeff behind the wheel of the No. 1 Carolina Ford Dealers Ford.

TOP: Jeff at top speed in the Fred Ede–owned No. 4 Silver Crown car, 1991.

His buddy Andy Graves, who had lived with the family for much of 1990, had taken a job in the chassis-building division at Hendrick Motorsports, which ran two teams in the Winston Cup. Jeff and Andy decided to share an apartment in North Charlotte.

On the track, Jeff seemed to have something diabolical in him. Two weeks before the Busch season started, he reeled off a major victory in Phoenix in a Silver Crown car owned by California-based Fred Ede, for whom he would race the entire 1991 season. And while he failed to qualify for the Busch season's first race at Daytona—the car was simply too slow, he said—he gradually began to find his footing. By his sixth race, in April at Darlington, he logged his first top-ten finish. He followed that up two weeks later with a second-place finish at Lanier, in Georgia, and then a fifth place fourteen days later at Nazareth, Pennsylvania. Three weeks after that, he finished second again at Dover.

Jeff clearly had the skills. To Rollie Helmling, his midget team owner, it was his ability "to control his emotions and instinctively make the best decisions." ESPN's Terry Lingner cited his penchant for keeping his momentum while carving through traffic. For race commentator Dave Despain, Jeff's calling card was his ability to gauge the evolving situation on the track, stalk, and make passes in half the time it took any other driver. Humpy Wheeler said that even then, Jeff was one of the best loose racecar drivers he'd ever seen. There was one thing nobody would deny: Jeff was fast. "He was a Tasmanian devil in disguise," says Wheeler. "He didn't look it. He didn't act it. But good lord, when that flag dropped, he became a different human being. It was almost like he was shot out of a damn cannon."

That speed would sometimes get the better of him. In all, Jeff would damage the No. 1 Carolina Ford Dealers' car seventeen times in the first season. "If you're going fast, you're going fast," Bill Davis says philosophically. "They're just cars. You fix them." Gail felt the same way. "He had to learn someplace. But he was fast, and we liked him. He was getting lots of attention."

He was getting plenty of attention off the Busch circuit, too, running Silver Crown cars—which are slightly larger than midgets—for Ede, as well as USAC midgets for Helmling, sprints for John, and he was still a major player on the ESPN *Thunder* series. It all made for some dizzying back-and-forth travel. On Friday, May 24, 1991, he flew into Indiana from Charlotte, won the Holman Trophy in a nighttime Silver Crown race at Indianapolis Fairgrounds, then flew back to North Carolina the same night, arriving at his apartment at 4:00 a.m. for a few quick winks before showing up bleary-eyed at Charlotte Motor Speedway at 9:00 a.m. for his noontime Busch race, in which he finished a disappointing eighteenth. Then it was a helicopter trip back to the airport and a 4:20 p.m. return flight to Indianapolis to make it in time for the "Night Before the 500" midget event, in which the two-time defending champion finished second. ESPN jokingly christened him "Air Gordon."

It was also the year he made his legendary two-wheeled pass in a midget race. He came together wheel to wheel at full speed with another racer, his car popped up on its two left-side tires, and he still managed to make the pass. "Just jaw-dropping," says Dave Despain. "Like, 'Oh my God, did you see that?'" Producer Terry Lingner recalls the ESPN announcers, Larry Rice and Gary Lee, "peeing their pants" with excitement. "They were just both shouting at the top of their lungs. It was awesome. That was an incredible moment."

Jeff wasn't just racing on all these different circuits—he was earning pay from each as well. But his facility with a checkbook was about as good as dirt. "I'd make trips down there for races," Carol recalls, "and I'd ask him, 'Hey, did anybody pay you lately?' And he'd go, 'Oh,

yeah, I think I might have a few checks in my helmet bag.' Wonderful. He probably still has some checks that never did get cashed."

"I like cash," Jeff admits. "Cash is always better. For whatever reason, you hand me cash, I can keep track of that. You hand me a piece of paper with a number on it, I seem to lose it." Even when he did have cash in hand, he didn't spend much. "He was the most frugal guy you'll ever meet," John says. "If he'd get carried away, he might buy a really nice pair of tennis shoes." And once in a while, he'd treat his friends to a little bit of fun.

Childhood friend Rod Sherry remembers Jeff showing up out of the blue after a midget race in California, carrying his brown briefcase. "I was like, 'Dude, why are you carrying a briefcase?' I mean, we were like eighteen. And I remember him opening it up, and he had some random stuff and like a fistful of cash in it. I was broke. I mean, I was living off Top Ramen and frozen burritos. So we found someone to buy us a case or two of beer." The party of two grew into a party of half a dozen.

Bill Armour, who handled marketing and PR duties for Bill Davis, says, "There were times I forgot he was nineteen until we'd be somewhere on a media tour or something and Jeff would say, 'There's a mall. Let's go to the arcade,' and then he would play arcade games for two hours. And I'd just think, 'Okay, well.'"

But when he was behind the wheel, the frivolity dissipated. By the end of June, after sixteen Busch Series races, Jeff had seven top-ten finishes and four top fives, including three second-place finishes, and he had captured his first pole at Orange County, North Carolina. But the summer was not kind. Over the next eight weekends, he registered only one top ten, a third-place finish at Bristol. The day before his twentieth birthday, at his home track of Indianapolis Raceway Park, he finished eighteenth. Sometimes the issues were driver related, and sometimes they were mechanical, but the team hung in.

"The 1991 season was not instantly successful," Lee Morse remembers, "but I kept the interest going with the Carolina Ford Dealers. They'd been used to having Mark Martin in their car, and Mark won a lot of Busch races for them. Now they were taking a chance on a new young fellow. I kept asking them to be patient and it would pay dividends."

Winning or losing, Jeff approached his work like a consummate professional. Veteran racer Dave Dion remembers Jeff's first attempt at Oxford Plains, in Maine. "He asked a lot of

TOP LEFT: Pulling into the winner's circle at the Holman Hundred, a hundred-mile dirt track race at the Indiana State Fairgrounds, 1991. TOP RIGHT: Jeff celebrating his Holman Hundred victory with the race promoter and Indy Car racing legend A.J. Foyt.

questions about the track, and he didn't do well the first day in qualifying. The next day, he came back and said, 'If you are willing to talk again, I'm willing to listen.' You could tell right then he was going to be a heck of a driver."

It was something a lot of people in the racing community saw. Jeff was a brilliant but raw talent who was willing to learn—he just needed some miles and molding. Cale Yarborough, the retired three-time Winston Cup champion, had been running his own Cup team since 1987. Midway through the 1991 season, he'd already fired Dick Trickle and Lake Speed and was looking for another driver to help lift the struggling program. He reached out to Jeff.

"I had a conversation with Cale, and I went and tested for him," Jeff recalls. It was Jeff's first-ever experience in a Cup car, and Yarborough was impressed enough that he asked Jeff to finish out the Cup season then and there. "I turned him down," Jeff says. "Partially it was because of Bill Davis."

"Bill was really pissed that Jeff had tested for Yarborough," John recalls. "I remember him saying, 'Don't do it for some team that's fading and pulling at straws. If you're going to do it, do it.'"

"And he was right," Jeff says.

The Yarborough test made it clear to Jeff that he still needed a bit more minor-league experience. To Bill Davis, it became clear that if he had any intention of creating a long-term future with Jeff Gordon, he was going to have to figure out a way to get to the Winston Cup himself.

Jeff came back from the three-week Busch series break a little heavier in the pocket, having won a $10,000 midget feature at Eldora Speedway in Ohio, and ready to gun for the Busch Series Rookie of the Year award. Despite his uneven showing so far, he was still in the running with four races remaining, but with subsequent finishes of thirty-fifth, nineteenth, and thirty-seventh, the prize seemed to be slipping from his grasp. And then bad news: Davis had no cars left. With Jeff's wreck in the second-to-last race on October 19, there was no way the team could have a ride set up for the October 27 finale at Martinsville.

As fate would have it, Bobby Labonte, a good friend and neighbor of Bill Davis who would win the Busch Series championship that year, happened to have an extra car. There

RIGHT: Jeff races door-to-door in the No. 1 Baby Ruth Ford.

was one catch: it was an Oldsmobile. The irony of a Ford Motor Company driver winning a major NASCAR award with the help of a General Motors car was not lost on Lee Morse, but in the end the Ford executive reasoned that any criticism would be outweighed by the prestige of Ford having a new Rookie of the Year.

Now all Jeff had to do was go out and get it. His eighth-place finish in Labonte's car kept him just ahead of David Green, who finished twenty-fifth, to clinch the rookie title. Between all the Busch racing, Jeff also managed to capture the 1991 USAC Silver Crown championship, becoming the youngest driver to ever win that title. For the second year running, he was named to the Auto Racing Writers and Broadcasters Association All-American Team.

It became clear the gamble by Ford, Davis, and the Carolina Ford Dealers had paid off. While he hadn't won a race, Jeff notched three runner-up finishes among his five top-fives, and he'd taken the checkered flag in the top ten in a full one-third of his races. Credit was due to the Davises, who for the first time ran a full schedule of thirty races in the Busch Series with a sponsorship that covered only about half that load. Bill Davis, his co-crew chief and engine builder Keith Simmons, and the rest of the team had poured their heart into the season, and Jeff's overall eleventh-place finish was reason to smile. The outlook couldn't have been better for 1992.

"Bill was great. He was super nice," Jeff remembers. "I liked Bill a lot, and I loved driving for him." Bill Davis, like Rollie Helmling, found himself developing a sincere fondness for this smart, unpretentious youngster. "Oh, he was a good kid. We had a great relationship. It was a whole lot more than just a car-owner and driver relationship," Davis says. "We loved him to death. . . . He was refreshing. He was funny. He was witty. He was sensible, had his head on straight. Never screwed anything up the whole time. And I knew that we had something we could build on."

★   ★   ★

The off-season brought some changes. For one, Jeff bought a house—or a third of one. Along with Andy Graves and Graves's childhood friend Bob Lutz, whose father owned some dirt tracks in upstate New York, Jeff put a down payment on a home in Withrow Downs, near Charlotte Motor Speedway. "We thought he was crazy," says Carol, who admits she was surprised her son even qualified for a loan. "We were like, 'You can't do that. That's a lot of responsibility, owning a house.' But I was actually quite proud of him for doing that at that age."

The other change was that John and Jeff negotiated a new Busch Series contract with Bill Davis. According to Davis, it was John who requested a contract. John recalls simply being sent a "Roush contract"—Jack Roush ran a Ford-affiliated team in the Winston Cup—"all Roush wording, with Bill Davis's name at the top of it."

"So I read through this big, long contract," John remembers, "and I called my friend Cary Agajanian," the attorney who had been instrumental in helping Jeff gain partial emancipation as a teen. "I'm not sure we really want to sign this thing," John told him, "but we don't have anything else."

Over the phone, they combed through the document and made several edits. The contract contained a clause allowing the team owner, at the end of one year, to either terminate the contract or renew it for an additional two years. According to Agajanian, it was not unusual in racing, but in what the lawyer today calls "the seminal legal moment in Jeff Gordon's career,"

TOP: Jeff, in his Carolina Ford Dealers firesuit, contemplates an upcoming race, 1991.

he and John inserted language that put Jeff on equal footing with Davis, allowing him the same discretion to terminate the contract at the end of a year.

At the time, it seemed like a trifle—they'd just finished a promising rookie season and were flush with good feelings. Bill Davis agreed to the alteration, along with a continuation of the fifty-fifty split. It wasn't long before that small change took on a much larger significance.

Bill Davis Racing started the 1992 season with new optimism and a new part-time sponsor, Baby Ruth, but they still weren't able to swallow Daytona. Just as in 1991, the team failed to qualify, but this time, Jeff snuck into the race on a "provisional"—a spot for non-qualifying racers who finished well in the previous season's point standings. Starting forty-fourth among forty-four cars, he completed 102 of 120 laps before engine problems ended his run. He finished twenty-third.

The opening-day disappointment was tempered by some encouraging news. "All through 1991, I was thinking to myself, Jeff needs Ray," John remembers. "He's the guy that could help this program." But during that first Busch season, not only did Bill Davis not need a new crew chief, but Evernham was racing modifieds on the East Coast. Midway through the modified season, Evernham was involved in a hard wreck. When he awoke the following day, doctors told him he had sustained a brain-stem injury. Although Evernham would compete six weeks later, winning his first race back, he realized he had probably taken his final checker. In December, he was offered a job crewing for Winston Cup racer Alan Kulwicki, and he took it. During qualifying for the Daytona 500, the headstrong Evernham and Kulwicki locked horns, and the two unceremoniously parted ways. Over time, John and Davis maintain different versions of what happened next.

John recalls that Davis didn't want to bring Evernham on, but John felt that if he could get Ford to cover half of Evernham's $50,000 salary, he would cover the other half. Davis remembers Evernham coming by to say good-bye, and thinking that if they could work out a deal with Ford for half his salary, they could hire him on. "Long story short, I agreed to pay Ray's salary through the race team to bring Ray on board as crew chief," Lee Morse says.

TOP: Jeff's No. 1 Baby Ruth Ford being worked on at Darlington Raceway, Darlington, South Carolina, 1992.

"And in my opinion, that certainly helped Jeff's 1992 season turn out to be as successful as it was in that Baby Ruth car."

Keith Simmons stayed on as the engine builder, and Evernham took over the crew-chiefing duties. "Ray and I, we immediately had that line of communication and rapport. It started very quickly," Jeff says. The results came equally as quick. Following Daytona, they won the pole at Rockingham and finished ninth. The next week, at Richmond, they qualified first again and finished eighth. One week later, in the Atlanta 300, they got their third consecutive pole position, and Jeff, after thirty-five races, finally broke through with his first Busch Series win in a dramatic, drive-the-wheels-off performance.

Bill Davis was thrilled. This was a team that had the potential to jump to the next level. "We wanted to go Cup racing," he says. "That was our plan." They were only four races into a thirty-one-race season, but the feelers were out there for potential 1993 Cup sponsors. The Atlanta race was pivotal for another reason. Andy Graves's employer, Rick Hendrick, happened to be at the speedway for a sponsor appearance ahead of the next day's Winston Cup race in which his two teams—the No. 5 Chevrolet of Ricky Rudd and the No. 25 Chevrolet of Ken Schrader—would be competing. He stopped momentarily to clock the action near Turn 4, just as Jeff came flying into the corner, smoke rolling off his tires. Hendrick recalls waiting for the wreck he was sure would follow, but it never came. Again and again Jeff came charging through that turn, right up against the wall, so loose he was nearly sideways, but he somehow never lost momentum.

"I saw his car control and his ability to drive over the edge and maintain control, and how fast he was," Hendrick recalls. "He was one of the best I'd ever seen. His God-given talent and hand-eye coordination was unreal. . . . I said this is a once-in-a-lifetime opportunity. I just felt this was my chance to have a Michael Jordan, to have a Larry Bird. It's like you own an NBA team or an NFL team and you just saw one of the most impressive quarterbacks you've ever seen in college football and you've got a chance to get him. You better get him now."

The North Carolina–based car-dealership mogul knew Jeff Gordon was the complete package. He was so convinced that, having never met the kid, he was prepared to build a new third team around him and run it out of his own pocket if necessary.

Back in the shop that Monday, Hendrick met with his organization's general manager, Jimmy Johnson, to explore the possibilities. When they heard that Andy Graves, then a crew member on Ricky Rudd's car, was Jeff's housemate, they called him to the office. "Jimmy and Rick were sitting in Jimmy's office," Graves remembers, "and evidently Rick was talking about Jeff. He said to me, 'It's a shame Jeff Gordon has a contract with Ford because I'd like to start a team for him.' I said, 'He doesn't have a contract.'"

★   ★   ★

In Winston Cup racing during the early 1990s, Hendrick Motorsports was among

TOP: Jeff and Bill Davis embrace in Victory Lane following his first Busch win at the Atlanta 300 Busch Series event at Atlanta Motor Speedway, March 14, 1992. LEFT: Jeff and the Davises happily pose with the first-place trophy following Jeff's first Busch victory, Atlanta Motor Speedway, 1992.

CLOCKWISE FROM TOP: A collection of Jeff Gordon Busch Series trading cards; An article from the *Evansville Press* paper announcing Jeff had signed with Rick Hendrick, Evansville, Indiana, June 3, 1992; Jeff racing the No. 1 Carolina Ford Dealers Ford.

Gordon looks like stock car racing's budding superstar

By Jim McLaurin
Knight-Ridder News Service

COLUMBIA, S.C. — If Jeff Gordon showed up on your doorstep one spring evening and asked if your daughter were ready to go to the prom, your first thought would be, "Is he old enough to drive?"

If he pulled beside you in an auto race, you wouldn't have time to ask.

"I was looking at the bumper of one of the best NASCAR drivers there is," Gordon said recently. "I was working as hard as I could to get by Dale Earnhardt. I didn't care how fast he was running. I wanted to run faster because he had come up to me the day before and said, 'Boy, you got your car running 32.50s consistently?' I said, 'No.' He said, 'You'd better, because I'm gonna run your butt down and blow you away.' "

Gordon allowed himself a half smile. "When I passed him," he said, "I waved."

The press box at Charlotte Motor Speedway erupted in a combination of laughter and applause. It's not often you get to see a five-time Winston Cup champion taken down a peg by a 20-year-old novice. It's rarer still you get to see a star being born.

Jeff Gordon could be the next great stock car racer. The duel with Earnhardt during the Champion 300 Busch Grand National race at Charlotte, N.C., on May 25, was mere byplay. Coming into the third turn on the 162nd lap of the 200-lap race, Gordon was trailing leader Dick Trickle and the lapped car of Phil Parsons.

Trickle, a 50-year-old champion of Midwestern short-track racing, wasn't about to get snookered, but he did.

"Dick was running strong," Gordon said. "I knew he was going to be hard to pass in the open, that I'd have to use a lapped car (as a pick). I was trying to run him as hard as I could and make him slip. Finally, he did, and I got underneath him."

Gordon got around Trickle as the two banged their way to the finish line. He took home the biggest winner's share in Grand National history — $113,844 — under a caution flag when Trickle and Todd Bodine wiped each other out fighting for second place with one lap to go.

Bill Davis "discovered" Gordon a couple of years ago driving on the open-wheeled USAC circuit. If it's possible to be a legend so young, Gordon was already one. The Pittsboro, Ind., resident had moved from his native California to the heartland of the nation so he could reach more races.

Gordon began racing when he was 6. He won three national quarter-midget championship, four national go-kart class crowns, the 1990 USAC national Midget Series title, and the 1991 USAC Silver Crown division national championship.

Also in 1991, Davis signed him on to drive his car on the Grand National circuit and he won the rookie of the year title.

Davis and Ford Motor Co. had pegged Gordon as a future superstar, and spent a lot of money on him. Two weeks ago, Gordon announced he would be driving a Chevrolet on the Winston Cup circuit next year for owner Rick Hendrick.

Davis was bitter, because he also lost crew chief Ray Everham, who also signed on with Hendrick. Accusations that Hendrick lured Ford's superstar away with a big up-front bonus and a multi-year deal were fired off; caught in the middle was this kid. Gordon admitted that if he had it to do over, he'd have handled it differently.

"I knew I was going to pay for what happened," he said. "But I felt I had to make the decision right now."

Hendrick's offer was too good to turn down. There was no "signing bonus," Gordon said, but it was a multi-year deal.

"It's a contract that means I'm going to be in Winston Cup racing for at least three or four years," he said. "All we can do is wait and see if I've made a good decision.

"I think everybody knows I'm here to race, but I'm also here to learn. Going into Winston Cup next year is another step and I'll be starting all over again, just like last year when I got into Grand National."

Gordon spent a troublesome season last year with no wins in his first season on the stock car circuit, even going back to open-wheel on occasion "just to remember what it was like to win," he said.

"The biggest thing was moving from a 1,400-pound car with 700-800 horsepower to a 3,200-pound car with 500 horsepower. Next year I'll be going to 3,500-pound cars with more horsepower."

Winston Cup racing is Gordon's ultimate step. But "the money is just a bonus," he said. "I want to be in Dale Earnhardt's shoes, Richard Petty's shoes. I want to be over in that garage and be successful for a long time. That's what it's all about."

And maybe wave goodbye to Earnhardt a couple more times, someone asked?

"I don't know," Gordon said. "Next year, he'll probably be waving at me."

a handful of powerful, resource-rich multicar teams. Launched in 1984, Hendrick didn't have a championship plaque on the wall yet, but they were a modern, well-funded, technologically aggressive operation that was knocking on the door. Tim Richmond, the colorful and bombastic playboy and Hendrick driver on whose life the movie *Days of Thunder* was loosely based, finished third in the Winston Cup standings in 1986.

It was in part Richmond's legacy that drove Hendrick's decision to pursue Jeff. "I've always liked an aggressive driver and a driver that had unbelievable car control. Tim Richmond was that kind of guy. When I used to watch Tim race and watch him make moves that I couldn't believe, I was so excited. And when I lost that and I saw Jeff come along, I thought, here's a guy with the same, maybe more, talent, and young. He can be the future of our company."

Jeff had heard a thing or two about Hendrick cars, the operation, and the facilities during evening conversations with Graves—all of it was "top-notch." So when Graves arrived home after the meeting and told Jeff that Rick Hendrick was interested in having him drive and had personally requested a meeting with him, Jeff balked. "He thought I was pulling a prank on him," Graves says laughing.

"It was just beyond my comprehension," Jeff recalls. "I mean, I'm on a team in the Busch Grand National Series, I'm not associated with any Cup team . . . And now I go from that to one of the top teams? To have one of those teams reaching out to me, I was just like, 'Are you kidding me?'"

It took a lot of convincing, but several days later, Graves finally convinced Jeff and dragged him into Rick Hendrick's office for a sit-down. Hendrick presented his vision. He had run three cars between 1987 and 1990 and was looking to do so again, as long as Jeff would agree to drive. He would have access to everything Hendrick Motorsports had to offer. And Hendrick was even willing to let him bring Ray Evernham on board as crew chief.

"I remember Jeff was super excited in thinking he'd have an opportunity to join an organization and get good equipment at such a young age," Hendrick says. "No young guy had ever gotten an opportunity to go with a big team, one of the top teams. It was unheard of. And I just told him that I felt like he was going to be a future champion, that he'd have a long career here and that I really wanted to work with him and see him blossom into a champion. I didn't have a sponsor, which was really out of character for me, but I just said, 'This kid is so good, we'll find one.'"

"Mr. Hendrick didn't sign him on the spot," Graves recalls, "but he basically gave him his word. He said, 'Let's figure this out. I want to start a team for you. I give you my word I'll find a sponsor. Please let's do it.' Rick has that personality and influence over people. He could sell Eskimos snow. He's such a charismatic person that you would do anything for him. And standing there in his office, Jeff agreed."

"Jeff called me immediately after leaving Hendrick," John says, "saying, 'Oh, this guy's the greatest guy in the world! This is what he wants to do, and he's going to put this car together and I'm going to be the third team.' I don't think I remember him ever being that excited before."

The whole arrangement was still just a word and a handshake. Graves had been a little off suggesting Jeff had *no contract*, but his deal with Davis allowed him to leave the team with proper notice. Legal and contractual details needed to be worked out. There were cars to be built and a team to assemble. To announce anything at that point would surely have scuttled any sort of deal. Hendrick still had his two other Cup drivers to focus on, and of course, Jeff

TOP: **Jeff signing autographs in Radford, Virginia, 1992.**

was still racing for Bill Davis, who was trying to turn his own dream of taking Jeff to the Cup into a reality.

"The more [Jeff] thought about it over the next several days," Graves recalls, "the more it started to weigh on him how difficult it was going to have to be to tell Bill Davis, who gave him his break, that he was going to leave. And from what I remember, Jeff was even wavering a little bit, just because the pressure of having to tell Bill was so stressful. . . . He felt a big obligation to Bill, and they had a tremendous relationship."

Over the next month, Jeff continued his high-level run for Davis, logging four more top-ten finishes, including two top fives and one pole. While the deal was still very much on the table with Hendrick, Jeff bided his time as Davis continued looking for a new sponsor for the Cup team while dumping his sweat into the current Busch season, where he was again attempting a full schedule with limited funds.

"But things were going really well, and Bill was like, 'We're going Cup racing! In '93, we're going Cup racing!' And I remember asking Ray, 'What do you think about this?' And he said, 'Oh, man, we're a long way from going Cup racing.' I mean, Bill had the making of it. He was building, but certainly not for the next year. And if it did happen in '93, it was going to be very small, and I didn't feel like it would be a very competitive program," Jeff says.

Meanwhile, the Hendrick folks were beginning to make preparations. John was hammering out contract issues and the business side of a potential deal, and Evernham had been invited to come tour the operation's facilities. "At that time, Hendrick Motorsports was not performing like it should," Evernham recalls. "I toured the facility with a man named Jim Johnson, who was the manager at that time. I went back to Jeff and told him it was an incredible opportunity. Everything you could ever ask for is there. I just don't believe they're using it properly." It was Ray's appraisal that sold Jeff on Hendrick.

As secretive as it all was, NASCAR was like a big family. Inevitably, rumors began circulating. "At the time, I was aware that Rick Hendrick had an interest in Jeff, but I didn't know that it was a serious interest," Lee Morse says. "But based on that, I initiated discussions with two of my top Winston Cup teams, Jack Roush and Junior Johnson, about hiring Jeff, and both of them indicated that they would consider it. I felt pretty positive that I could make that work."

Still, with it being so early in the season, Morse didn't feel any great sense of urgency. If he pressed too hard, word might get back to Davis that Ford was trying to find a new home for Jeff behind his back. It likely would have been easier for Ford to support Davis in his own Cup aspirations. "One of the reasons I didn't actively pursue it as soon as Bill started talking about it was that I didn't feel that program would be the best program for Jeff," Morse admits. "They were successful, but it's a much bigger deal than what Bill knew to go from Busch to Winston Cup."

Ultimately, over the following weeks, Ford's big boys—Jack Roush and Junior Johnson— did reach out to Jeff, along with a number of other teams, including the Stavola Brothers team. But none were willing to take on Ray Evernham, the one selling point Jeff and John were insistent on, and a demand Hendrick had already agreed to.

By the first week in May, Jeff was ready to sign the deal. But his excitement was nearly smothered by the knot growing in his stomach. He just wasn't sure how or when to break the news to Bill, the only party who had been left completely in the dark. "Jeff knew it was going to be a big letdown, a big problem," John says. "But at the same time, he had to think

TOP: Jeff in front of the No. 1 Baby Ruth Ford.

June 30, 1992

From: Jeff Gordon
        Jeff Gordon, Inc.
        RR1 Box 117A
        Pittsboro, IN 46167

To: Bill Davis
        Bill Davis Racing
        11 Robbins St.
        Thomasville, NC 27360

Pursuant to paragraph 6 of the agreement between Jeff Gordon, Inc., and Bill Davis Racing, dated February 4, 1992, the undersigned herein notifies Bill Davis Racing that Jeff Gordon hereby exercises his option to terminate said agreement.

Signed: *Jeff Gordon*   Date: 6-30-92

Jeff Gordon for Jeff Gordon, Inc.

about his career. He had to think about the fact that Bill had no sponsor, he'd never run a Cup team, and it was already May and he had no Cup cars built."

To make matters worse, the week Jeff, John, and Ray met with Jimmy Johnson of Hendrick Motorsports to put pen to paper, Bill Davis called with what he thought was the news they'd all been waiting for. It looked like they had a Cup sponsor. A big one.

On May 6, with the ink still drying on the Hendrick contract Jeff had signed the day before, he, Davis, and PR man Bill Armour boarded a plane for Minnesota for a meeting with Target executives. Armour's friend Henry Rischitelli, who was head of motorsports for International Management Group and had helped set up the talk, joined them. Rischitelli had worked with Target in Indy racing and was eager to bring them into NASCAR; Jeff Gordon, with his youth, charisma, and clean-cut image, seemed just the right person for them.

"Jeff was perfect in that meeting," Armour recalls. "I wasn't surprised, because he was so impressive in those situations." Yet none of them had any inkling of the secret he was harboring.

"To me, the news was not going to go well, regardless of when it came," Jeff says. "And I really got my mindset behind going to Minneapolis because I wanted what was best for Bill. I really wanted him to get that sponsorship. But it wasn't going to change my decision."

"That was as good a meeting as I was ever in," Davis recalls. "They were very interested in NASCAR. As I recall it, they were more interested in a limited schedule, maybe run eighteen races or something. . . . It probably wouldn't have been a bad starting point for us at that time. . . . I would say there was probably a very, very, very good chance they would have done it."

Jeff saw it all a bit differently. "I remember Bill being excited about how the meeting went. I had a different impression. I felt their interest level was minimal and their knowledge of NASCAR was also minimal, so it would be a long shot if it happened and a long way from getting it done if at all."

On their way down in the elevator, Jeff told Davis they needed to talk. Once they reached the lobby, the two of them split off. Jeff remembers first explaining to Davis that he didn't think Target was anywhere close to coming on board. Then he delivered the news. "I said, 'I hate to tell you this, but I've made a decision that I'm going to go work for Rick Hendrick.' And

TOP: Jeff's resignation letter to Bill Davis, June 30, 1992.

he was floored. He was absolutely floored. He fought a little, like it wasn't quite a done deal yet. . . . And he just sunk down, you know, and went into a shell, like I stabbed him in the heart."

"He said, 'I'm a Hendrick driver next year,'" Davis recalls. "It was quite the moment. I'll never forget it. I was in such shock. There wasn't a red-faced curse match or anything. It was lots of stunned silence, disbelief. Man, it was real ugly. Just hurt, resentment. 'My god, how unfair. How could you?'"

With the race in Nazareth, Pennsylvania, coming up in a few days, Davis flew home alone to get the car and hauler, while Rischitelli returned to Cleveland. Armour and Jeff spent the night at an airport hotel before flying off to Pennsylvania the following day. Armour still remembers vividly the two of them sitting on the corners of their hotel beds as Jeff ran through the story. "I remember Jeff crying," he says. "That was one of the few times I felt parental with him. Because it hit me: What else was he supposed to have done?" They got John on the phone, who helped further explain the situation to Armour and calm Jeff down.

"I knew it was happening," John says, "and I felt for him. It's really hard to tell a guy that has basically been the catalyst for your dream as a racecar driver that you've got another opportunity. But you've got to think of your own career versus Bill Davis's dream. And you're basically going to disrupt his dream. It was very hard on him. I think it's maybe one of the hardest things he's ever had to do."

After the race at Nazareth, in which Jeff completed only eighty-seven of two hundred laps due to engine trouble, he called Lee Morse. The bitterness was so harsh that no one had yet told Ford what was happening. "Jeff knew he had to make that call, and I certainly understood it was a very difficult call for him," Morse remembers. "He was very emotional about it, and he was feeling bad. Jeff was young, and he wasn't a hardened individual. He was just a nice person." Morse tried everything he could to dissuade him. He again raised the topic of potential opportunities with Roush and Johnson. But Jeff was adamant. "In hindsight," Morse says, "I should have talked to him about those opportunities much earlier on. We talked for a long time . . . He knew I wasn't happy, but he understood that I understood. And in the end, if it ended up being what Jeff told me Rick offered him, there was nothing I could have come up with that would have matched it anyway."

Not everyone was as understanding. When the news officially broke, there was an uproar beyond anything Jeff could have anticipated. "Ford Brass Fuming after Being Spurned," read one headline. The article went onto state, "Officials of Ford Motorsports in Detroit reportedly feel angry, disappointed and betrayed that Jeff Gordon has spurned them and signed . . . to drive Chevrolets for Winston Cup team owner Rick Hendrick."

Morse's boss, Michael Kranefuss, told any media willing to listen that Jeff was, in essence, an ungrateful punk who had repaid their faith in him with out-and-out betrayal. Race commentators, other drivers, crewmembers, and Bill Davis came down hard on him. It was like getting "kicked in the teeth," Davis told one television reporter.

"When Jeff announced to Bill that he was leaving us, oh my gosh, the media was just up in arms," Gail Davis says. "It was the first bad media he'd ever gotten. And that was hard."

"The way he was treated by the media who decided to take Bill Davis' side tortured Jeff," John recalls. "I mean, just literally, newspaper article after newspaper article just crucifying Jeff for his decision."

Jeff tried to hold it all together. He tried to be philosophical and take the high road. He didn't whine or complain or hit back in the press. "It was probably one of the worst times

TOP: As hard as it was, Jeff and Bill Davis continued working to win races through the rest of the season, 1992.

of his life," Carol says. "He was down there in North Carolina, and he had Bill Davis and all of his people calling him everything in the book. . . . Jeff called up one day and said, 'Mom, I can't take it anymore. John has to come down here. I can't handle this.' He just needed some positive reinforcement."

Ray Evernham was leaving Davis, too, but he wasn't "Ford's fair-haired boy, its favorite superstar-in-waiting," as the press had dubbed Jeff. "My feeling was that Jeff was treated unfairly through some of that because of other people's emotional reaction," says Evernham. "Bill Davis was really good to me, a fun man to work with, but feelings were hurt. Bill's an emotional guy. . . . He felt like he gave Jeff a shot and Jeff should've stuck with him no matter what. But the reality was—and this is even where Michael Kranefuss, I think, got emotional—Ford really didn't have that much for Jeff."

To be fair, there were people in the racing community and media who understood Jeff's decision and supported him. Both ESPN's Dave Despain and Terry Lingner remember thinking that come hell or high water, he had made the right decision.

The situation with Bill Davis couldn't have been more uneasy. Jeff was still his driver, and they had another twenty races that season. But when he got in the car, it was as if none of the acrimony had transpired. The first race after the announcement was on May 23, 1992, at Charlotte, which offered a $100,000 bonus for any team that could capture the pole and win the race. Jeff went out and did both. But the bitterness had reached such a level that Armour recalls Davis approaching Michael Kranefuss and Lee Morse after that win and asking, "You're not going to have a problem with me firing him in Victory Lane, are you?"

By the time the season was over, Bill Davis Racing was fourth in the standings and had put up the best numbers they had ever achieved. "We put everything into it, and '92 was an incredible year," Gail Davis says. "We won three major races. We still hold the record for the most poles won in that series. We led the most laps, won the most money. It was quite the year."

The success didn't do anything to soften the Davises' resentment; it was a feeling that would last the better part of two decades. In the end, they *would* make it to the Winston Cup in 1993, but with Bobby Labonte in the driver's seat and a sponsorship from Maxwell House coffee.

"Jeff did help take it to another level," Bill Davis admits today. "And we probably wouldn't have gone Cup racing without the experience of two years with him. It certainly worked out for both of us."

On November 15, one week after he took his final Busch race, Jeff climbed into Hendrick Motorsports's No. 24 Chevrolet for the first time. Rick Hendrick wanted to give the twenty-year-old a taste of Winston Cup racing before they went whole hog on the 1993 season. Symbolically, Jeff's presence on the starting grid at Atlanta Motor Speedway couldn't have been weightier. He was back where Rick Hendrick had first seen him sliding through the corners en route to his first NASCAR victory. More importantly, he was lined up against seven-time champion Richard Petty, who would be running the final race of his long and storied NASCAR career. Nobody knew it then, but one racing era was drawing to a close, and a brand-new one was dawning.

TOP: Jeff Gordon posing with the race sponsor after he captured the pole and win at Charlotte, May 23, 1992.

5
RISE OF THE
RAINBOW WARRIORS

"AT THE AGE OF TWENTY-FOUR, OUR next guest won an impressive seven races on his way to becoming the NASCAR Winston Cup Series champion," David Letterman trumpeted on the December 1, 1995, *Late Show*. "Ladies and gentlemen, here he is, the Boy Wonder of NASCAR, Jeff Gordon!"

With that, Jeff came flying down Manhattan's West 53rd Street in a replica of his No. 24 Chevrolet Monte Carlo, leapt out the window, and bounded into the Ed Sullivan Theater to the strains of "Life in the Fast Lane." If the show's 4.5 million viewers hadn't already seen his image on a cereal box or toy-car package, they were getting their first glimpse of the young man who was quickly becoming the new face of professional auto racing. But absent were the worn-down cowboy boots, belt buckle, and blue jeans. Everything about Jeff exuded youthful pep and polish, from the casual suit without a tie, to the freshly blow-dried hair and radiant smile.

"Look at you," Letterman chuckled, "you're just a kid, for heaven's sake." Jeff grinned good-naturedly, laughed, told stories, and made jokes. He did everything right, and the tiniest drop of boyish awkwardness that seeped through seemed to make him all the more endearing.

Later that evening, he and his then-wife, Brooke, a former Miss Winston model, would attend NASCAR's year-end banquet at the Waldorf-Astoria, where he would accept his first championship trophy. He would then party late into the night with the 240 guests that had flown up from Charlotte before heading to ABC the following morning for a guest spot on *Good Morning America*. The whirlwind week in New York—the TV appearances, the parties, the sightseeing, the courtside tickets to the Knicks, hobnobbing with Spike Lee and NHL great Mark Messier—was part of his newfound status.

In a mere three years, his life had outpaced his dreams. He'd made millions and was poised to make many more. He seemed to have it all. "It should be illegal to be that young, that good-looking, and that talented," Dale Jarrett famously quipped that year. Jeff was doing

OPPOSITE: Jeff in his No. 24 DuPont Chevrolet Lumina leading the field at Martinsville, Virginia, April 25, 1993.

his best to enjoy the fruits of his hard work and good fortune, but by his own admission, everything was blazing by at such warp speed that his head was spinning.

*   *   *

Jeff's rocket rise to stardom began just thirty-four months earlier, when, as a twenty-one-year-old, he first rolled onto the track at Daytona in his DuPont-sponsored Chevrolet. If Hendrick Motorsports was trying to get their rookie noticed, the flashy No. 24, with its eye-catching rainbow paint scheme, did the trick.

A few competitors had gotten a quick peek at Jeff in the final race of 1992 in Atlanta, when he first sampled the Cup waters. Jeff had gotten into the wall mid-race. In their hurriedness to repair the damage, his pit crew accidentally left a roll of duct tape on his deck lid. Once he was back on the track, the tape rolled off and lightly damaged championship contender Davey Allison's car. Jeff wound up finishing thirty-first.

But that was already forgotten. Daytona was the real coming-out party. There was a buzz around Hendrick's new third-car team, and the racing world was eager to see what kind of waves these newcomers in their flamboyant fire suits might make in 1993.

In the first 125-mile qualifying race, Jeff stunned everyone by taking the checker, becoming the youngest driver to win a Daytona 500 qualifier and earning third position on the starting grid. He then survived a wreck-strewn afternoon to jockey into second place behind Dale Earnhardt with twenty laps to go, before both were overtaken late by Dale Jarrett. Jeff ended up fifth, but it was a very impressive showing. It was clear the No. 24 team was there to compete.

Now all they needed was a map. "We didn't even know how to get to half the racetracks when we left the Hendrick building," Ray Evernham laughs. "Jeff and I used to drive together sometimes, and I remember we'd ask each other, 'Where do we go?' 'I don't know, I thought you knew.' . . . The good news is that we faced a lot of the challenges with our inexperience in NASCAR racing together."

Most of those challenges were racing related—learning the tracks and the surfaces, understanding how they affected fuel mileage and tire wear, finding out how loose a bigger, heavier Cup car could get during a race, and determining where a track's fastest groove was, what lines to take, and which marks to hit. Except for their brief tenure in the Busch Series, neither of them had any stock-car experience, which was unheard of for a driver–crew chief combination in the Winston Cup.

TOP: Jeff's 1993 Winston Cup test badge. RIGHT: Andy Graves douses Jeff in Victory Lane after winning the Gatorade Twin 125's at Daytona, February 11, 1993. At the time, Jeff became the youngest winner of a Gatorade 125-mile qualifier.

"The way I looked at it, I was like a baseball player coming into the NBA," Jeff says. "And they looked at me as an outsider. A lot of the other younger drivers, they grew up racing one another as they progressed up through the ranks. Well, I had come from a totally different type of racing, and I was having to break in and find my place."

Jeff and Ray had to gain their bearings culturally as well. You simply couldn't get farther afield from NASCAR's nerve center than the San Francisco Bay Area and New Jersey.

QUICK FACTS

CAR NUMBER	24
SPONSOR	Du Pont Automotive Finishes
COLORS	Red and blue, trimmed in yellow and green
CAR MAKE	1993 Chevrolet Lumina
TEAM NAME	Hendrick Motorsports
OWNER	Rick Hendrick
GENERAL MANAGER	Jimmy Johnson
DRIVER	Jeff Gordon
CREW CHIEF	Ray Evernham
SHOP OFFICE MANAGER	Michael Landis
CREWMEN	Darryl Bobbin, Andy Graves, Edward Guzzo, Michael Landis, Charlie Libby, Eddie Nawrocki, Andrew Papathanassiou, Corrie Stott, Brian Whitesell
SCORER	Gary Wall
CHASSIS	Hendrick R&D Chassis
ENGINES	Hendrick Engines
MEDIA CONTACT	Performance PR Plus (704) 896-8683
SHOP LOCATION	5325 Stowe Lane Harrisburg, NC 28075 (704) 455-3400

Performance PR Plus, Inc.

CLOCKWISE FROM TOP: The cover and fact sheet from the Hendrick Motorsports press kit introducing the No. 24 DuPont Chevrolet and new star Jeff Gordon, 1993; Jeff's No. 24 leading off at Charlotte; Jeff prepares to race in his first-ever Daytona 500, February 14, 1993.

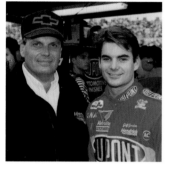

"I remember going into that drivers' meeting," Evernham recalls of their first encounter with the predominantly Southern racers. "And here's some kid from California wearing high-top freakin' Michael Jordans and some guy from New Jersey, and we're sitting there with all these guys from Georgia and North Carolina."

On the track, however, racing was racing. It made no difference whether your name was Petty, Jarrett, or Gordon, or whether you came from Appalachia or the moon. Jeff built on his promising performance at Daytona with a sixth-place finish at Richmond and a fourth-place finish at Atlanta. But then he wrecked, and wrecked, and wrecked again.

Darrell Waltrip, the three-time Cup champion, remembers speaking with Rick Hendrick that season and telling him he was skeptical about the youngster's ability to hack it in the big time. "He said, 'So what do you think about my young hot-shoe?'" Waltrip recalls. "And I told Rick I didn't think the kid was ever going to make it. I mean, seriously, he hit everything but the pace car that year."

"I think he wrecked about seventeen times," Hendrick chuckles. "But he had the speed. I knew he could do it. He'd get in the wrong spot and get tangled up in a wreck, but I knew it would come."

In the end, despite the crashes, handling problems, and occasional engine blowups, the No. 24 logged some strong finishes, including runner-up performances at Charlotte and Michigan, as well as their first pole. They didn't have a points-race win, but eleven times—in more than a third of the races—they finished in the top ten. Ultimately, Jeff came out of the season with the Winston Cup Rookie of the Year trophy, just shading Bill Davis Racing's Bobby Labonte.

What also came out was that, for the entire season, Jeff had been secretly dating Miss Winston model Brooke Sealey, one of the Southern beauties tasked with presenting trophies to Cup drivers. "There was a rule that Miss Winston could not date a driver," says Jeff's friend and housemate Andy Graves, who worked for the No. 24 team. "They didn't want to get caught, and she didn't want to get in trouble. So that first nine months, they had to do it in secret."

Their connection had started in February 1993, when the two made eyes at each other in Victory Lane as Jeff celebrated his Daytona qualifier win. Their budding romance quickly assumed the air of a cloak-and-dagger comedy, as they found themselves having to slip out the side doors of restaurants, stagger their entrances to hotels, and use Graves as a buffer to avoid the prying eyes of the NASCAR community. The charade was successful enough that Dale Earnhardt jokingly inquired whether the young, handsome, and inexplicably single rookie driver was gay.

But the confusion didn't end there. With Brooke frequently lingering on the edges of the No. 24 car camp, at least one crewmember was convinced that Cupid's arrow was aimed squarely at *him*. "We had a guy who would drive the van and clean the cars," Evernham recalls. "And he would always tell us, 'Yeah, she's hanging around here because she likes me.' Jeff and I talked a lot, so I knew what was going on, but this guy would keep telling us, 'Hey, I think she's sweet on me.'"

TOP LEFT: Front page of the Jeff Gordon Newsletter from June 1994, reporting his win at the Coca-Cola 600. TOP RIGHT: The No. 24 DuPont Chevrolet leads at Charlotte Motor Speedway. BOTTOM LEFT: Rick Hendrick and Jeff pose before a race.

Jeff was serious enough that one year after they met, he proposed to Brooke at Daytona. He then went out and won the Busch Clash, a non-points invitation race for the previous season's pole winners. In that race, he pulled off a bold move to the inside on the second-to-last lap to beat Brett Bodine, Dale Earnhardt, and Ernie Irvan. A week later, in the Daytona 500, he finished fourth. But the No. 24 team was still looking for that first win. In the season's third race, Jeff came close, finishing third at Richmond, but soon slid through an ugly six weeks in which he finished no better than fifteenth and failed three times to crack the top thirty.

Coming off that, few expected him to challenge for the Coca-Cola 600 at Charlotte, the season's longest race and one of the most grueling. Still, the No. 24 team won the pole, just as they had in the October race the year before, and although Jeff led the first lap, he quickly got shuffled back. The lead changed hands twenty-five times that day. With eighteen laps to go, the race leader, Rusty Wallace, pitted for fuel and a four-tire change. Geoff Bodine, who was running second, did likewise. Evernham called for just two tires, and the quick stop put Jeff back on the track ahead of both of them, with only Ricky Rudd, now running first, to pass. To the announcers, it seemed a fool's gambit. What they didn't know was that Evernham and Jeff had run two-tire stops in practice and discovered they could muster around fifteen good, fast laps. When Rudd eventually had to pit for fuel, Jeff took the lead and never looked back. After he crossed the finish line, Earnhardt pulled up alongside him and gave the first-time winner the thumbs-up.

Jeff pulled into Victory Lane in tears, a rare display of emotion for a Winston Cup driver. "This is the greatest day of my life. I don't know what to say," he stammered, then regained his composure and thanked his team. When he finally climbed out of the car, the grandstands erupted, and he broke down again. "My emotions showed how much that meant to me that day," he recalls. "It just all came out. I couldn't hold it back.

"I hadn't even dreamt of being in the Cup Series, and there I was, realizing how much I wanted to be a part of it and how hard I had worked and how much I had wanted to be successful at it. So that moment was a relief, but at the same time, it was just the pure joy and excitement of winning at that level. To me, that was the ultimate level."

His win at Charlotte set the stage for what, just eight races later, would become one of the greatest performances of his twenty-three-year career. For the first time in history, NASCAR would be running at the cathedral of car racing, the Indianapolis Motor Speedway,

TOP LEFT: Jeff is overcome with emotion as he celebrates his Coca-Cola 600 win with his crew in Victory Lane. TOP RIGHT: Jeff receives a congratulatory hug from his mother, Carol, following his victory.

the most storied track in all of motorsports and the Holy Grail to Jeff's childhood hopes and ambitions. He never imagined he'd get there as a stock-car driver, but the unthinkable had come true. "If ever there was a dream, that was the dream," he says. "Just to be racing at Indianapolis, just to drive onto that track as a racecar driver, competing."

The 1994 Brickyard 400 would be the most anticipated stock-car race in history and would far surpass any NASCAR event in attendance, television viewership, and prize money. The buildup had been so big, and the potential payoff so huge, that racers from every corner lined up to join the current Winston Cup regulars gunning for a starting spot. The eventual field of forty-three would include 1985 Indianapolis 500 winner Danny Sullivan and the iconic four-time Indy 500 champ A.J. Foyt, who would make it the final race of his career. Even during pre-race testing, the crowd was so hyped that at least one fan tried to scale the grandstand's chain-link fence for autographs. "And on race day, it was packed—350,000 people," Jeff recalls. "You just knew that whoever won that race, it was going to be a huge moment in history."

Evernham was brimming with confidence from the outset. "I was enjoying the fact that it was square one, it was a level playing field, we were all going there for the first time. Not even the Indy guys had an advantage," he says. When the No. 24 car qualified third, he felt good enough about their chances to skip the final practice.

"We showed some speed at the test," Jeff recalls, "but when that race started, I knew immediately we were—wow—we were fast, we were one of the top three cars, I felt. And by the halfway point, it seemed to be between just me and Ernie Irvan. We were racing hard, going back and forth." Each time one of them would take the point, the other would come up strong, take the air off the lead car's spoiler and loosen him up, then pass. It went on and on. "We had a great battle."

But with five laps left, Jeff, running second, moved down to pass Irvan in the turn. Irvan suddenly dropped off the pace, the victim of a cut tire. "When he fell out, I remember Brett Bodine coming on pretty strong; I was worried a bit because he was catching me, but I felt confident. I had a pretty good lead." He told himself: *Concentrate. Just don't make any mistakes, hit all your marks. And then the white flag: the final lap.* "That's when I started getting chills up my

TOP: A pair of tickets to the qualification and practice, 1994 Brickyard 400 Inaugural Race at Indianapolis Motor Speedway. RIGHT: The No. 24 DuPont Chrevrolet speeds past the grandstands during the Brickyard 400, 1994.

spine," Jeff remembers. "I was thinking, 'Oh my god, this is really happening. This is real.'"

Evernham barely remembers Jeff crossing the finish line. "It didn't hit me until we got to Victory Lane and I realized we had done it," he says. "And at the time, the whole stage used to go up in the air. And they raise it up, and you look out at Indy, the front stretch, and I'd never seen that many people. It was just wall-to-wall people. And you realize, 'Holy shit, this is Indianapolis.'"

After soaking up the crowd's adulation, fulfilling his sponsor commitments, signing enough autographs to get hand cramps, and talking to more reporters than he could count, Jeff trudged back to his nearby hotel with Brooke, drained. "I was starving," he remembers, "and I wanted something quick and easy." He rang up Pizza Hut and ordered a pepperoni and pineapple pizza for delivery. But when he gave them the hotel's address, he heard a sigh. "Uh, yeah, that's going to take a while," they told him. "A couple hours. They just had a big race out there, and there's a lot of people, lot of traffic."

"And I thought, if there's ever a moment to pull the card, it's now," Jeff laughs. "I said, 'Yeah, I'm aware of the race. Would it help if I told you I won it?' And they're like, 'Excuse me?' I said, 'Yeah, I'm Jeff Gordon. I won the race. I'm staying here at the Brickyard Hotel.' They said 'Okay, we'll see what we can do.'" Jeff hung up, skeptical the pizza would arrive any time soon, but thirty seconds later, the phone rang. It was the front desk calling. "The desk clerk asked, 'Did you just order a pizza? I've got Pizza Hut on the other line and they're wanting to confirm it.' I said yeah, tell them it's me and to please get the pizza here as fast they can. That thing was there in thirty minutes. I think I gave them a $100 tip."

The post-Brickyard insanity provided a good snapshot of what Jeff's life would become from that moment forward—the media, the fans, the hangers-on, the public appearances, autograph signings, the hospitality events for his sponsors, and a host of other obligations.

"That's when it really took off, when he hit the Brickyard," says Ron Miller, Jeff's DuPont public relations representative. Miller remembers thinking toward the end of 1992 that in a matter of years, "his name, Jeff Gordon, will be a household word." It was happening sooner than Ron, or Jeff, had imagined. "There's nothing that can prepare you for the media attention or the fans or the demands on your time," Jeff says.

Jeff's friend from Vallejo, Rod Sherry, was stupefied the first time he got a glimpse of the spectacle surrounding NASCAR's new star. "I knew he raced, but I didn't know anything about racing," Sherry admits. Jeff invited him to an appearance at a DuPont distributorship near Vallejo following the Indy victory. Sherry, who agreed to give Jeff a lift back to his hotel after the event, says security guards instructed him to back his '78 Chevrolet Nova up to the rear of the building so he'd be able to make a quick getaway when his friend was through. The precautions struck him as unnecessary. "I just thought these guys were way over the top," he says.

"So we hear him finishing up, and then Jeff comes walking out with three security guys around him, and he hops in the car and I'm like, 'All right, so where are we going?'" Before Jeff could answer, a throng of fired-up fans swarmed around the back of the building and

TOP: The No. 24 DuPont Chevrolet races to victory at the Brickyard 400, 1994.

converged on the Nova. "People started climbing on my car. People started climbing through the windows. I couldn't believe it. I had a guy climbing over my lap with a die-cast car he wanted Jeff to sign—climbed right through the window, over my lap, and handed Jeff the car. . . . And he finally said, 'Just go, just go, just gas it.' . . . And that's when it hit me. I was like, 'Wow, dude, you are actually big-time. This is serious.' I had no idea."

That was nothing compared to race days at the track, when armies of admirers would descend on him for autographs. "I've been in situations with Jeff where I was actually worried about his safety," Evernham remembers. "People would get around him and I'm thinking, 'Wait a minute, now, they're going to trample him, poor guy.' So I would grab him out of the middle of something and he'd have Sharpie marks on his shirt, his face."

As Jeff navigated the waters of his newfound celebrity, he also embarked on an equally transformative journey in his private life. Religion had never been big in the Gordon-Bickford household. Neither John nor Carol were churchgoers, and for most of his life, Jeff didn't seem to have an ecclesiastical bone in his body. That all changed when he got to the Cup Series and met Brooke, who had been raised a strict Baptist.

"I was really influenced by Christianity at the time, because that's what surrounds North Carolina and NASCAR," Jeff recalls. "I saw a lot of people talking about God, praying, having church services at the racetrack. I had friends inviting me to Bible studies. I was curious and had questions about the Bible, about Jesus. And Brooke was one of those people that had a fairly good knowledge of it from her upbringing, so she facilitated a lot of that and sort of led me in that direction. And it just grew from there."

Soon he and Brooke were spending time with other devout racing couples and discussing scripture with Rev. Max Helton, who ran the traveling chapel at the Winston Cup tracks. They hosted Bible studies and prayed together each night. At the time, it helped Jeff find some kind of peace, both in the race car and amid the growing bedlam outside of it.

After the end of the season, in which Dale Earnhardt won his seventh championship and Jeff finished eighth in the point standings, he was baptized at Brooke's family church. On November 26, 1994, they took their wedding vows.

★   ★   ★

Since he'd first arrived at the Hendrick Motorsports facilities the spring of 1992, Ray Evernham had been a transformative presence. Not one to keep his ideas bottled up, he quickly took stock of the operation. "I saw resources and people willing to do stuff and just incredible opportunity that wasn't being used," he recalls. "They had all the right things to go into the 'new' way of racing, but they were very much old-school. It had nothing to do with Rick Hendrick's dedication. It was about understanding that it takes more than a big motor and a fast driver to win races."

To Evernham, that new way of racing was a much sharper focus on engineering, on car handling, on weight and chassis design, on aerodynamics, on springs and shocks, and on struts

TOP: A ticket to the Winston Pole Night at the Charlotte Motor Speedway, October 5, 1994.

and tubing. He set about building a program for the No. 24 that incorporated every engineering advance he knew of. "I had to fight pretty hard to get some of the things done that I wanted to have done," he remembers. "But I think they started to realize, 'Wait a minute, these guys are on to something here.'"

What they were on to sometimes ran up against NASCAR regulations, as Ray pushed the envelope for any competitive advantage. There were the occasional fines and sanctions, but most of the time, there was a genuine collective awe at his unbridled creativity and at the results on the track. "That was a time before NASCAR could build a box around everybody, and there was a lot of gray area," Hendrick recalls. "And boy, Ray knew how to work that gray area."

"I remember the days when we kept the penalty notices on index cards and kept them all in a file box—and you could say Ray maybe had his own file box," jokes NASCAR vice chairman Mike Helton. "We look at it as part of the sport. We lay down a rule and the first thing everybody will do—in particular, a guy like Ray Evernham—is figure out how to work around it."

Ray's innovative approach brought changes to the crew as well. He revolutionized pit stops by hiring athletes to helm his over-the-wall team and drilled them like marines to maintain their fitness and speed. But it was his leadership in the shop, and his willingness to boot anyone who didn't share his relentless work ethic, that shaped the team into an unbeatable force. By 1995, Ray had sacked some sixty crewmembers but had finally found the twenty-five-man combination he was looking for.

"It was a culture that we had in there. I felt like I set some of that example," Ray says. "A lot of people are willing to do whatever it takes, as long it doesn't make them get home late for their favorite TV show or miss a family barbecue. But the No. 24 team was really committed, dedicated. I've never been associated with a group of people, before or after, that was willing to sacrifice as much for a team as that group."

And for Ray, there was no one but Jeff who could have completed that prize-winning package. "I always had one hundred percent confidence that he was the best guy I could put in the seat of that car," he says. "He's just one of those guys that can get more out of a car than somebody else."

LEFT: Jeff and Ray Evernham discuss the No. 24 pre-race at Dover International Speedway, 1995.

TOP: Jeff Gordon proudly holds his and Hendrick Motorsports's first-ever Winston Cup Championship trophy following the race at Atlanta Motor Speedway, November 12, 1995.

While the behind-the-scenes domain was Evernham's, the track belonged to Jeff, who continued to climb the Winston Cup learning curve, absorbing lessons from each of his sixty-three races. "It didn't take him long to figure out what he needed," says Hendrick. "As time went on, he put the combination together—the talent, the experience, being smart enough to know when to race, how to race, and how to save the car. I've been doing this a long time, and you can have the best equipment out there, but if you don't have somebody in that seat that can do it, you're not going to be successful. And as good as Jeff was as a driver, Ray was just as smart as a crew chief. So you had a dynamic duo there."

As in anything where passions run high, the two of them had spats in 1993 and '94. They were incidents both of them in hindsight chalked up to a variety of factors including exhaustion, dehydration, and Jeff's exposure to carbon monoxide in the car—an issue the No. 24 team was able to fix by 1995. "One of the side effects of that," Jeff says, "is a quick temper and being short about things and being easily frustrated."

"He could be a little bit childish sometimes," Evernham says. "You'd ask a question during a race and he'd give a smart-ass answer, and I knew everybody could hear us on the radio, and that was embarrassing to me. But I felt like I was doing a good job with him, because rather than grabbing him by the collar and shaking him, I'd just sit him down and say, 'Look, I've got to be able to ask you a question without you biting my head off.'"

With a fourteen-year difference between them, their relationship could be sometimes characterized as a brotherly bond, sometimes as a father-son dynamic. And while they never had much social interaction off the track, they communicated about racing at a level that was so intense and intimate that there were times, Ray admits, when it seemed something akin to a marriage.

"Whether it's a marriage or a crew chief and driver, I will say that trust, honesty, and respect are the biggest things," he says. "If Jeff would've come in and said, 'Look, I really need you to cut the roof off this thing and turn it backwards,' we would've seen how fast we could do it."

For Jeff, it was as much a matter of loyalty as trust and respect. "I had a responsibility to him, and to the team," he says, "because they were sacrificing so much, and I didn't want to let them down." All either one expected was that they give everything they had to each other and to the team.

When February's Daytona 500 was interrupted by rain a third of the way through, Jeff was leading the pack, with Sterling Marlin and Dale Earnhardt rounding out the top three. When they got back to racing two hours later, he continued to dominate. At the race's halfway mark, Jeff came into the pits under caution. And then a bad blunder ruined their day. "We dropped the car off the jack, tore the left fender up," Evernham recalls. The miscue put Jeff a lap down, and the aerodynamic damage to the car's body never allowed him to get back in contention. He would end the day twenty-second.

The crew chief waited for the inevitable verbal onslaught from his dismayed driver, but it didn't come. "Instead of him acting like a child or yelling or screaming at us," he recalls, "[Jeff] said, 'Look, we have a fast car, we're going to have plenty more Daytona 500s, we're going to have plenty more shots to win. We've got to put this behind us.'

"I always look back at that race as a major turning point, like okay, now we have a leader.... That was a key moment. Our team matured, and Jeff matured. And I think that day made us a championship-caliber team."

They showed up to Rockingham the following Sunday wearing "Refuse to Lose" T-shirts and made good on the promise, capturing the pole and the race. Two weeks later, they won at

Atlanta and then grabbed a victory at Bristol. In the space of a single month, they'd won more races than they had the previous two years. By the season's midpoint, sixteen races in, they'd added two more victories and five top-five finishes. That momentum carried through the season's second half, as they captured two more wins and finished outside the top ten only twice.

By the final race in Atlanta, Jeff had the title all but sewn up, having to finish just forty-first or better, or lead for a single lap to claim the championship over Dale Earnhardt. Early in the race, he jumped out to the front and held on long enough to clinch. But the car had been plagued by handling issues most of the race. "The steering box had debris in the valve," Evernham recalls. Jeff found himself fourteen laps down before the finish. With nothing to lose, during his final pit stop, an elated Rick Hendrick hopped in to do windshield-cleaning duty, while Evernham changed a tire. "We had some fun with it," Jeff laughs. "Obviously, it was a very slow pit stop." Jeff won his—and Hendrick Motorsports—first-ever Winston Cup trophy with a thirty-second-place.

"To me, it was all happening at the speed of light," Jeff remembers. "The whole thing— moving to Charlotte in 1991, Busch Series Rookie of the Year, getting signed by Hendrick, winning the 600, the Brickyard, the championship. I couldn't believe the way it was ramping up and going full steam ahead at a steep climb."

At the year-end banquet in New York, Rick Hendrick recalled looking over at the young driver he'd hired three years earlier in the hopes of finally landing a title, who was now the youngest racer to ever win the Winston Cup championship, and saying to him, "God, we're going to win a lot of these things.

"And I said, 'Do you realize, at your age, you'll be the greatest that ever did this?' I was just so proud of him for what he'd accomplished."

TOP: The No. 24 team celebrates their first championship in a champagne shower.

79

6
A FAMILY DIVIDED

JEFF'S WINNING OF THE CHAMPIONSHIP was certainly one of the proudest moments of John's and Carol's lives, but it wasn't one of the happiest. "It was a difficult time because of all the things that were going on with us on a personal level," Carol remembers. "He was married to Brooke at the time, and that wasn't the most pleasant experience."

The relationship between Jeff's parents and his wife had been strained since his wedding day, and Carol in particular felt as if Brooke was gradually trying to push them out of Jeff's life. Although they still, in essence, worked for Jeff—John had been overseeing all of his financial, scheduling, and contractual issues—things had quickly become cold and distant.

In April, in the midst of the 1995 championship run, they got a call from Jeff stating that he no longer wanted them to have a hand in his financial and business affairs. It was a demand initiated by Brooke, but Jeff felt it was necessary to support her. "It didn't bother me that they were involved," he says, "but it bothered the person I had partnered with, and that was a commitment I was making. I didn't want to have that issue. And so when it became clear to me that it was an issue, I was going to try to fix it. And they were hurt."

In some sense, a split was natural, and perhaps inevitable, with Jeff being newly married and starting a fresh chapter in life. It was understandable that a young wife might not be keen on her in-laws inspecting their marital finances. "The problem Brooke had was that she felt like they had a little bit too much access to our lives," Jeff says. "Some of the financial things they questioned were expenses related to her, so I think she just felt like a little bit of privacy and discretion was not there. And I think she felt like she was being judged, which was understandable."

Both John and Carol understood that on principle. But it was harsh news when coupled with the already frosty relationship, and harsher still because Jeff didn't seem to grasp what the change would mean. John and Carol had dedicated much of their lives to Jeff's progress—they'd moved from Pittsboro to Charlotte to be closer to him and NASCAR—and for the past ten years, the business side of Jeff's career had been their primary source of income. Now, at forty-eight years old, John would essentially have to start life over again and look for a job.

"It was harsher than I intended it to be," Jeff admits. "It could have been handled better. I should have said, 'Hey, guys, let's work out a transition here. I'm growing up, I'm getting older,

OPPOSITE: Jeff preparing to get back in the car at the Mountain Dew Southern 500, 1997.

and I want you to still be a part of all this, but not in the way you are currently.' But Brooke was fed up with a lot of it. And I had hinted to my parents a little bit, but it wasn't happening at the rate she wanted it to happen."

Ultimately, there was little John and Carol could do. "I didn't want to be the source of pain in my son's life," Carol says. "I kept telling John, 'He's going to figure it out. We've been his parents his whole life. There's no reason why we can't continue to do that, but we don't need to work for him.' And that was definitely hard on John."

John eventually found a replacement for himself in Bob Brannan, a former Charlotte-area banker who had been working in the motorsports licensing industry. And while Brannan assumed the title of vice president and general manager of Jeff Gordon, Inc., John set out to find a new role for himself without Jeff Gordon.

★   ★   ★

First, there was "Wonder Boy." Then there were headlocks and hat twistings and all manner of jibes about Jeff's youth. Throughout 1995, a season in which Dale Earnhardt, the Intimidator, was contesting for his third consecutive Winston Cup championship, Earnhardt wore Jeff out. When the rugged racer from Kannapolis, North Carolina, won the 1995 Brickyard 400, he crowed about being the first *man* to do it. When he was asked about No. 24's chances of winning the title that year, he cracked that the kid would "have to toast everybody with milk" at the awards ceremony.

"Dale loved to play it up," Jeff remembers. "And he had the ability to play it up like that, on and off the track. He would just make comments about everything. Me, I've always been too serious to take that on. I was always worried that if I went there, it was going to take away from my ability to focus on what I wanted to accomplish."

Jeff was not a joking showman, but he did have enough of a sense of humor and pride to tweak Earnhardt back once in a while. When he got up on stage to deliver his championship address at NASCAR's year-end banquet in 1995, he took the veteran at his word, saluting him with a champagne glass full of milk.

"Sorry, man," Jeff went on. "You've been having so much fun with me all year. I had to loosen up a bit. And I hope you didn't mind what I said about you on *Letterman* the other day."

Earnhardt clearly enjoyed the moment, and Jeff graciously highlighted his vanquished rival's immense contributions to the sport. Dale hadn't earned his sinister nicknames by being a gentleman on the track. He was exceptionally fast, exceptionally intelligent, and tough as hickory bark. He had few qualms about aggressive banging and pushing and scraping, and if you saw his No. 3 car knocking on your back bumper, it was generally a good idea to scoot aside. That abrasive, bare-knuckle style had earned him a lot of respect on the track, and more than a few enemies. It had also helped him win seven championships and made him a blue-collar, honky-tonk hero to legions of hardcore fans. And then Jeff Gordon showed up.

As early as Jeff's rookie season, it was clear the kid had an unusual gift for driving, but more importantly, he wasn't going to be cowed by Dale's on-track antics. "Dale Earnhardt would not have respect for anybody who was a pushover," Evernham says. "Drivers know who can drive and who can't, and I think Dale was like, 'Holy shit, this kid's the real deal.'"

During 1994 and 1995, they raced each other sixty-two times. Each had nine victories. Each won a championship. Over the course of their careers, they would line up together in

TOP: Jeff toasts Dale Earnhardt with a champagne glass of milk at the 1995 NASCAR banquet.

258 points races, with Jeff taking fifty-two of them and Earnhardt twenty-three. Every time they raced, they knew it was going to be a war.

"When it came to basic competition," Evernham recalls, "they'd wreck each other for a dollar. It was all about winning with them two. They'd even wreck cars on us in practice just screwing around with one another. If they were leaving the parking lot at the same time, stand back, because it was going to be a race. Whether it was getting to the airport, getting home, practice, getting to the best seat in the drivers' meeting, it didn't matter."

Throughout the mid-1990s, that rivalry grew, especially after Jeff wrested the Cup title. Frosted Mini-Wheats even featured the two competitors on a cereal box above a legend that read, "The Kid and the Champ." The more Earnhardt talked it up, the more people wanted to see the two of them go at it week after week. And once the press and the fans got a hold of it, it turned into something far bigger and more symbolic than Jeff and Dale on the racetrack: it became old versus young, working class versus middle class, plainspoken versus media polished, southerner versus outsider.

In many ways, it came to encapsulate the cultural clash of "old" NASCAR, the longtime regional Southeastern pastime, and the "new" NASCAR, the major national sport with wide appeal. "Jeff came in and was decidedly everything Dale wasn't," says PR and marketing man Bill Armour. "And Rick Hendrick knew he had the guy who was going to break the mold of the traditional mid-South, good-ole-boy driver. [Jeff] was going to transcend into the mainstream, as far as having the personality to break through to the American consumer. He would transcend the stereotype."

And while Earnhardt was by then a millionaire several times over, what he exuded was also what he was—a rural, hardscrabble son of the South who had done his time as a mechanic, mill worker, and welder before finding a Cup ride. "Earnhardt played that farmer deal. Every time you saw a picture of him, he was in the chicken coop, on the farm with cows," Hendrick remembers. "I knew there were pictures of him with his fishing boat down in the Bahamas on the weekends he wasn't racing. . . . But to his fan base, he played that good-ole-boy, roll-with-it guy."

TOP: Jeff and Dale Earnhardt share a laugh, 1995.

Earnhardt, perhaps more than anybody, understood that that kind of black-and-white battle is what made the money tills ring. It was good for him, good for Jeff, and good for the sport. Just as the Larry Bird–Magic Johnson rivalry helped resuscitate an ailing NBA in the 1980s, the Gordon–Earnhardt duel bolstered NASCAR's appeal among fans and sponsors.

"It was very much Ali–Frazier—both of them knew that their rivalry would put asses in the stands and sell plenty of T-shirts," Evernham says. "And when you've got sold-out events with 150,000 people and your TV ratings are up, the price of real estate on the side of that car goes up."

"I think that's why not just the fans but NASCAR loved Dale so much," Jeff says. "Because he got it. There aren't many that get it the way he did, and he used it to the advantage of himself and the sport." But his dedication to the fans and the sport sometimes meant he played up his "black hat" role a little too much for Jeff's liking.

"There were times," Jeff says, "when he either felt like he was in control of a race or like he couldn't win a race, so he would play it up. Like, 'My only chance of winning is to hit this person or make his life very difficult.' And he'd say, 'Oh, yeah, the fans love that.' He'd say that all the time, 'Oh, the fans eat that up.' And I'm like, 'Well listen, it cost me the race, so I didn't eat it up.' And he'd say, 'Ah, you'll get over it. It's good for the sport.'"

Earnhardt had very loyal and very vocal fans—and a lot of them. Add to them the supporters of forty or so other racers and things could be difficult for Jeff, and his team. When Jeff had started out in the Cup Series, when he got his first few victories, everybody loved it. When he won at the Brickyard, the crowd went berserk. Even through the first part of 1995, there were far more cheers than heckles. But that started to turn, quickly, as his success continued. It was something Rick Hendrick assured him was simply part of racing.

"When a young kid steps in and first starts winning or starts running good, all the fans applaud him," Hendrick says. "But then he starts beating their guy, and some turn against him. And then, when he starts winning a whole lot, you get the boo-birds."

But the rivalry between Jeff and Earnhardt took that natural progression to an outrageous and vitriolic level. "It got to where they would announce two people at the racetrack," Carol recalls, "and everybody there would know who those two people were because one would

TOP: Jeff and Dale Earnhardt share a moment at the 1996 Daytona 500.

have the biggest applause and one the biggest boos. There were probably rivalries before, but the one between Dale Sr. and Jeff was unique."

"People would throw beer at us, and it was pretty nasty for a while," Evernham recalls. "We'd work and do something really cool, win a race with two laps to go with a great pit stop or something, and then you'd just get booed. I didn't like it. I think it bothered me more than it bothered Jeff. At least on the surface, he kind of used to let it roll off. He just seemed like, 'Look, that's part of it. At least they're cheering, too.' But it was brutal."

With their rivalry surrounding the races, most fans would have been horrified to learn that not only would Jeff occasionally pick Earnhardt's brain about licensing and marketing issues and how to handle the race game, but the two were in business together. Even Humpy Wheeler, the head of Charlotte Motor Speedway, nearly lost his lunch when he found out the pair had purchased a piece of property together in Charlotte.

"They were business partners and they were competitors," says Dale Earnhardt Jr., who remembers his father introducing him to Jeff in 1993 and saying Jeff was going to be one of the greats. "And the fact that Dad would go into business with Jeff, and that he worked with Jeff on that side of the sport, the souvenirs and what have you, I felt that was probably a bigger compliment than 'This kid is awesome' or 'He's one hell of a racer.' I think for Dad to feel that comfortable about him as a person to go into business with him, that was saying something."

None of that, however, diminished what went on at the track. And while there were plenty of boos to be heard, Jeff had built up a large fan base of his own. Since winning the Brickyard in 1994 and shooting for the championship in 1995, everything had grown, and at times, it seemed everybody wanted a piece of him.

During the week, there were endorsements to negotiate, photo shoots, commercials, merchandising issues, board meetings, media interviews, and sponsor appearances—all of that *outside* the actual competition, which required testing, practicing, qualifying, talking with the team, and debriefing with the crew chief. But Sundays at the track presented the biggest challenge.

In NASCAR, unlike other sports, sponsors cover the drivers' salaries in return for a prominent display on the car and a driver's commitment to sling their product in public and put smiles on the faces of consumers and their VIP customers. A lot of that hobnobbing happens on Sunday, and in many cases, it lasts until the moment a racer straps into his car and puts his helmet on. Over the years, Jeff warmed to the reality that the tidal wave of supporters was part of what made the NASCAR world go round. He would even be recognized for his indulgence of fans on race day, but there was a short period in 1995 when the young champion needed a few words of helpful advice.

"He did have a crushing amount of fans," Hendrick recalls. "And at one point, he had surrounded himself with an entourage—usually at the track—to protect himself, and it looked like he wasn't the Jeff Gordon I knew and loved. They were trying to convince him, 'You've got to build a wall around yourself.' And that's not Jeff Gordon. Jeff Gordon is more comfortable walking among the people. He doesn't want to act like a superstar."

LEFT: Jeff surrounded by eager fans.

His business manager, Bob Brannan, remembers shooing well-wishers away and trying to insulate Jeff from the demands on his time and attention. "People would go directly to him, sometimes at inappropriate times," he says. "He's getting ready, he's sitting in the car, and somebody wants to ask him a question. And there was a point when Jeff, particularly before a race, would want to spend time in the transporter with his team, get changed into his uniform, all that. And people wanted to pop in: 'So-and-so is here and wants to say hi to Jeff.' And that got to be a distraction. So Jeff said, 'I just don't really want to be interrupted from this time forward, and I really don't care who it is.'"

Rick Hendrick felt Jeff was becoming too inaccessible. "And for anybody who had the success he had and the following he had, it was easy to do, but keeping him grounded was important. I talked to him about it, and I told him about his look when he walked by sponsors, and how you don't have time for this and you don't have time for that—and part of that was his manager. We had to rein it in a little bit. But as soon as you say something to Jeff, he gets it."

"I accepted the fact that the fans, the sponsors, the media, all those things are part of how this process happens," Jeff says. "And if you accept it, you can be more comfortable and open and have more enjoyment in life at the racetrack. It makes life easier."

★   ★   ★

Naturally, after his 1995 title performance, expectations were huge for 1996. Jeff didn't disappoint, winning a Cup-topping ten races, to go along with twenty-one top-five finishes. He and Evernham, after taking the competition to school on the track, were even invited to Princeton University to guest lecture on race engineering and communication.

But 1996 was more memorable for what he did not achieve—namely, a second championship. The trophy, which had been close enough to taste, was yanked away by his Hendrick teammate, Terry Labonte, who despite tallying just a pair of wins, had been slightly more consistent. Labonte narrowly slid past Jeff in points in the last few weeks of the season to edge him out.

"Yeah, it was disappointing," Jeff says. "I mean, I liked Terry, and I loved competing against him. But we were disappointed that we didn't get it done. Those near misses drive you. You're like, 'Okay, I know what it's like to win. Now I know what it's like to lose, and I don't want to lose.' In my experience, some of the greatest lessons were learned from the losses, more than the wins. And I thought that was a great lesson, a great year to go wrong. We came back with a vengeance the next couple years because of that loss."

But at the time, it didn't just bother him that he'd lost by a hair's breadth—it galled him. "He's just one of those guys; he is really competitive," Evernham says. "I remember we had a basketball machine and a pinball machine in the No. 24 shop, and Jeff had the high score on those. If anybody beat him, he would stand at those machines until he got the high score back. I saw him stand at that basketball machine for two hours one day until he got the high score."

On the team plane, he'd play poker and acey-deucey with the crew until he'd amass giant stacks of their per-diem cash and Evernham had to make him return it so they wouldn't starve. And nearly twenty years later, he would pass Evernham in a friendly go-kart race and feel the need to put him into the wall. "I said, 'You're Jeff Gordon,'" Evernham recalls. "'Do you really get that much enjoyment out of beating *me*?' He's laughing, and he said, 'Yeah, I really do, I really do.' You don't want to gamble or race with Jeff Gordon because chances are, you're not going to win. He's just that competitive."

TOP: Jeff and Ray Evernham celebrate in Victory Lane at Watkins Glen, New York, August 10, 1997. BOTTOM: Jeff and Evernham speaking on campus at Princeton Unversity, 1996.

So by February 1997, it was no surprise that he was nearly jumping out of his skin to get back on the racetrack at Daytona and rectify the 1996 bust. It had taken him some time to master the art of restrictor-plate racing, that special understanding of how to "draft," or exploit the cars' aerodynamics to his advantage during the bunched-up, pack-style runs at Daytona. "We had cars fast enough to win the first time we went there," Evernham says. "He just had to learn the drafting part of it." By 1997, with wins at Talladega and in Daytona's shorter Pepsi 400 under his belt, Jeff felt he had every tool he needed to finally crack NASCAR's signature race.

And if he required any extra incentive, his ailing boss, Rick Hendrick, who had recently been diagnosed with life-threatening leukemia, had responded to Jeff's offer of help by telling him to "just go out and try to win that race and try to win a championship."

During the first half of the 500, Jeff slowly worked his way up from deep in the pack, and by the race's later portion, he had settled into a battle up front with Bill Elliott, Dale Earnhardt, Dale Jarrett, Mark Martin, and Ernie Irvan.

With twelve laps to go, Jeff and Earnhardt were running side-by-side behind the leader, Elliott, coming out of Turn 2. Jeff made a quick passing move to the inside. Earnhardt's No. 3 suddenly hit the wall on the back straightaway and skittered off. Contact with Dale Jarrett's No. 88 sent Earnhardt flipping up into the air and barrel-rolling over Irvan's No. 28, sending Irvan's hood reeling off into the grandstands. The battered No. 3 then slid across the track and onto the infield grass.

"It was an intense battle," Jeff says. "I got aggressive on his bumper, and he washed up the racetrack. As I got underneath him, he went wide, hit the wall, and he bounced off the wall into me. Jarrett made contact with him and turned him upside down. I actually never touched him until after he hit the wall and bounced into me."

ESPN's Dave Despain claims Dale took a slightly different view of things. "Probably the next week, I happened to be alone with Earnhardt, and so I said, "What happened at Daytona?" And he got this glint in his eye, and he got that lopsided smile on his face, and said in a hushed tone, even though there was nobody around, 'The [expletive] wrecked me and never touched me.' And it was with admiration. It was wonderful, because Earnhardt knew more about wrecking

LEFT: Jeff and Dale Earnhardt battle side-by-side at the 1997 Daytona 500.

people than anybody in the business, and the old dog had learned a new trick from the young kid."

Earnhardt may have been giving the incident more than its due, but whatever the perception, the move pushed Jeff into second, and over the next few laps, his teammates Terry Labonte and Ricky Craven crept up behind him. With six laps left, he dove low into Turn 1 to pass Elliott as Labonte and Craven moved by on the outside to take over the second and third spots. A wreck near the back of the pack, a lap and a half later, brought out the caution flag and ended the race. It was a sweep for Hendrick Motorsports, and Jeff, at just twenty-five years old, was the youngest driver, at the time, to ever win the Daytona 500.

In Victory Lane, having made good on his promise to Hendrick, he spoke to his boss by cell phone. "Did I tell you we were going to do it or what? I told you, man . . . We love you, and this one's for you." He then thanked God for throwing out the timely caution and embraced his wife.

Jeff may have been the biggest name in racing at the time, but he was just a guppy in a giant pond of celebrity, still shy enough to be starstruck. Just weeks after the Daytona win, Hendrick reached out to Tom Cruise and producer Jerry Bruckheimer, whom he had become friendly with during the filming of the 1990 racing movie *Days of Thunder* in Charlotte, and landed Jeff and Brooke an invite to *Vanity Fair* magazine's exclusive post–Academy Awards party in Los Angeles.

"It was the A-list of who's who in Hollywood," Jeff remembers. "We were like, 'How the heck did we get here?' I'm sitting there, and nobody really knows who I am, and everywhere I looked I'm seeing every major actor, director, and entertainer in Hollywood—I mean, they're just standing right next to us. It was amazing."

He and Brooke tried to cozy up to Cruise, who had been nominated for a best actor Oscar for *Jerry Maguire*, but the megastar had a line of VIPs a mile long just waiting to shake his hand. They joined the queue. "Mr. Cruise is not taking any more visitors at this time," his security detail eventually told them. "No problem," Jeff said. "Can you just pass along a message that Jeff Gordon and Rick Hendrick say hi?" Then he and Brooke turned to go. They hadn't gotten more than a few steps before he heard someone shout his name. It was Cruise, waving them back.

"He sits us down in this booth and says, 'Oh my god, this is awesome. It's such a pleasure to meet you.' He introduces us to Nicole [Kidman]," Jeff recalls. They were flabbergasted. He and Cruise talked about racing, about Hendrick Motorsports, about the track at Darlington, where he'd raced the previous day. "He couldn't have been nicer."

But the kicker for Jeff was when they passed twenty-two-year-old Leonardo DiCaprio on the way out. "He had these purple sunglasses on, two glasses of champagne. I said, 'Leonardo, I

TOP: (left to right) Terry Labonte, Jeff, and Ricky Craven, along with Hendrick Motorsports teammates, dedicate the 1997 Daytona 500 race to Rick Hendrick.

know you're probably not a NASCAR fan, but I'm a NASCAR driver and I love your work, and congrats on everything.'

"I'll never forget, he looks at me and goes, 'Ah, man, I don't follow NASCAR, but if you're in here, you must be somebody.'"

*   *   *

After the initial Daytona victory, No. 24 only got hotter. Heading into the 23rd race, they'd already amassed eight wins and seventeen top-fives, but the Southern 500 at Darlington topped them all. According to Evernham, it was "the best race we ever executed as a team."

Jeff wasn't just racing for a win that weekend; he was shooting for the Winston Million, the $1 million bonus R.J. Reynolds offered to any team that could capture three of the Cup's four major races—the Daytona 500, the Winston 500 at Talladega, the Coca-Cola 600 at Charlotte, and the Southern 500—in a single season. Jeff had already nabbed Daytona and Charlotte, but from the get-go, it looked like Darlington was going to be a bust.

"We went and tested and we struggled with the car, and we came back and cut it up, put a new snout on it, did all these things," Evernham recalls. "We worked on it all day. It was probably a fifth-place car." From the green flag, Jeff wrestled with the No. 24, and the crew continued to hack and hammer away to keep him in it.

"We made all kinds of pit stops—spring rubbers in and out, change this, change that. He bounced off the fence; we kept fixing it. The guys were good, the pit stops were good, but I mean, Jeff drove his ass off." Jeff managed to get close enough to make a run on the leader, Jeff Burton, who had a much stronger car. "And with two laps to go, we're leading the race with this car that shouldn't have been running fifth, a car that's freakin' destroyed because he hit the fence with it so many times."

The two cars touched coming around Turn 4 to take the white flag side-by-side, with Jeff holding off a hard-charging Jeff Burton. After four and a half hours of knockdown, drag-out battling, Jeff—who Rick Hendrick and Ray Evernham always said could do more with a mediocre car than any driver they'd seen—crossed the finish line just ahead of Burton. "Yeah! Yeah, we did it! Holy cow!" he shouted into his radio. It had been an incredible team effort, but it had taken Jeff Gordon to bring it home. "We were out of tires and the pit crew guys were worn out," Evernham recalls. "My box of tricks had been empty for a hundred miles." But just as their loss in the 1995 Daytona 500 had brought the No. 24 team together, the 1997 Southern 500 showed what they were capable of overcoming.

And with that pivotal win, Jeff captured the points lead back from Mark Martin, put the hammer down, and didn't let up. Nine races later, he was in Atlanta and aiming to seal the deal. "That final race in Atlanta was one of the toughest of my career," Jeff declares, "a nail biter all the way to checkered." Ultimately Jeff prevailed and was once again crowned Winston Cup champion.

*   *   *

The January 25, 1998, Super Bowl between the Green Bay Packers and Denver Broncos made for stirring competition, but Jeff was far more interested in what was going on during the ad breaks. With more than ninety million people tuning in each year for the big game, the Super

TOP: Jeff proudly holds up the 1997 Daytona 500 Championship trophy.

TOP: Jeff triumphantly holding up the 1997 Winston $1 million check. BOTTOM: Jeff proudly stands next to his second Winston Cup Championship trophy, Atlanta Motor Speedway, November 16, 1997.

Bowl's commercials—then costing about $1.3 million for a thirty-second spot—had become a something of a show in themselves.

That year, between ads by Budweiser, American Express, MasterCard, and Doritos, with stars like Jerry Seinfeld and boxer Oscar de la Hoya, people saw a Pepsi commercial featuring Jeff Gordon. From a personal branding standpoint, it was a huge boon. "I'll tell you, Jeff has got a super-smart business head," says Rick Hendrick. "And not to have been educated in business, he's got a God-given sense for it."

Indeed, up until a year before the Super Bowl ad aired, Jeff had a Coca-Cola sponsorship, even appearing in a Coke commercial back in 1995. But in surveying the athlete-endorsement landscape and understanding that NASCAR was now reaching out to a broader audience, he felt like the company could be doing more for him and benefiting more from his image and cache.

"They almost treated it as a regional sponsorship, which was fine at first," Jeff says. "But as things were progressing, I hoped for more, especially after winning the first championship. And they did a little bit more. But, at least in racing, they never really wanted to put a lot behind one driver.

"And I wasn't trying to be arrogant or selfish, but if you have a consumer product, you tie yourself to someone who is doing well. You could see that in other sports, where they'd tie themselves to an athlete and promote that athlete with their brand."

In late 1996, with Rick Hendrick's blessing, Jeff decided to test the waters and approached Ron Faust, a friend of Brooke's family who worked for Pepsi, about setting up a meeting with company executives. It was a bold move for a twenty-five-year-old racecar driver. Within days, Jeff, armed with a "wish list" he had prepared with the help of his financial adviser Bob Brannan and marketing consultant Hal Price, was on a plane for PepsiCo headquarters outside Manhattan. A top priority on that list: a Super Bowl commercial.

"It was all the things we were wanting Coke to do that we didn't think they were doing," he says. "And everything we asked for, Pepsi said, 'Yes, we're going to do that, yes, we're going to do that, yes, we're going to do that.' And they brought in all the key people to say hello. They were well prepared. And they basically agreed to everything."

Having signed a letter of intent with Pepsi, Jeff and his team then set up a meeting with Coca-Cola in Atlanta, where Jeff hoped to let them down easy. But the marketing folks seemed to have gotten a whiff that something wasn't right in Gordonville and had a presentation ready to go. And while their new plan offered more than it previously did, there were two deal breakers: they wanted Jeff to be part of a group of NASCAR drivers they hoped to promote, and no Super Bowl commercial.

"So I told them, 'Listen, this is great and I appreciate it, but we came here because we wanted to inform you that we're going to make a change.' They were pretty taken aback. . . . I could see the look in their eyes," he remembers. "They were like, 'We can't let this happen. We're going to lose our jobs.' And they just started throwing out anything and everything." Jeff stopped them. "Guys," he said, "I'm sorry, but the decision has been made. It's done, and I'm sorry." Then he thanked them for everything they had done for him the last few years and walked out.

"It was a difficult decision," he says, but just as he'd done four years earlier, when he signed with Hendrick, he realized it would pay off in the long term. "I loved the way Pepsi was thinking about things. They were thinking big picture, and they believed in it." Jeff's

10/21/96
Pepsi

Objectives

Ⓐ • Develop long-term partnership with select corporations that can deliver the following assets to Jeff and the #24 Team:

1. National "mainstream" exposure via
   - Electronic & print media
   - In-store POS and merchandising
   - Special Events (Rock N Jock, customized)
   - Promotional programs which capitalize on targeted JGI initiatives. (TV specials, Video, etc)

Commit min. one National
TV Spot per year
1) NCAA Final Four
2) World Series
3) NBA Finals
4) Olympics?
5) NFL games
   Super Bowl

2. Fan Building programs via:
   - National Fan Club (15,000)
   - World Wide Web Chat Sessions @3¢
   - Tie-in programs which offer licensed merchandise
   - Youth related program(s)

3. NASCAR related programs / sweepstakes to capitalize on 50TH Anniversary (Tie-in with Pepsi Tracks, History of Championships)

4. Participation in long-term initiatives like
   - NASCAR Speed Park
   - Sanctioned Youth League Racing
   - Sponsor Summits
   - International Exhibitions

5. Performance Incentive Programs with Ray Evernham and Team

6. Charity related programs
   - "Racing for a Reason"

patience—looking for the right opportunities and playing the long game—is something he admits picking up from his mother and John over the years. "I knew I was doing the right thing," he says. "I just felt it."

From a sponsor's perspective, Pepsi couldn't have been happier, and their relationship with Jeff turned into the longest-running endorsement deal the company has ever had with a spokesperson. "They lived up to everything they said they were going to do. They had me plastered all over billboards and soda-machine fronts," he says. "And we did a Super Bowl commercial."

The Super Bowl ad itself featured Jeff, in the midst of a race, attempting to retrieve a rolling can of Pepsi from the floor of his car. Oblivious to his nearby competitors, he goes up on two wheels, drives over the tops of other cars, spins 360s, flips end over end, and eventually drives backward across the finish line, winning the race. In the name of amusement, the moves he pulled were clearly unbelievable and ridiculous. But they were only slightly more ridiculous and unbelievable than what would actually happen on the track in 1998.

TOP: An actual page of the handwritten notes Jeff and Hal Price prepared before the Pepsi meeting in 1997.

7

DON'T STINK UP MY SHOW!

THE 1961 NEW YORK YANKEES, the 1995–96 Chicago Bulls, Secretariat in 1973, and Martina Navratilova in 1983. In the history of sports, there have been those seasons in which individuals and teams suddenly seem to be invincible. Every ball just falls their way; every mistake somehow turns out to their benefit. That was 1998 for Jeff Gordon and the No. 24 team.

It had a rocky start, though. Jeff was sleeping soundly one morning in his Lake Norman home, near Charlotte, when the phone rang. It was his PR person wanting to know if he was coming to the Charlotte track that day. "Of course," he told her.

"And she said, 'Okay, well you realize practice starts in five minutes,'" Jeff recalls. "I hang up the phone. I'm just, 'Oh crap, oh crap, oh crap.' I either forgot to set my alarm before I went to sleep or didn't set it correctly. Regardless, I was freaking out. Threw clothes on. Got in the car. I was doing ninety miles an hour the whole way to the racetrack, and it's a thirty-minute drive. And I get to the track, and I'm mortified. Mortified."

Sitting up on jack stands was his No. 24, damaged. When he hadn't shown up for practice, Evernham had asked Terry Labonte to take a few laps so he could get some feedback and information on how the thing was running. Labonte had blown a right front tire and hit the wall.

"I just knew there was going to be hell to pay," Jeff says. "I tried to avoid [Evernham] because I knew the wrath that was about to be put on me. . . . And it wasn't cussing me out. Like with John, it was just all about respect. . . . Evernham said, 'You let the team down. These guys work their butts off.' And I told him, 'I know. There's no excuse.' It just made me feel this big," Jeff says, holding his fingers an inch apart. Jeff personally apologized to everyone on the crew.

He more than made up for it. After the crew got the car fixed for the race the next day, Evernham says, "That's when he got on that tear." Of the year's twenty-two remaining races, he won ten of them, including another Brickyard and another Southern 500, for a season total of thirteen—a modern-era NASCAR record. He finished second in five of them and third three times. He won four races in a row, becoming the first driver to accomplish that feat since Earnhardt, twelve years earlier. Jeff was so far ahead in the point standings he wrapped up the

OPPOSITE: Jeff drives under the checkered flag, waving to the cheering crowd at the 1998 Brickyard 400 for his second Brickyard victory and thirty-fifth career win.

93

championship before the season reached its final race.

It wasn't just that they won the races, it was the way they won them—by twenty, twenty-five car lengths or more, by lapping drivers multiple times on road courses. "Jeff was literally ten feet tall," recalls Brian Whitesell, the No. 24's team engineer at the time. "Just brimming with confidence and aggressiveness. . . . You would really get a feel throughout the weekend that when he walked in on Sunday morning, unless something came out of left field, this is ours."

"I'd be out there with a four-, five-, six-, eight-second lead, just on

cruise control," Jeff remembers, "and I'm like, 'Hmm, man, what am I going to have for dinner?' And then I'd have to say, 'Okay, stop that, stop that. Pay attention.'"

The muscle they showed on the track had all the other teams trying to emulate whatever they did, to no avail. "I'm telling you," says Evernham, "for a while I felt like, 'How could this much good stuff keep happening to us?' One time, we were leading, we pit, he goes back out and runs three or four laps, and then says, 'I think I got a flat tire.' So he comes down pit road all by himself. Sure enough, flat rear tire. We change tires, go back out, and we're in last place. All of a sudden, everybody else panics because we came in and put on tires. So they all pit, and it puts us back in the lead."

NASCAR did not like what was happening. The organization was in the business of providing entertainment, and when the competition got too lopsided, they feared fans of the other forty-two drivers would stop paying attention, stop coming to the track, and shut their television sets off.

"If you get a distinct advantage," Jeff says, "a big part of their job, at that time, was to find that advantage you have and take it away from you to even out the competition. Back then, NASCAR would adjust things if they felt it necessary. As a competitor, it sucked, but that's the world we lived in."

"Jeff and I got direct orders from Bill France Jr., 'Don't stink up my show this week,'" Evernham recalls. "He said, 'You guys need to slow that thing down a little bit or I'll slow it down for you.'" Both Evernham and Jeff found it flattering.

Still, none of the new rules or regulations that had been designed to curb the No. 24 seemed to work. Other owners accused them of cheating, but NASCAR couldn't find any evidence. "It's every competitor's job to build the best race car they can within the rules, and we did a great job at that," Jeff contends. "We were a cohesive team, communicated well, executed well, and did our homework. We just had a slight edge in all of these areas."

The team ultimately began to slow themselves down. "We had our own theories that NASCAR had a cutoff, where if you got more than a three- or four-second lead on the field, they were going to find a way to throw a caution, because they knew people were tuning

TOP: The well-tuned Rainbow Warriors make quick work of a tire change at Martinsville, 1999.

out," Jeff says. "And so what we would do is, if we had that strong a car and got a run, Ray would say certain things to me on the radio so that I would let off and slow the pace to try not to get too big of a lead."

"We got accused of sandbagging a lot," Evernham says, "and the truth is, we were. We still won every race we could, but we didn't get the lead and go out and lap the field."

When a race team's biggest problem becomes how to slow down, it's clear they are in a pretty good place. Back in 1994, Evernham had posted a checklist on the shop wall that read, "From Nobody to Upstart—From Upstart to Contender—From Contender to Winner—From Winner to Champion—From Champion to Dynasty." By 1998, with three championships under their belt, the first four of those had been crossed off.

Although they started the 1999 season by winning the Daytona 500 for the second time in three years, the bar had now been set so high that even the slightest deviation from perfection cast an outsized shadow. In the first dozen weeks, they racked up three wins but also had two thirty-ninth-place finishes, along with a thirty-first, a thirty-eighth, and a forty-third-place finish.

There were races they should have won and didn't. There were handling problems, suspension issues, tire issues, a crash, and a broken transmission. They hovered around fifth in the point standings for most of the first half of the season, but that was no longer acceptable. Second would have been a letdown.

"We had a few months where things hadn't gone great on the track," Jeff says. "We weren't as competitive in 1999 as we wanted to be. [Ray and I] were battling a little bit on the radio about what I think we need with the car, and he's telling me what he thinks we should do. And we just weren't in sync like we had been."

"Our communication was starting to fall apart," Evernham agrees, a trend he traced back, at least in part, to Jeff and Brooke's move from North Carolina to Highland Beach, Florida, at the close of 1998. "When Jeff moved to Florida, we saw him a lot less. I don't think that helped." But whereas in previous years the pair's pit-road jawing sessions would end in a

TEAM #24 CHECKLIST

- ☑ **From Nobody To Upstart**
- ☑ **From Upstart To Contender**
- ☑ **From Contender To Winner**
- ☑ **From Winner To Champion**
- ☑ **From Champion To Dynasty**

TOP: Ray Evernham's checklist for the No. 24 team on the shop wall at Hendrick Motorsports. LEFT: The team celebrates winning their fourth straight Pepsi Southern 500 at Darlington, as well as claiming the Winston No Bull million dollars.

laugh, or at least a brotherly agreement that they both wanted what was best for the team, things seemed different now—less constructive and more biting.

"As a crew chief, I needed to talk to Jeff the way I needed to talk to him," Evernham says. "But Jeff didn't need a guy like that anymore. We'd won three championships, he'd won all these races. . . . It's like you coach somebody to get them to a certain level, and once they're at that level, you've got to coach them a little bit different. . . . I think if we'd talked about it, I could've done that."

But the reality is that the squabbles and tensions were indicative of even deeper, more profound frustrations behind the scenes. In some sense, Jeff and Ray, and the entire team, had become victims of their own success. They were without question the premier operation in NASCAR. Individually and collectively they had lucrative offers from other owners, from agents, from anybody and everybody who saw dollar signs and wanted a piece of the pie. The team was perched like Humpty Dumpty, and it seemed like all it would take was a stiff breeze to make it fall.

If anyone had his eye on the horizon, it was Evernham. "I think he was yearning for more," Jeff says. "We'd had a lot of success, and I think he was looking for the next challenge, whatever that may be."

Whitesell saw the same thing in the shop. "Ray had done all he wanted to do as a crew chief. He didn't necessarily want to stay and click off eight championships so he could say he won the most ever as a crew chief. He had aspirations of bigger, better things for himself."

Evernham's restlessness was no secret. As early as the March race at Darlington, he was interviewed by ESPN about how much longer he planned to soldier on through the day-to-day grind of crew chiefing. "As long as it's fun," he replied. "And right now, it's still fun." A politic answer, perhaps, but in a word, he wanted control, whether that meant a greater hand in steering the Hendrick ship or an opportunity to own his own team.

The fact is, he already *was* an owner. In late 1998, he and Jeff had launched Gordon–Evernham Motorsports, a Busch Grand National team sponsored by the Pepsi-Cola Company. For Jeff—who, along with Rick Hendrick's son Ricky, raced the No. 24 Pepsi car on a limited schedule in 1999, his first time in the Busch Series since 1992—it represented a business opportunity, a co-branding arrangement from which both he and Pepsi could benefit. For

TOP: Jeff leads the pack at the 1998 Brickyard 400. RIGHT: Jeff and Ray nearing the end of their storied partnership, 1999.

Evernham, it was a chance to escape the "politics and counterpolitics" of being a Hendrick employee and run things his own way without bureaucratic interference.

"Right away, after a couple races, I saw how much he liked it," Jeff says. "He loved that it was his race team, his name was on it, and he was able to be in control of what happened. I was happy for him. But I will say I was a little concerned what it meant for his future at Hendrick, because I saw he wanted to be more than a crew chief. So when the Dodge thing came along, it wasn't surprising to me at all that he wanted to do it and was going to do it."

With the rise in NASCAR's popularity and revenues in the mid-1990s, DaimlerChrysler was looking to return its Dodge brand to racing after a quarter-century absence. And who better to shepherd the project than Jeff Gordon and Ray Evernham? Early in the season, the company had quietly approached the pair with an invitation to start and own two new Dodge teams and build the reentry operation from the ground up. It was a major offer, and for Evernham, as an ambitious, meticulous, and domineering nuts-and-bolts field commander, it seemed especially appealing.

They mulled it over for months, even as Rick Hendrick, still battling leukemia and unaware of the deal, floated the idea of Evernham assuming an executive position with more oversight over company operations. But it was too little too late. By the end of summer, Evernham had already made up his mind that Gordon or no Gordon, he was going with Dodge.

"When Ray came and told me he was going to do this," Hendrick says, "he still had another year on his contract, and at first I was kind of bitter. At the time, I was still sick. But I let him out of his contract. And I was concerned, because the rumors were that Jeff was going to go with him. But I talked to Jeff, and he said, 'I'm going to stay, I want to stay here.'"

The driver-crew chief-owner partnership that seemed as if it could last forever was over. Seven years. Three championships. Forty-seven victories in 216 starts. A spectacular climb from rookie upstarts to the height of NASCAR. And while the Dodge deal was ostensibly the wedge that drove them apart, the groundwork had been laid by all those incendiary elements that lurk in the depths of any competitive team—ego, pride, and vanity. Who deserved the most credit for their success? It was a question that had been pondered and dissected for years in the press and among fans. Was it Ray? Was it Jeff? Was it Hendrick's equipment and resources? Could they survive, and thrive, apart, or was it all just a synergistic tapestry?

"It's the same things that tear rock bands apart, or any great team," says Evernham, who admits there were times when he felt he wasn't getting his due. "You start to get like, 'I'm the one that's working a gazillion hours with these guys.' And that's when you start to drift apart, you lose communication, you get to the point where all of sudden it's about *me*, I'm not getting enough. . . . Our pit crew guys started to do that, too. And then the Dodge people came to me, and I was feeling underappreciated. I'm thinking, 'Man, Jeff is making $25 million a year, and I'm making $1 million.'"

That perception of disparity was, like a cancer, slowly eating away the heart of the team. And if he could pinpoint a moment when the edifice began to crumble, Evernham says, it would be when Jeff's financial manager, Bob Brannan, came to him after the 1998 season to get his rubber stamp on the blueprint for that year's championship ring. Evernham had some ideas of his own that would have cost a little more, but he figured he and Jeff could chip in to make it happen. Brannan, he recalls, wasn't listening.

TOP: The logo for Gordon-Evernham Motorsports.

"Was it really a terrible request, for all the hours I was putting in?" Evernham remembers thinking. "And Brannan said, 'This is the ring design, this is the way it's going to be, this is what we're paying, and that's the end of it.' When he said that to me, I said to myself, 'Here's my two choices: I can punch him square in the face, or I can just go find something else to do.' And right then is when I think it really changed for me, that day."

The Dodge offer was a once-in-a-lifetime chance for forty-two-year-old Evernham to prove his worth to himself and to all the doubters. "In some ways, I think Jeff wanted to try it without me," he contends. "I think Jeff, really deep down inside, wanted to be his own person. John had guided him all the way here, and then I had picked him up and guided him to three championships. I don't mean that Jeff wanted to get rid of me, but I think, honestly, it was time."

It was a fair assessment. Despite everything, it gnawed at Jeff that there was a notion his success had always been orchestrated by "masterminds" and "handlers." This was his moment to stand on his own and show his merit. "I would never say that anyone doesn't deserve the credit," he says. "Ray did. But I wanted to feel that my contribution was significant as well. And I knew I would never get that with Ray being my crew chief—and that's only a credit to Ray."

The two ran their last few Cup races together in early fall, culminating with the MBNA Gold 400 in Dover on September 26, where Jeff finished a disappointing seventeenth. On September 28, Hendrick and Evernham officially announced Ray's departure to the media. The following day, as the story broke, Ray cleared the last of his items from the shop and walked out, taking the No. 24's chief mechanic, Ed Guzzo, and two other crew members with him and leaving a giant vacuum in his wake.

"There was huge concern," Whitesell admits. "They'd had all this success, they'd done all these things, and now the spoken leader had left the building. . . . It was a big deal, like 'Oh my god, the world is going to fall apart, what are we all going to do?'"

They did the only thing they could do. They moved forward. Jeff and Hendrick installed Whitesell as the interim crew chief, they hired several new employees, and the shop began readying the car for the NAPA AutoCare 500 on October 3. By the time they rolled into

RIGHT: Jeff and Brian Whitesell pose with the trophy after their momentous win at Martinsville, October 3, 1999.

Martinsville that Sunday afternoon, the news about Evernham was all anyone could talk about. "Never in modern-day motorsports," said ESPN commentator Jerry Punch, "has so much attention been paid to the separation of a driver and crew chief." Everyone was wondering what would happen next for the No. 24 team.

Within a few hours they had an answer, as Jeff took the checkered flag just ahead of a charging Dale Earnhardt. The hard-fought effort was punctuated by Whitesell's gutsy decision not to pit under caution with twenty-eight laps left and Jeff running third behind

Earnhardt and Bobby Labonte, both of whom went in for fresh tires. That gamble put Jeff in the lead on the restart, and he did a masterful job of holding off the wolves for the win.

The team went crazy, hooting and high-fiving, and hoisted Whitesell onto their shoulders. As a teary-eyed Jeff pulled into Victory Lane, he leaped out of the car and doused his new crew chief with water. "I've never wanted to win so bad in my life, I tell you," Jeff said in the post-race interview. He praised Whitesell's effort. He thanked God. He thanked his sponsors. And he thanked Ray Evernham. The thirty-five-year-old Whitesell, who had been with the No. 24 since the team's inception, also had praise for his former captain. "Ray Evernham taught us well," he said. "He's the reason we're here—ain't no doubt about it."

A week later, the No. 24 team repeated the feat, surprising everyone with another emotional victory at Charlotte for their Cup-leading seventh win of the season. If they were looking for a sign that the ship would continue to float, they had it.

"The first person that texted me after those victories was Ray," Jeff recalls. "He said, 'See, you don't need me after all. You're going to be just fine.' And I sensed in those conversations I had with him that he was happy for me, but in a sort of sad way. It was like he saw his child moving on."

For Jeff, those wins, "were very gratifying because so many people said, 'Well, it's all Ray.' And it was nice to go do something without him. And yet I didn't want to shout that out to the world, because he was my friend and I respected him."

Those wistful and fraternal feelings between Jeff and Evernham took a hit a few weeks later, when after winning a Busch race in the Pepsi car at Phoenix, Jeff told his former crew chief they were going to have to disband Gordon–Evernham Motorsports. There was just too big a chance that proprietary information might slip from Chevrolet to Dodge if they continued.

"That didn't go over too well with him," Jeff says. "It was kind of ugly. Here we are posing in Victory Lane, and he was not happy with me. He hated me at that time. I was a little harsh in the way I told him, and I just didn't handle it the way I wanted to."

In hindsight, Ray says, "I think if we'd talked through some things, we probably could have stayed together." Whitesell agrees, "You know, a little bit of love here, a little bit of love there, and everything would have been textbook."

As the 1999 season drew down, the euphoria of the two wins at Martinsville and Charlotte faded. They had gone from the most dominant force in racing just twelve months earlier to a sixth-place team. And when the famed Rainbow Warriors over-the-wall pit crew announced they were leaving Jeff to work for the new champion, Dale Jarrett, it only compounded the sting.

If there was a silver lining to any of it, it was that Rick Hendrick decided to sign Jeff to a lifetime contract with Hendrick Motorsports and give him an equity stake in the No. 24 team, something Jeff had hinted at earlier in the year.

"Jeff was so close to me, and he had done so much for us that I just wanted to give him an opportunity to do what he wanted and be part of the company," Hendrick says. "I just cared that much about him that I felt like he could help me run the company after he retired. And I wanted to reward him for what he'd done and have him not have to worry about negotiating again."

Their first move as partners would be promoting Whitesell to team manager and choosing a permanent replacement for Evernham. They found their man in thirty-three-year-old Robbie Loomis, a crew chief from Richard Petty's Cup team.

TOP: Jeff celebrates the No. 24 team's second consecutive victory at Charlotte Motor Speedway, October 10, 1999. BOTTOM: Jeff and Rick Hendrick signing the lifetime agreement, October 6, 1999.

8

THE END OF ONE ERA, AND THE START OF ANOTHER

NOT ONLY WAS ROBBIE LOOMIS STEPPING into some enormous shoes, he was going to have to wear them in their previous owner's home. Loomis was the first outsider to take the helm of the No. 24 team. The guys in the shop had gotten used to doing things a certain way—Ray's way—and not everyone was ready for a change. Commanding an Evernham-level of respect was going to be a tall order.

"I told him the week he came on board, 'The first thing I want you to do is go in and fire two people,'" Jeff recalls. "'You need to find the weak links and fire them. If you want to grab hold of this team and get their attention and make sure they respect you, that's what you need to do.'"

Loomis never did. That wasn't how he learned to crew chief, and it wasn't in his blood. He wanted to build relationships, earn the team's trust. The reluctance to bring the hatchet down irked Jeff. "I felt like we suffered that first year because of it," he says.

There were other issues, not the least being the Ford Taurus's clear aerodynamic advantage over the new Chevrolet Monte Carlo. In the season-opening Daytona 500, Fords swept the top five spots and continued to dominate the next few races before NASCAR allowed midseason changes to achieve more parity. The No. 24 body shop had to adjust quickly to the new design. Still, Jeff managed to reel off five top-ten finishes in his first eight races heading into Talladega.

Starting from way back in thirty-sixth position, he waged a knock-down battle with Mike Skinner over the last six laps to grab the fiftieth win of his career, snapping a thirteen-race winless streak and making him only the seventh driver in history to achieve a career Grand Slam—wins at Daytona, Charlotte, Darlington, and Talladega.

But through the spring and summer, the highlights were few and far between. He mustered a win at Sonoma in June, his record-setting sixth straight road course victory, but he also, for the first time in his career, stumbled through a four-race series in which he couldn't crack the

OPPOSITE: Jeff Gordon celebrates another win at Sonoma Raceway, June 25, 2000.

TOP: The No. 24 DuPont Chevrolet in the lead at Talladega, April 16, 2000.

top twenty. It wasn't what he wanted his first post-Evernham season to look like. He was at least reassured by DuPont's announcement that they would sponsor the No. 24 through 2006.

As the year wore on, Jeff and Loomis struggled to find the right connection. Loomis wondered how much encouragement Jeff needed. Should he be a rah-rah guy or keep it cool? How far should he push it if they disagree? Should he ask *him* to help rally the troops when they were down? For Jeff's part, he was still concerned over whether Loomis could develop into the team-leading hard-ass he felt his crew chief needed to be.

"Ray always had the right metaphors and the books and the leadership skills and all these things," Jeff says. "I didn't have to do anything other than go win races." But now he found himself showing up to the shop more often, throwing out some positive words. After all, he was no longer just the team's driver—he was also a co-owner. But it was a struggle. Eventually, he would finish ninth in points, his worst performance since 1994.

Yet despite the overall mediocrity of the 2000 season, as summer had rolled into fall, something seemed to gel. They got a fourth place at Dover, then a win at Richmond, and they kept rolling. They posted eleven top-ten finishes—six of those were top-fives—in the final twelve races. Except for a momentary stumble at Daytona in 2001, their hot streak continued. By summer 2001, sixteen races in, they had finished outside the top five only five times, had wins at Las Vegas, Dover, and Michigan, and were sitting atop the point standings.

No one could deny something special was happening. "I think Jeff really felt the cohesiveness of the team and the guys," Loomis says. "We got our communication together, and the guys in the shop started accepting the 'new guy' and that I was asking for things differently."

"To my surprise," Jeff admits, "Loomis's more conservative approach worked in 2001."

There was certainly a burgeoning sense of destiny, but the No. 24 team's excitement was tempered by two tragedies. On February 18, on the last lap of the Daytona 500, Dale Earnhardt had been involved in a wreck that took the forty-nine-year-old legend's life. For Jeff, losing the competitor and mentor who had in many ways defined the early part of his career was a heavy blow. The loss left everyone starkly aware of their own mortality.

But Earnhardt's death was more than a monumental loss for racing; it left Bill France Jr. and the NASCAR front office without their back-channel connection. For years, when something in the sport needed fixing, Dale would walk among the drivers, get a consensus, then march over to the NASCAR trailer, sit down with France, and hammer out a solution. It might not have always been what everyone wanted, but by sheer force of personality, he was able to make it stick. With Earnhardt gone, some eyes turned to Jeff to fill that role. It was not something he wanted.

But by virtue of Dale's absence, Jeff was now "the face"—no other driver even approached the same public notoriety. Rick Hendrick remembers that soon after Earnhardt's crash, France told Jeff he would now have to be NASCAR's true and sole figurehead. "He was a man of few words and an iron fist," Hendrick says of NASCAR's CEO, "but he told Gordon, 'You will have to be the flag bearer for this sport.' Jeff didn't say a word. Then he said, 'I'll do my best.' He didn't make a big deal about it."

LEFT: Jeff (left) and Robbie Loomis pose with their trophies in victory lane at Talladega, 2000.

TOP: (left to right) Jimmie Johnson, Rick Hendrick, and Jeff Gordon meet with the press.

What he did do was what he'd done from the beginning—present a clean image and make the fans and sponsors happy. He was also busy clearing the decks at Hendrick Motorsports for his new protégé, a young Busch Series racer and fellow California native named Jimmie Johnson, whom he had encouraged Hendrick to hire as the new fourth-car team in 2002, a team Jeff and Rick would co-own. But most of all, he kept winning races.

In August 2001, he gave himself a thirtieth birthday present with his third career victory in the Brickyard 400. The next week, he won at Watkins Glen, then had three more top-ten finishes and a pole, before tragedy struck again on September 11. Racing, along with nearly all professional sports, was canceled the following week as the nation mourned those killed in the terror attacks. When NASCAR returned on September 23, Jeff joined Bill Weber and Benny Parsons on NBC's pre-race broadcast and was asked, as "a leader in the garage," about the atmosphere among the race teams, many of whom had been busy raising money for the victims.

"That's what I love so much about our community within NASCAR," he told them. "The drivers, the crew members, the car owners, NASCAR itself—everybody in this garage area has always supported those in need. And right now, there's a lot that we can do, and that we are doing . . . to donate toward these needy causes out there. I'm not only proud to be an American, but I'm proud to be a NASCAR Winston Cup driver." If Bill France Jr. had been looking for a flag-bearing performance, he couldn't have gotten a better one.

After finishing fourth that afternoon, Jeff went on to win again the next week in Kansas. It was looking like the No. 24 juggernaut was going to be hard to beat. By that point in the Cup season, Jeff was already nearly 400 points ahead of second-running Ricky Rudd, with just five races to go. He finished sixth that weekend in Phoenix, then had poor showings at Rockingham and Homestead, but by the time he reached Atlanta on November 18 for the season's second-to-last race, he only needed to finish thirty-second or better to claim his fourth championship in seven years. It was everything he'd worked for and dreamed of since that fateful fall of 1999, and he capped his two-and-a-half year crusade with a sixth-place finish, finally stuffing a sock in the mouth of all the naysayers.

"It wasn't until that championship that my stock and respect as a driver went to another level, because everybody realized, 'Oh, it wasn't just Ray,'" says Jeff. For him, it was the most personally gratifying of the four titles he had won. Standing on the stage that day in Atlanta to accept the trophy, "was an awesome moment," he remembers. "In my opinion, at that moment, life could not be any better."

But in an instant, it all came crashing down. Amid the celebration, the confetti and champagne, the team photos and interviews, Mike Helton suggested that they bring Brooke in for a few pictures. When Jeff beckoned her to the stage, she glared. Her response was sharp and steely. "It's about time you asked me to come over," Jeff remembers her telling him. "I thought you were just going to leave me over there. Is this celebration just about *you*? Is that what it's all about?"

Her bitterness caught him off guard. "It hit me like a ton of bricks," he recalls. One moment, he was rejoicing in the greatest accomplishment of his Winston Cup career, and the next he was being raked over the coals for his selfishness. "Did I kind of forget about her in that moment? I kind of did," he admits. "But at the same time, I wasn't intentionally trying to." Still, his inattention was telling, especially for a man who, season after season, race after race, was regularly greeted in Victory Lane by a kiss from his wife and was seldom seen outside her company.

"She was pissed," Jeff says. "And she stayed like that all the way back to the airport." Finally, Jeff couldn't hold his tongue. "I stopped her in her tracks," he remembers. "I said, 'Hey, I'm sorry you feel that way, but this moment's not about you. This is about me and my race team and what we just accomplished. I'm proud of that, and I'm not going to let you ruin it.'"

It was one of the first real fights they'd had in nine years together, but it was a watershed. "We always got along pretty good, but that was mainly because I went along with pretty much everything she wanted to do," Jeff says. "I was easygoing." Now, it was as if a switch had been thrown, and he found himself dwelling on the slights and resentments, the petty jealousies, and all the slings and arrows he felt he'd absorbed good-naturedly over the years for the sake of marital harmony. And the one topic he kept coming back to was family.

TOP: (left to right) Rick Hendrick, Brian Whitesell, Robbie Loomis, and Jeff on the stage in Atlanta to accept the 2001 Winston Cup Championship trophy, November 18, 2001.

"In all honesty, if I had to look at one single thing that was the biggest factor, I'd say that was it," Jeff says. "The fact of the matter is that she had a problem with my parents. She had a certain picture of the way we were going to live, and my parents didn't fit into that." The wedge that had been driven between Jeff, Carol, and John in 1994 and '95 had only gotten worse over the years, particularly after Jeff and Brooke moved to Florida. Over time, Jeff watched as his parents were shunted further and further to the periphery while Brooke's mother and stepfather, who lived part-time in a home Jeff and Brooke purchased for them near Highland Beach, assumed a much larger role in the couple's lives. It weighed on him.

"That separation from my parents, I always carried that on me, every day, every year," Jeff says. "I didn't like what had happened, but it had happened, and at that point a 'sorry' was not going to repair it. And I kept a lot of it to myself."

"There were times when I just wanted to go over and strangle Jeff," Carol admits. "Like, 'What are you thinking?' I mean, it's okay to not have your parents running your business. I understand that. You're married. You need to have that independence. But it was the way that he was being manipulated—and he has to live with that."

Jeff agonized over being pulled in opposite directions, attempting to please everybody. He knew that acceding to Brooke's wishes would hurt his family and that pushing the issue would damage his marriage. "I think my mother and me and Jeff are very sweet people," says Jeff's sister, Kimberly, whose first marriage, like Carol's marriage to Billy, had ended in divorce. "And we went looking for people who were controlling, because we're not controlling. So we found people that were controlling, but they weren't nice and didn't treat us well, you know?"

With his emotions still roiling, things came to a head during Christmas as he waited at the local private airport to pick up Brooke's relatives, who were being flown in for the holidays on the couple's jet. Jeff's clan had been relegated to two days during Thanksgiving—Brooke said she couldn't tolerate them for more than that—and suddenly the unfairness of it all hit him. "And I just said, 'This is bullshit,'" he recalls. "What am I doing? This is crazy. I have no friends, I have no family that I have any real relationship with, and my life has become all about what happens on the racetrack and with Brooke and her family. I mean, it was nuts. That was just not the way I envisioned life to be."

Shortly after New Year's, Jeff met with a divorce attorney. Then he moved out. "I think I had held so much in for so long that when it hit me, I was done. We went through therapy,

TOP: The entire No. 24 team celebrates their fourth Cup championship in Victory Lane. Jeff is standing at the top of the stage with Rick Hendrick on his right and Brooke on his left. Atlanta Motor Speedway, November 2001.

but it was too late. All these things added up, and when I finally accepted that the marriage was not working, it came flooding out."

Not long after, Jeff made a trip up to Charlotte to visit Carol and John. Both of them remember having suspicions that something wasn't quite right. He spent the night, and in the morning he asked his mother to show him the pond they were building on the property. "I'll never forget this. It was starting to sprinkle," Carol recalls, "and we drove down in his car, past the shop, and he parked on the grass and we started to get out. Then it started raining a little bit harder, so we got back in the car. He turned the car on, then he turned the car off. I just kept waiting for those words, 'We're going to have a baby.' But he said, 'Brooke and I aren't living together.' Oh my God, I was so relieved. I just said, 'Jeff, I'm so sorry.' I mean, I didn't know whether he was devastated. So I said, 'You know, maybe this is just a temporary thing, maybe you guys can work it out.' And he said, 'No, Mom, we're not going to work this out. I know what I want.'"

He also dropped in on Rick Hendrick. "He came to talk to me, and he was sweating so bad," Hendrick says. "And I don't know what it is, but he's got some bad news, something is wrong, something is big-time wrong. And I was almost relieved when he told me he was getting a divorce. I thought, 'God, I'm lucky he's not divorcing me.' So I said, 'Listen, I'm going to give you some advice. Here are the three things you don't do: You don't hit her, you don't leave her, and you don't get caught with your pants down.'"

In the months to come, Jeff's romantic intrigues—which he was adamant began after he separated from Brooke—would become fodder for the tabloids. But two out of three ain't bad. "He didn't hit her," Hendrick jokes.

Fresh on his own, Jeff joined Robbie Loomis, Jimmie Johnson, and Johnson's new crew chief, Chad Knaus, on a private flight to Las Vegas that January, where they planned to test for the upcoming season, less than a month away. The Friday departure gave them four free days before their scheduled speedway session. "I had a feeling we were going to go out there and have some fun," Johnson says, "but I didn't know what kind of fun Jeff was planning on having." Would he drink? Would he gamble? Would he hole up in his hotel room reading Bible verses? "I didn't think our fun was going to match up."

Shortly after the plane took off, Jeff got up to go to the bathroom, and Johnson quickly cracked open a bottle of rum, poured some into his half-empty Pepsi, and passed it around for the others to do likewise. "Hurry up, pour it, pour it, pour it," he urged. They weren't fast enough. Jeff returned to find Loomis clutching the open jug of Captain Morgan. His crew chief fixed him with a hangdog look and pointed his finger at Johnson like a guilty teenager. "He brought it." But any fears that they were dealing with a stiff-necked schoolmaster dissipated once they saw Jeff's approving reaction. When the plane landed in Sin City, the party was on.

LEFT: Jeff looking confident as he wraps up his championship season.

107

9

LIVE FROM NEW YORK . . .

IF BEING ON HIS OWN WAS AN ENTIRELY new experience for Jeff—"Brooke and I were apart no more than seven days during our entire marriage," he says—it was also a little jarring for the fans.

To them, racing's royal couple was as inseparable as biscuits and gravy, and the smooching, hand-holding, clean-living pair had become as much a NASCAR institution as the pre-race prayer. So when Jeff arrived for the 2002 season absent his other half, the question on everyone's lips was: Where's Brooke? Is she sick? Is she pregnant? The rumor mill began churning, but Jeff, and everybody else who knew, stayed tight-lipped.

On Friday, March 15, just before the fifth race of the season, Brooke filed for divorce. In her petition, she asked for alimony, exclusive use of the couple's Florida beachfront home, several automobiles, and access to their boat and jet. Boiled down, she was looking for a fifty-fifty split.

The racing world was shocked. But even more astonishing than the breakup itself was Brooke's filing that Jeff might have been unfaithful. The truth, though it wasn't known publicly at the time, was that nothing had occurred until after Jeff moved out of the couple's home for good. In his mind, the marriage was over at that point, even if he wasn't legally separated.

The idea of NASCAR's golden boy philandering, let alone divorcing, was so at odds with his public persona that the newspapers had a field day. As for the public's reaction, it remained to be seen whether the news might win him additional fans or earn him the cold shoulder from the moral majority.

Throughout the NASCAR garage, Jeff got a lot of support. If anybody took pleasure in his misfortune, they weren't saying so. Jeff himself stuck to the high road. "People don't understand that every once in a while, things are going to happen in my life just like everybody else, because I'm human," he told reporters. "I don't like what we're going through, but I want it to come out with us being friends in the end." His one request to the media was this: Don't use this divorce as a reason for why I'm off to a slow start.

But while Jeff explained every lurch and blunder on the racetrack in terms of mechanics, track conditions, caution flags, or driver error, the situation with Brooke, and the media scrutiny, did have an effect. When Jeff countersued, claiming he should retain more than half of the couple's estate because he risked his life to earn it, the legal battle kicked into high gear. He would race on Sundays, his head filled with anxiety about his legal strategy and stacks of

OPPOSITE: Jeff delivering his opening monologue as host of *Saturday Night Live*, January 11, 2003.

depositions. The messy negotiations would drag on for sixteen months. "I was paying as much per month in lawyers' fees as I'd made in salary my entire rookie year in 1993," he ruefully recalls.

Ultimately, he decided that for his own peace of mind, he needed a change of scenery. He'd been shuffling between Charlotte hotels, Rick and Linda Hendrick's house, and spare rooms in the homes of Ricky Hendrick Jr. and Jimmie Johnson, but now he chose a location where he felt he could enjoy himself with some degree of anonymity: New York City. He quickly fell in love with the place.

"New York had a lot of energy," he recalls. "It was an exciting town. There were always things happening, and fun. And at that time, that's what I was looking for, that's what I needed, that's what I didn't have for many, many years, and I wanted to enjoy that opportunity in my life."

Jeff soon developed a close network of well-connected friends there who were eager to show him all the city had to offer. Throughout 2002 and 2003, he soaked it up. There were dinners at the swankiest restaurants, weekends at East Hampton estates, and late nights at exclusive Manhattan clubs like Serafina and Pangea. It didn't matter if he had to compete in a 500-mile race on Sunday; the second he climbed out of the car, he was on his way to the airport. "Those places were open on Sunday nights, so when I'd come back from a race, I would go there," he says. It was tons of fun.

"I'd spend a few days there, then go to the next race, maybe come back to New York or go back to Charlotte, depending on what was going on. If I had a weekend off, I was going to the Hamptons with friends or I was going on my boat in the Bahamas. Wherever the fun group was, that's where I was going."

Jeff and Johnson developed a fast bond, the first time in his career that he'd allowed himself to get close to another driver, teammate or not. Become too sociable and the competitive flame may flicker, he'd always thought. But in Johnson he saw a kindred spirit, and after years of living in virtual marital solitude, he yearned for friendship. It wasn't long before the two were hanging out and carving up the Big Apple together.

He was also enjoying the freedom of playing the field and dated a number of women that season, most of them models or aspiring actresses. As a single man, he was unquestionably NASCAR's most eligible bachelor. The running joke around the garage was that the nation's number-one pickup line was "Hello, my name is Jeff Gordon."

Some would say he was making up for lost time. "I would call it experiencing life as I never had before," Jeff says. "But yeah, I made up for it. I wasn't young and single. I was older and single, and I did it maybe even to a bigger, better level because I got to include New York and St. Bart's and Paris."

For once, he had no one to answer to. There was nobody else's respect to earn, no one's ego to care for, no dread of disappointing someone, or pressure to please anyone else. In 2001, he proved he could race, and win, on his own merits. Now he was crawling out from beneath his oppressive, carefully manufactured image—squeaky-clean "Jeff Gordon," the championship racer, the prized product pitchman, the role model, the God-fearing churchgoer, the dutiful husband—and reconnecting with the person he felt he had always been.

"What sunk in," he says, "is that I really didn't care what other people thought. It's what's going to make me happy. I learned a lot through that experience, and one thing I learned was to be more me. I don't want outside influences to steer me away from me being me, or away from what's going to make me happy. Life's too short and life's too good. I mean, I had thought my life was amazingly perfect, and I realized it wasn't at all. There were good moments and a

TOP: Jeff walking solo at the track in 2002.

lot of great things happening, certainly on the racetrack, but there's a lot more than just that. And for many, many years, that was all that mattered to me."

In November, Jeff and Johnson hit the road for Europe, where the two of them, along with motorcycle racer Colin Edwards, were to compete in the international Race of Champions, a team-based contest held annually on the Canary Islands, featuring racers from NASCAR, Formula 1, Indy, and a number of other formats. Busch Series driver Casey Mears, who would start his rookie Cup season the following year, also joined them. Their journey took them first to Paris, where Jeff knew friends who showed them the City of Lights—"the coolest nightclubs in the world, with hot models everywhere," Johnson recalls—and then on to Madrid, where they sampled the sights and were given front-row seats to Cirque du Soleil. Finally, they jetted down to Gran Canaria, off the coast of Morocco, where they won the Nation's Cup during the three-day Race of Champions (ROC) competition, making it back to the States just in time for NASCAR's year-end banquet in New York.

It was there, during the ceremony, that an NBC employee slipped Jeff an envelope, which he dutifully tucked into the pocket of his tux and forgot about. Later that evening, while out for dinner with friends, he remembered it. Everyone's curiosity was piqued.

"It's an invitation to host *Saturday Night Live*," Jeff told them.

"You're shitting me," said one of his friends. "You're going to do it, right?"

"Hell no," he responded. "I'm not an actor. I'm not worthy of doing *Saturday Night Live*."

The show had been after him for a year, ever since NBC began broadcasting half the NASCAR season in 2001. In fact, they'd offered him the hosting spot then, but he shrugged it off. "There was no way I could do it," he remembers thinking at the time. "I laughed at them. I never responded." It's not that acting intrinsically scared him. Over the preceding few seasons, he'd starred in episodes of *Spin City* and *The Drew Carey Show*, and had even cohosted

TOP: Jimmie Johnson (left), Colin Edwards, and Jeff celebrate their victory at the 2002 Race of Champions—Nations Cup.

Live! with Regis and Kelly three times in Regis Philbin's absence (he'd go on to do it eight more times). But *SNL*, with the pressure to be funny for an hour-and-a-half on live TV, was far outside his comfort zone.

"Let me tell you something," his friend said. "I don't care what you are capable of or what you think you're capable of. If you get an invitation to do *Saturday Night Live*, you're doing *Saturday Night Live*."

"So I said, 'All right, I'll do it,'" Jeff laughs. He had five and a half weeks till showtime.

*   *   *

When Jeff showed up at Rockefeller Center in the cold rain the week before his scheduled January 11 appearance, he was oblivious of what to expect. After some brief introductions, they plunked him down on a sofa and dropped a gargantuan stack of fifty or so scripts into his lap. Read these, he was told. "Some of them were funny," he recalls. "Some of them were pretty out-there." He hadn't gotten anywhere near the end of the stack when someone fetched him and brought him into a conference room where the show's producer, Lorne Michaels, the writers, and the cast—which at the time included Tina Fey, Jimmy Fallon, Tracy Morgan, Amy Poehler, and Seth Meyers—were gathered.

Jeff, shaking in his boots, took the one free seat, next to Michaels, who welcomed him and thanked him for hosting that week. "This is where we go through all the scripts," Michaels began. "All right, let's go." Jeff started off with the first, which, unfortunately, required him to howl like a wolf. 'Do I just say it, or do I act it,' he wondered. "Nobody's giving me any direction," he says, "and I'm scared shitless." He gathered himself. "So I do the whole howl, I do it very, 'Aaaaoooooooh!'" The next "line" was a cast member's howl. "And they're like just over-the-top selling it," Jeff says. "And I realized I've got to step up my game." His howling grew louder each time. "It was awkward," he admits. "I was out of my element." Michaels made it easy on him and cut the sketch.

By the time they'd worked their way through the immense stack, Jeff was more unsure than ever. "I was overwhelmed," he recalls. "I was seriously concerned at this point." One of the cast members assured him that he was doing fine and they'd have plenty of time to work through everything in rehearsals. "Still," he says, "that was one of the most frightening experiences of my life, because I had no direction, no idea what to expect."

TOP: Jeff reviewing his script in the green room before *Saturday Night Live*, 2003 RIGHT: Chris Parnell (left) and Jeff Gordon (right) in the "The Terry Funck Hour" skit on *Saturday Night Live*, 2003.

As the week progressed, he lightened up and eventually began to enjoy himself. During rehearsals, Carol remembers him calling her. "They were on a break or something, and he was like a little kid in a candy store," she says. "So he's got me on the phone, and one of the guys comes in and says the F-word, and Jeff goes, 'This is my mom I've got on the phone!' And the guy goes, 'Oh God, tell your mom I'm sorry.' It was just funny. I could tell how much he loved doing that. He was having such a good time and was so happy . . . even though he was going through all the stuff with Brooke."

On the night of the live show, he was on the verge of a coronary as he waited to be introduced by Don Pardo. And then he stepped on stage—a cooler, edgier Jeff than most NASCAR devotees were used to, sporting a dark, open-necked shirt, a black leather jacket, and spiked-up hair.

His opening monologue ran with that idea of image. A couple cast members planted in the audience played "typical" rowdy NASCAR fans—replete with No. 24 paraphernalia, pork rinds, and beer koozies—who interrupted Jeff by shouting clichéd racing phrases in mock-Southern accents. "Drop the hammer, Jeff!" "Yeah, open 'er up, dog!" At first, he brushes them off. But they lay it on so thick he finally stops and says, "You can't possibly go to a NASCAR event and act like that . . . because a real NASCAR fan would've killed you by now."

The moment was telling. On one hand, it was a defense of NASCAR's image. On the other hand, it was a nod to the fact that the sport had outgrown its regional roots, and that even then, the stereotype of the old-time stock-car fan was an overblown myth. It also showed just how far away Jeff, the sport's best-known personality, stood from that long-held image. It was a subtle PR coup for everyone, and it was hilarious.

For the rest of the show, Jeff played a variety of characters, as both a straight man and a ham, and nailed them all. "It was a huge adrenaline rush, such a blast," Jeff says of the *SNL* experience. "You realize you can't fail. It's one of those situations where it could be a terrible skit, and you could go in there and mess it up and make it look funny. It's so much fun that it's hard to mess it up."

The same could have been said of Jeff's life at the time. He couldn't fail. The issues with the divorce had done nothing to lessen his popularity, his profitability, or his attractiveness to sponsors. The appearance on *SNL*—which added him to a short list of athlete-hosts that included Joe Montana, Michael Jordan, Wayne Gretzky, and Walter Payton—only boosted his public profile.

Since his rookie season, his face had emblazoned millions of cereal boxes, Pepsi cans, and a number of other consumer products, not to mention the millions of hats, T-shirts, posters, die-cast cars, bobbleheads, and other licensed goods. He'd been in TV commercials, sitcoms, and talk shows. He'd even been name-checked in a chart-topping hip-hop song and christened one of *People* magazine's "Sexiest Men Alive." Throw in the increasingly frequent mentions in gossip pages, and at times he seemed to be everywhere. When people thought of racing, they thought of Jeff Gordon. But the *SNL* show sealed his status as a crossover superstar and his place in American popular culture.

"I got goose bumps the night he did *Saturday Night Live*," Rick Hendrick recalls. "I mean, you get good drivers, guys that have a lot of talent, but they couldn't do *Saturday Night Live*. They couldn't do *Regis and Kelly*. But Jeff Gordon is a guy who took this sport to another level . . . elevated us to another level in the fans' eyes, and brought in new fans that weren't from the Southeast."

"Jeff ushered in an era of sophistication," NASCAR vice chairman Mike Helton says. "He brought with him a persona that crossed into more areas than we may have been in previously, and he led the charge [with his] cross-generational, cross-genre personality."

Jeff's profile and the sport had exploded together. As NASCAR expanded from its Southern base, building new tracks in big media markets like Los Angeles, Chicago, Miami,

TOP: Jeff Gordon (left) and Tracy Morgan (right) on *Saturday Night Live*, 2003.

TOP: Jeff standing beside the trophy
after winning the Atlanta 500,
October 28, 2003.

Las Vegas, and Dallas, event attendance skyrocketed by nearly sixty-five percent. By the new millennium, the Winston Cup races each weekend had more TV viewers than any sport except NFL football. Sales of NASCAR and driver-related products rose from roughly $80 million a year in 1990 to nearly $1 billion by the decade's end. By the early 2000s, NASCAR had become a $2-billion-a-year business.

How much of that was a result of Jeff's success and popularity is difficult to say. But one thing is clear: You don't sell a product unless you've got personalities. The fresh look and attitude that Jeff brought to the sport, along with his skills in a race car, attracted new fans—older fans, to be sure, but also younger fans, female fans, and fans from parts of the country NASCAR hadn't touched before. That shift brought with it new advertisers and sponsors who saw an opportunity in the burgeoning sport.

"It didn't take long," Helton remembers, "for NASCAR, Winston, Chevrolet, and others to identify Jeff as one they had great respect for as far as being the face of our products." And the market push that Jeff had given not only NASCAR, but his sponsors, was immense. By 1999, Lou Savelli, head of DuPont automotive finishes, was attributing a phenomenal twenty percent, or $100 million, of his division's fifty percent growth in the 1990s to their association with Jeff and Hendrick Motorsports. With returns like that, it's no wonder Fortune 500 companies were falling over each other to get a piece of a NASCAR race team.

But if there was a "Jeff Gordon Effect" on the business and marketing side of NASCAR, there was an equally discernible Gordon effect on the racing side. Since his sensational successes in the mid and late 1990s, everyone was searching for the "next Jeff Gordon," that new youthful super-talent who could anchor a race team, drive the wheels off a car, please the sponsors, and bring home a boatload of money.

"Jeff was what I'd call our first Pop Warner race driver," Humpy Wheeler says, referring to the early-youth football league. "He set the stage for young people racing. Before Jeff Gordon, it didn't exist where you had a multitude of drivers seven, eight, nine, ten years old racing. It just didn't happen. Jeff Gordon started it all."

It wasn't only his youth, though. It was where he had come from and the cars he raced. NASCAR broadened its horizons after folks saw what Jeff—one of the first to have raced open-wheel cars on short tracks before joining the Busch Series—could do on a stock-car oval. Scouts fanned out to sprint, midget, modified, and Silver Crown tracks across the country. Within a few years, the various NASCAR series were teeming with former open-wheelers and off-road racers, hailing from Nevada, California, Wisconsin, and Indiana. And some of them, like Tony Stewart, the 2002 Winston Cup champion, were already starting to blow the doors off the place.

"Nobody from open-wheel ever got a chance in this sport," says Hendrick. "Jeff opened the door, and everybody followed. . . . More than anybody else, he revolutionized the sport. If it wasn't for Jeff Gordon, all the other guys that have come along from outside the sport would've never gotten a shot. And so they owe him a ton."

The entry of all those new drivers ushered in a sea of change that altered the geographical face of the sport. But as far as the next Jeff Gordon, some, at the time, argued he had already been found—by Jeff Gordon. Jimmie Johnson was among that new crop of young guns who had followed in Jeff's footsteps and were starting to come into their own. And that's who Jeff would be up against in the years to come.

Kellogg's Frosted Mini Wheats is a trademark of Kellogg North America Company, used with permission.

CLOCKWISE FROM TOP: Jeff on Apple Jacks and Frosted Mini-Wheats cereal boxes; A Jeff Gordon bobble-head; No. 24 car leading at Martinsville, April 13, 2003; Jeff on a four pack of Pepsi.

10

A "NEW" JEFF GORDON

JEFF'S 2003 SEASON STARTED MUCH like 2002, an up-and-down series of races highlighted by a couple runner-up finishes and his fourth career win at Martinsville, where he also won the pole. But no team was running away with it, and by mid-June, the No. 24 found themselves sitting third in the standings.

And then, on June 12, Jeff's sixteen-month divorce nightmare came to an end. In an effort to avoid an ugly, drawn-out battle in court, Jeff, who was by then NASCAR's all-time leading race-earnings winner, settled with Brooke for the publicly reported amount of $15.35 million, one of the most expensive divorces in sports at the time. In an effort to ward off further publicity, the parties elected not to file the settlement with the court, but today Jeff scoffs at that number. "That was just a fraction," he says. "The real number was actually way more than double that, and I had five years to pay it. That's insane. The lawyers on her side said, 'Listen, he has the ability to recoup.' And I'm sitting there going, 'I'll never recoup that much!' But luckily, my best-earning years were after that. To this day, I dislike the system—I dislike the lawyers involved, hers and mine. But I'm not bitter," Jeff chuckles.

As his bank balance began plummeting, so did his performance on the track. In the six races between late July and late August, he had one top-five finish, but otherwise finished no better than 28th. Worse still, he wrecked four times and nearly put himself out of title contention.

Robbie Loomis chalked up a good measure of the team's temporary implosion to his own difficulties in navigating the crew chief–driver relationship with what he termed the "new Jeff Gordon," the Jeff who continued jet-setting between the track, the Caribbean, and New York. The Jeff who was getting friendlier with some of his fellow racers and who at one point took a golf-cart tour through the Watkins Glen infield and came upon a motorhome dripping with anti–Jeff Gordon slogans, and promptly hopped out, signed some autographs, and posed for pictures with the vehicle's gobsmacked owner. It was that Jeff, Loomis says, that he didn't recognize.

"Up until the end of 2001, the guys on the team and myself had always had more of what I would call a 'working relationship' with Jeff," he says. "But I think when he was getting divorced, he was experiencing a whole new side of life out there. And I think for me, I was seeing a whole different Jeff than the guy I knew. He was getting real close to a lot of guys on the team, and I was getting closer to him from a friend standpoint. That was a big change for all of us. . . . looking back on it, I probably could have been more influential in helping keep the focus on the racecar."

It also worried Loomis that as Jeff became more sociable with some of his competitors, the veneer of power and invincibility he'd possessed for so long—something he felt gave the No. 24 a distinct psychological advantage—seemed to chip ever so slightly. "Before, there was a little edge or mystique when Jeff had beat [a competitor], because they really didn't know him; they didn't think he was human," Loomis says. "Then, all of sudden, they're out with him on a Wednesday night and they look at him and go, 'This guy's just like us, there ain't nothing special about him.' But at that time in his life, he was really enjoying becoming Jeff Gordon the person rather than just Jeff Gordon the winner."

From a statistical standpoint, that air of complete dominance began eroding before Jeff ever shared a couple rounds with his rivals. In the years between his 1995 and 1998 championship seasons with Evernham, he'd averaged nearly ten wins a year. In his four seasons with Loomis, even with the 2001 title, that mark had dropped to just under four. While he may have been slowly coming down from Everest, Jeff was still a threat and led all other Cup racers over that four-year span in wins, top-five, and top-ten finishes.

As Jeff began to emerge from his cloistered existence in the hauler, the mansion, and his marriage, people *did* see a new side, one that those closest to him had always known—the one they described as down-to-earth, humble, generous, friendly, a normal dude, good people. Things were changing. And perhaps one of the most obvious changes was that "God" seemed to have fallen out of Jeff's post-race vocabulary. Once considered one of NASCAR's most stalwart Christians, who would race with psalms taped to the dashboard and give the Lord top billing before his sponsors after every win, Jeff appeared to have distanced himself from NASCAR's worshipping community.

"They used to see me in Victory Lane thanking God first for everything," Jeff says. "And I wasn't trying to be fake or phony with it. That's where I was in my life at that time. And

RIGHT: Jeff's outlook on life began to shift in 2002.

I'm glad I had those experiences with Christianity; I'm proud of that experience. It taught me a lot about life, about religion. But what I learned from it also is that, ultimately, shouting it out to the world is not really me. That's not who I am."

The fact that he had been led to the Christian life primarily through Brooke made it harder for him to hew to the faith following their breakup, especially when the community of folks they had been close to turned against him. "When I went through that divorce, the people I had confided in, the ones that had influenced me to pray and follow Jesus, were not very supportive," he recalls. "They didn't believe in divorce. And because they didn't believe in it, they didn't believe in what I was doing, and they didn't support me. And that turned me off, I'll be honest."

He still believed in God, and he still prayed. But he felt more comfortable with a broader spirituality, one that incorporated elements of different belief systems rather than a single one. It was an evolving approach he no longer felt compelled to wear on his sleeve.

In the wake of their disappointing summer, the team managed to put the pieces back together and salvage some sense of competitiveness. "When things were breaking on his divorce, he carried that team on his shoulders," Hendrick says. "He never flinched. He just marched right on. He can shoulder a lot, and people don't really know that about Jeff Gordon. Even with all the tabloids on him and he wasn't running as good, he just marched right on, and we fixed it."

From that fall onward, they showed what they were really made of. In the season's final nine races, Jeff finished in the top-five seven times, including back-to-back wins at Martinsville and Atlanta, the eighteenth time he'd followed one win with another. At the end of the season, the No. 24 settled for fourth in the standings, but for Jeff, it felt like that last series of races was the beginning of something great.

★   ★   ★

The 2004 season brought with it a truck-load of changes, not the least being a new Cup series sponsor, Nextel, and a revamped championship format called "The Chase," which was designed to boost fan excitement by means of a playoff-style competition. Rather than tally the points after the entire thirty-six-race season and crown a king, NASCAR would now select the top ten drivers after the first twenty-six races, reset their points, and have them compete against one another in a ten-race showdown for the trophy. Everyone outside that ten-team group would still race alongside them for prize money and bonuses but would not be eligible for the title.

Among the other changes was the return of John Bickford. Nine years after Jeff and

LEFT: Jeff hoists the trophy over his head after winning the Dodge Save Mart 305 at Sonoma Raceway, June 27, 2004.

his stepfather severed their business relationship and Bob Brannan took over the helm of Jeff Gordon, Inc., Jeff decided it was time for a change and approached John with an offer to run the company. It wasn't an easy sell. While Jeff, John, and Carol had reconnected since the divorce, feelings were still a little raw over how things had played out in 1995.

"I knew John loved the cars and being a part of a race team, but I had no idea how much the business side of it meant to him, so I didn't realize how much it was going to impact him, but it did," Jeff says. "He thought I saw him as somebody who just liked to carry wrenches, and, in a way, that's true."

Since then, however, John had built a hugely successful career as a business consultant and executive with Action Performance, a company that manufactured and distributed licensed die-cast cars and assorted memorabilia for NASCAR and other racing leagues. There wasn't a soul in the race game who didn't see John as one of the more astute business minds in the sport. And Jeff had ultimately seen that, too.

Jeff wanted John to come back and run his business. He ran the idea by Carol first. "I thought about it," she says, "and I told him there probably would be nothing better in my mind than for that to happen. 'But you need to talk to him. I'm not sure how he's going to feel.'"

Getting him to agree, Jeff soon realized, was going to be like getting a mule to dance. John declined. Jeff asked again. No deal. John no longer felt his personality would be the right fit for Jeff. He was too direct, and he wasn't willing to schmooze people the way he thought Jeff wanted. Jeff asked again. Negative, he replied. It wasn't until after the March 21 race at Darlington, in which Jeff wrecked and finished forty-first, that John's stubbornness gave way and he finally made the decision to come back on board.

"Everybody has that point they get to, and I just said, 'You know what? It probably makes sense. I should do that,'" John says. "I was really tired of where I was at."

It wasn't easy news for Brannan to swallow, but he bowed out gracefully. "Following the divorce, I sensed that Jeff wanted to have more of his family involved with him in a more positive role," he says. "And for whatever reason, me being there and John being there at the same time wasn't going to work out from their standpoint. So I had a nice nine-year run with him, and hopefully I helped Jeff build what he wanted around him from a business standpoint."

Four days after Darlington, Jeff Gordon, Inc. issued a press release announcing that John would replace Brannan as the company's vice president and general manager. His first order of business? Selling the Highland Beach mansion to help pay off Brooke.

Perhaps it was that together-again feeling, or the high he was riding from the end of 2003, but after his crash at Darlington, Jeff had six straight top-ten performances, with a couple more wins back-to-back. After a relatively poor showing over the next four weeks, he strung together his best streak of the season: six straight top-five finishes, with three wins and three poles. It was in the midst of that run that Jeff reconnected with New York–based, Belgian model Ingrid Vandebosch.

The two had dated briefly in 2002, and while they quickly

RIGHT: Camilla Olsson, Ingrid, Jeff, a friend of the group, and Chandra Janway (now Chandra Johnson, Jimmie's wife) at the New Hampshire race, 2002.

developed a special bond, Jeff felt he wasn't quite ready at the time for a committed relationship. "I was separated and going through my divorce, and I was carrying too much baggage," he says. "Ingrid was a quality person and somebody I could see myself dating seriously, but I knew I was going to ruin it if we started then."

"After a couple months, I knew I couldn't do it anymore," Ingrid recalls. "It hurt. So I told him, 'You go have fun, and I'll go my way.'"

They had parted on good terms. "I was just hoping that at the right time, she and I would reconnect," Jeff says. "And it just so happens that it worked out perfectly." In the spring of 2004, after bumping into each other at a Manhattan restaurant, they arranged to have Ingrid—along with her sister, brother-in-law, and nephew from Belgium—come to the Fourth of July weekend race at Daytona. Jeff won the pole and the race that weekend.

"She came to that race," Jeff recalls, "and I was like, 'What's wrong with me?' What I wanted was right there in front of me. We sat in the bus and just started talking. I remember that at that moment, I knew we needed to reconnect." Before long, the romance rekindled, and their relationship would fast become one of the most important in his life.

In the meantime, he qualified for the first-ever Chase, leading all drivers in the standings, a slim five points ahead of his teammate Jimmie Johnson. Adding to his ever-growing list of accomplishments were a fourth career victory in the Brickyard 400 and a win at Sonoma that solidified his position as NASCAR's greatest road racer of all time. A fifth championship was beginning to look like a real possibility and a fitting way to cap Hendrick Motorsports' 20th anniversary in the sport.

Jeff started the ten-race playoff decently enough, finishing seventh at Loudon's New Hampshire Motor Speedway and third at Dover International Speedway, which was enough to maintain his first-place standing in the Chase. But the team struggled in the following two races, at Talladega and Kansas, before picking up a second-place finish at Charlotte. By that point, though, both Kurt Busch and Dale Earnhardt Jr. had overtaken him in the Chase standings.

LEFT: Jeff holds up four fingers to signify his fourth career Brickyard 400 victory, August 8, 2004.

121

With five races left, he was hoping to make up some ground the following Sunday in the Subway 500 at Martinsville Speedway. And he did. Even with a ninth-place finish, he managed to move up a position, overtaking Earnhardt, who crashed and finished thirty-third. Jimmie Johnson got the win, his series-leading sixth victory. But there were no celebrations. "Instead of heading to Victory Lane, we were all told to stop on pit road," Jeff remembers. "I could tell something was wrong." Then came the tragic news. A Hendrick Motorsports' plane that had left North Carolina earlier that day for Martinsville had crashed into a foggy hillside in southern Virginia.

"The first thing I thought of was whether John was on board," Jeff says. "Thank God he wasn't. At the same time, there were a lot of people who were close to me and, more importantly, close to Rick on that plane. You're just in shock and disbelief and devastated, but there's also this little glimmer of hope that maybe they'll find someone alive. Then reality started setting in, and that wasn't the case."

The tragedy took the lives of ten Hendrick family members, friends, and associates, including Rick Hendrick's son, Ricky, his brother and team president, John, John's daughters Kimberly and Jennifer, the team vice president and general manager, Jeff Turner, chief engine builder Randy Dorton, DuPont executive Joe Jackson, racer Tony Stewart's helicopter pilot, and the plane's two pilots.

Even with the countless woes and misfortunes that had befallen the NASCAR community since its beginnings, no race team and no team owner had ever suffered a tragedy of that magnitude. Jeff could hardly comprehend what Hendrick was going through, but he did his best to be there for him.

"I didn't know what to do, but I knew that he was hurting, and I went over to his house that night," Jeff recalls. "You just want to be there supporting someone you care so much about who is going through so much, even if you can't really understand how big that loss is to him. That night, it was just devastation and loss and trying to understand and accept and mourn. It was very difficult."

In the face of the tragedy, the grieving Hendrick operation stepped up and swiftly got the team's cars ready for the following weekend. That next Sunday, in an emotional tribute at Atlanta Motor Speedway, where the flags were lowered to half-staff, Hendrick's four drivers—Jeff Gordon, Jimmie Johnson, Terry Labonte, and Brian Vickers—rolled up to the starting line in cars bearing the names and images of the crash victims. When Johnson took the checkered flag, his third straight, all the Hendrick drivers and crews gathered in Victory Lane, hats worn backward in memory of Ricky Hendrick, for a tearful celebration.

In the long run, bouncing back was much harder. The crash had decimated the organization's upper management and gutted its prized engine program, which outfitted not only the Hendrick teams but many of their competitors. On a personal level, the question was whether to go on at all. Rick Hendrick, after burying four members of his family, wavered over hanging it all up and shuttering the organization after two decades and six championships.

TOP: The commemorative decal created to honor those who died in the Hendrick Motorsports plane crash, October 24, 2004. BOTTOM: Jeff and Jimmie Johnson wearing their hats backwards in honor of Ricky Hendrick at Atlanta Motor Speedway, October 31, 2004.

"It was two weeks after the crash," he remembers, "and I didn't think I'd ever be able to come over [to the Hendrick Motorsports complex] anymore because we lost so many people—all of my family. And so I walked into the team center and Jeff was the first person I saw. He was crying, and we cried together. And when I saw him, it connected me to this place and this family. My relationship with these people here and with Jeff—I knew that for the honor of the family, I had to go on. I've always called it a family. All of our employees are like our extended family, but Jeff is special in that deal.

"You know, he's very caring and he's got a big heart," Hendrick says. "I'll always remember the embrace we had after the crash."

Ultimately, the organization rebounded and became just as strong. But in 2004, there were still three races to be run, and Jeff, after finishing thirty-fourth in Atlanta, was now sitting in third place in the Chase. He raced his heart out, claiming third place in each of those final races, but it wasn't enough. The standings stayed as they were, with Jeff in third, just eight points behind the runner-up, Johnson, and a mere sixteen behind the champion, Kurt Busch.

In any other year, Jeff Gordon would have been crowned NASCAR's Cup champion. In terms of sheer points for the season, Jeff was at the top of the board; Busch finished fourth. But because of the new Chase format, the driver who performed best over the final ten events won. There would be no fifth championship. It was a bitter pill to swallow.

TOP: Jeff's No. 24 DuPont Chevrolet car with the "Always In Our Hearts" decal on the hood at Atlanta Motor Speedway, October 31, 2004.

11

TEAM OF RIVALS

"WHEN I STARTED OUT, I DON'T THINK I fully appreciated the magnitude and significance of the Daytona 500, because I didn't grow up with it as a kid," Jeff admits. "For the guys who grew up in the stock-car world, the Daytona 500 was the ultimate race. Where I grew up, the Indy 500 was the ultimate race."

But by 2005, after twelve years in the Cup series, Jeff no longer harbored any dreams of trying his hand in Indy or Formula 1 racing. "I still loved the Indy 500, but once I went down the stock-car path, I stuck with it and gave it everything I had," he says. "I really thought stock cars were far more for me than Indy cars because of the way the cars drove and the oval tracks. I could draw from my experience racing sprint cars. For the most part, Indy cars were rear-engine road-racing cars.

"So I had wanted to learn more of the history of the Daytona 500 and give the race the respect it deserved. I can't say I fully grasped it the first time I won it, and maybe not even the second. But by the third time I won it, I did."

On February 20, in a race that saw four lead changes in the final nine laps, Jeff, at thirty-three years old, became only the fifth driver in NASCAR history to win the Daytona 500 three or more times, edging out Kurt Busch, for his seventieth career victory. On the radio, during the cool-down lap, Rick Hendrick chimed in: "Dedicate this one to the families . . . buddy, okay?"

During the Victory Lane festivities, after his tribute to the victims of the Hendrick plane crash, Jeff made it clear that the kid who had dreamed of the Indianapolis 500 had truly been converted. "This is the Daytona 500," he said, "and it just doesn't get any sweeter than this."

Unfortunately, it was an accurate assessment of the season to come, one in which his cars just didn't seem as fast, his qualifying average dropped, his average finish fell six spots behind the previous year, and he wrecked eight times. He ended up with fewer top-fives and top-tens than at any point since 1994. The only thing gaining momentum that year was frustration.

After a wreck in Chicago, one that Jeff felt was caused by a careless move made by driver Mike Bliss, he boiled over. "To me, it was just ridiculous," Jeff remembers. "I was really angry, and I said that if I get to the airport and see him, I'm going to knock the shit out of him. Sure enough, he was there. And I'm a man of my word."

OPPOSITE: Jeff driving under the checkered flag to join an elite group of repeat winners at the Daytona 500, February 20, 2005.

125

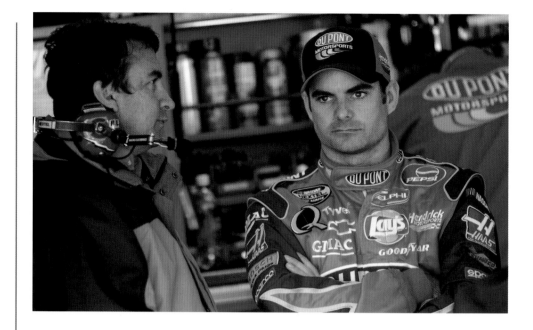

Jeff approached Bliss on the tarmac, "and I clocked him. And it felt great. Later, I felt bad about it, because I like Mike. But it was stupid what he did, and based on the fact that he didn't retaliate, I think he knew it. I don't think he disagreed with me."

At the same time, the disappointments on the track only compounded the personal turmoil in crew chief Robbie Loomis's life. He and Jeff had put together some fantastic seasons in 2001 and 2004 and had shared some good times, but they never really found that spot where instinct took over and they were at their competitive best. When Loomis's mother fell ill toward the end of 2004 and didn't seem to get better, he started to lose focus and to question his own dedication to the sport.

Jeff had seen what was happening, and Hendrick saw it, too. And while they had planned to shake things up at season's end, the No. 24 team's failure to qualify for the 2005 Chase convinced them and Loomis that it was best to part ways then and there.

With ten races still remaining, they brought up twenty-six-year-old Steve Letarte, who as a teenager had been hired by Ray Evernham to sweep floors and run errands, and had worked his way from tire specialist, to mechanic, and finally, to car chief for the No. 24. It was a position they had been grooming him for. The season was no longer salvageable, but the final races under Letarte—including a win for Jeff at Martinsville—gave the team a chance to get up and running in preparation for 2006.

By May the following season, Jeff was sixth in the standings, but in his personal life he was closer to the top of the world. He and Ingrid Vandebosch had been in a serious relationship for more than a year. "He was so wheels-off over her," recalls Jimmie Johnson, who in 2004, had married Chandra Janway, someone Jeff had known from his time in New York. "There was some definite magic in the air with those two."

But while Ingrid was keen on marriage, the word itself had become loathsome to Jeff. He felt he had been so badly burned by the divorce that he'd never again step to the altar. "I had a chip on my shoulder," he admits. "I wanted to be in a committed relationship, and I knew we both wanted to have children. My only hang-up was the whole marriage thing."

Yet on Mother's Day, after his race at Darlington, he finally popped the question. "I thought it was really cute," says Ingrid. "I don't remember exactly what he said, but it was

TOP: Communication began to break down between Robbie Loomis (left) and Jeff (right), 2005.

126

something like, 'Well, I think we should get married. What do you think?' And I said, 'Yeah okay,'" she recalls with a laugh. "It wasn't the most romantic proposal. But when you've gone through what I went through, it takes all the romance out of it. But I knew being married to each other was ultimately what we both wanted. So I guess my focus was on a lasting relationship, and not so much on a big over-the-top proposal or event."

He and Ingrid decided to keep their engagement under wraps.

Less than a month later, Ingrid got a pretty good primer on the life of a NASCAR spouse when Jeff suffered one of the most violent wrecks of his career. Heading into Turn 1 with eleven laps to go at Pocono Raceway in Pennsylvania, his right-front brake rotor went, and he lost control. The car skidded through the infield, then back onto the track and slammed driver's-side into the retaining barrier at nearly 150 mph. "That is a bad crash," Darrell Waltrip said from the broadcast booth as the crowd waited for signs of life. "I don't like the looks of that at all." Memories of Dale Earnhardt no doubt flashed through many people's minds. So there was a general sigh of relief when Jeff climbed out of the badly mangled vehicle some forty-five seconds later.

"It was significant, probably the scariest crash I've ever been in," Jeff says. "They suspected I had a head injury. Did I have a minor concussion? Maybe. I was a little loopy when I got out of the car."

What he *did* have was an order from NASCAR to undergo an MRI before he could be cleared to race again. When he and his worried fiancée flew home to New York after the race, they immediately went to the hospital for an examination. In Charlotte, it would have been a 1-2-3 deal in an MRI unit, in and out, very efficient and very clinical. But this was New York City, and it was a mess.

"You take an elevator to an intensive-care floor where there's a lot of people that have had accidents and significant brain trauma. And then I walk up to the desk and tell them I'm there to get an MRI. They don't know who I am at all. They're looking for the file."

Jeff recounts the conversation:

"What's your name?"

"Jeff Gordon." They look.

"All right, well, where's the patient?"

LEFT: One of the most violent wrecks of Jeff's career at Pocono Raceway, June 11, 2006.

"I *am* the patient."

"It says here the patient was in a high-speed crash, with a head injury."

"Yes, that's me. I was in a high-speed crash in a racecar."

"How fast were you going?"

"I don't know, one hundred forty, one hundred fifty miles per hour."

"Well, that's not possible."

"That's what they told me. 'That's not possible.'"

It took a bit of explanation from Jeff about helmets and safety gear before they fully grasped the situation. Then he had to wait. And wait. He and Ingrid had food delivered to the ICU. And then, finally, he got his MRI.

"It was very funny and really sad at the same time," says Ingrid, "because we were in intensive care, and all these people went through really bad accidents, way slower than Jeff, but they're hooked up to machines and probably will never walk again."

A week later, he was back behind the wheel at Sonoma. On Saturday before the race, Ingrid and Jeff gathered family and close friends at Meadowood Napa Valley resort. After several games of croquet, the couple announced their engagement. "I was just so happy and feeling great about life," Jeff says. The next morning he called his PR man, Jon Edwards, and his crew chief, Steve Letarte, to tell them both about the engagement, and then he told them something he had never said before a race: "By the way, we're going to win today."

"I went out and led about half the laps and got my fifth Sonoma victory," says Jeff. "I can't even describe the emotions that day. First the engagement, and then my first win of the season. I got pretty choked up in the car after I got the checkered flag. I guess it suddenly hit me, everything that was going on. It all came together that weekend," says Jeff.

He followed his win in Sonoma with another at Chicago and three top-fives just before the Chase selection, he grabbed the ninth playoff spot. But a fuel pump problem, a crash, and an engine issue over the next three races effectively ended any chance he had of pulling off a surprise ending.

He and Ingrid did, however, pull off a surprise wedding—and in costume, no less—in a secluded gazebo in New York's Central Park on Halloween. With a judge dressed as a witch, Ingrid in a tutu and crown as the black swan from *Swan Lake*, and Jeff clad as a polo player next to their cowboy hat–wearing dog, Valentino, the happy couple took their vows. "Normally, a guy forgets his wedding date, but I was afraid I'd forget—I'm no good with dates," Ingrid says. "So I said, 'Let's do it [Halloween] so we'll never forget.'" A week later, on November 7, they tied the knot again in front of their friends and family at a ceremony in Mexico.

But the biggest surprise came a week and a half before their Halloween nuptials, when

TOP: Friends and family pose after their croquet game at Meadowood Napa Valley resort where Jeff and Ingrid announced their engagement.
RIGHT: Jeff and Ingrid, dressed in Halloween costumes, wed in a secluded gazebo in New York's Central Park, October 31, 2006.

Jeff returned to Manhattan after his race in Martinsville. "He comes home with his luggage and he's tired, and I made him dinner," Ingrid remembers. "He was just taking his sweet time, and I'm like, 'Can you hurry up?'"

"'What's the rush?'" Jeff recalls saying. "She said, 'I have something for you. It's on the pillow on the bed.'" Resting there was an envelope with a ribbon. Jeff opened it. Inside was a sonogram. They were having a baby. "We were both so happy we started crying. It was just a very happy moment we shared that I'll never forget," Jeff says.

*   *   *

The end of the 2006 season brought Hendrick Motorsports its sixth Cup series championship. It had taken a few years, but the young driver Jeff and Rick Hendrick brought on back in 2001 had come into his own. Jimmie Johnson had won twenty-three races since his 2002 rookie season, and in 2006, he, his crew chief Chad Knaus, and the rest of the No. 48 team captured the Cup series championship.

As the car's part owner, a member of the Hendrick team, and as a friend and mentor, Jeff was thrilled. "Shades of Gordon and Evernham" buzzed about the Johnson-Knaus pairing, and in many ways it was true. Like Jeff, Johnson had been a talented but unproven driver who had come into the league with the highest-quality equipment and the backing of a top-notch racing organization. And in Knaus, he found an Evernham-trained partner who even Jeff admits "was like Ray on steroids." But there was one difference: Jimmie had Jeff. And that meant he had the experience of four championships and decade's worth of top-level racing to draw on, not to mention a goldmine of track and set-up knowledge. Whatever Johnson needed, Jeff had been happy to oblige.

"Chad and Jimmie, I mean, let's face it, they came in and stepped into Jeff's equipment," says Hendrick. "And the chemistry there between Jimmie and Chad got to what he and Ray used to have."

Johnson, to his credit, always acknowledged Jeff's role in his success, and Jeff, likewise, was quick to give Jimmie his due. "Jimmie doesn't always get the credit. You'll hear people say that if it hadn't been for me, he wouldn't have gotten the opportunity, which isn't completely true," he said. "You have to give Jimmie credit for knowing the right questions to ask. He's very talented, and he was going to have success and prove himself eventually regardless of my involvement," Jeff maintains.

Just five weeks into the 2007 season, Jeff took over the top spot on the leader board, and for the next twenty-one races, no one could touch him. The numbers he put up were the most impressive he'd posted since the late 1990s, and not even his 2001 championship season or his brilliant 2004 effort could match them. Twenty-one times in twenty-six races he finished in the top ten, and fifteen times he was a top-five finisher. Among his four wins were back-to-back victories at Phoenix and Talladega in which he tied Dale Earnhardt's record of seventy-six wins. He then broke that record, taking over the sixth spot on NASCAR's all-time career victories list.

Following the twenty-sixth race, at Richmond, where he finished fourth, he was still the season leader, more than 300 points ahead of second-place Tony Stewart. But with a newly reformatted Chase, in which each of the twelve qualifiers had their points reset and were then awarded ten extra points for each victory up to that point, he found himself seeded second,

TOP THREE: Jeff and Ingrid wed in Mexico, November 7, 2006. BOTTOM: Jeff and Ingrid after his win in the Dodge Save Mart 350 at Sonoma Raceway, June 25, 2006.

twenty points behind the win leader: Jimmie Johnson. The 2007 Chase for the Nextel Cup would be a battle for the ages.

Jeff got off to a good start in the Chase's first contest, at Loudon, where his second-place finish put him in a tie with Johnson, who ran sixth. At Dover, Jeff logged an eleventh-place finish, still better than Johnson's fourteenth, which allowed him to hold the lead. But by the third race, Johnson's third-place finish was enough to put him back on top, with Jeff, who finished fifth, just behind him. From there on out, it was the Jeff and Jimmie show.

At Talladega the following weekend, Jeff hung around the back of the pack most of the day before making a move with about seven laps to go. A lap later, he was running second, in an inside draft line, nose to tail behind Johnson. With two laps left, they remained that way, and it looked like Jeff wouldn't be able to find his way around the No. 48. But with just half a lap to go, Jeff popped out from behind Johnson, received a good push, and took the lead, dropping down to block Johnson through the final turn and take the checkered flag. It was a thrilling, virtuoso performance, and it put Jeff back in the Chase lead.

It was expected Johnson would dominate the following week at Charlotte. Jeff's last trip to Victory Lane at that track was in 1999. Jimmie led ninety-five of the 337 laps, before spinning unexpectedly on lap 231. That's when Jeff picked up the lead, trading it with teammate Kyle Busch and Clint Bowyer. After an oil spill by Jeff Green, Jeff and Kyle began experiencing fuel pickup problems. Fearing a wreck, owner Rick Hendrick told Kyle to "race Gordon clean." Ryan Newman attempted a "bump and run" on Jeff, giving Newman the lead until he spun out with three laps to go, putting Jeff back in front to take the win. Jimmie finished fourteenth. "Man, I don't know where to start," Jeff told reporters after the race. "I'm so fired up about this."

"Looking back, Charlotte gave us a lot of confidence," Jeff recalls. But it wouldn't last long. Johnson roared back the next Sunday to take the checkered flag at Martinsville, and repeated the performance the following week in Atlanta, cutting deeply into Jeff's lead. Considering that there were ten other Chase competitors—including Hendrick driver Kyle Busch—and

RIGHT: Jeff's No. 24 takes the lead over Jimmie Johnson's No. 48 in the race at Talladega, October 7, 2007.

forty-three total racers on the track, the fact that the two teammates had now claimed four victories in a row was a testament not only to the depth of the Hendrick Motorsports operation but to Jeff and Johnson's individual skill.

It was difficult not to flash back to 1996, when Jeff, who had put together a similar monster season, was edged out in the final few races of his drive for a second championship by then-teammate Terry Labonte. "Back then, we were outperforming Terry on the track, but we had some failures," Jeff reminisced after the Atlanta race. "In this situation, it's hard to say. Jimmie has won the last two races; we won the two before that. He might be outperforming us just a little bit, but we've got the consistency like Terry did."

With three races left, Jeff and Jimmie were separated by only nine points. It was still anybody's title heading to Texas Motor Speedway. Throughout practice, Jeff struggled and wasn't completely happy with the car's handling. In the end, he logged a seventh-place finish. Jimmie capped off a dogfight with Matt Kenseth in the final few laps for a third straight victory, catapulting him to the top of the standings—thirty points ahead of Jeff.

Jeff knew that if he had any hopes of a fifth championship, he would have to summon a masterful performance at Phoenix International Raceway to hold off the surging No. 48. His victory there earlier in the year gave the team some confidence, and his third-position qualifying run, three spots ahead of Johnson, was reason for optimism. Still, he didn't start off well. But by the eightieth lap of the 312-lap contest, he had found his composure and was running fourth, just behind Johnson; the two of them soon moved up to second and third. They continued dueling among the top five racers, and by the halfway mark, Jeff had worked his way into second, with Johnson sitting fourth. But a dozen laps later, Johnson caught and overtook him, then surged ahead of Matt Kenseth for the lead. After being kicked back following pit stops, they both grappled their way up again through slower traffic, but Jeff was becoming increasingly frustrated with the car's handling. With forty-five laps to go, he was in tenth position, trailing the sixth-place Johnson. And then, after they both pitted a final time, Johnson turned it on. He blasted his way up from sixth place to take the lead with twenty-three laps left, as Jeff continued to fight with his car. When the checkered flag fell, it was Johnson who claimed his fourth consecutive victory, nine spots ahead of the limping No. 24, effectively slamming the door on Jeff's best season in a decade.

"Whatever they've got, we're missing," the disheartened four-time champion said during the post-race interview. When asked about his chances of rebounding at the Homestead-Miami Speedway race, he was blunt. "It's over," he said.

If there was any silver lining in Miami, where he finished fourth to the now-two-time champion Johnson's seventh, it was that he posted his thirtieth top-ten of the season, setting a new modern-era NASCAR record. And for those scoring pre-Chase style, it was Jeff who again walked away with the "shadow" title, just as he had in 2004. In terms of overall points, he had crushed the competition that season, finishing 353 points ahead of Johnson, the largest margin between a first- and second-place driver in Cup racing since Jeff's 364-point besting of Mark Martin in 1998.

As for Jimmie Johnson's impressive ten wins that year, you would have to go back to Jeff's 1996, 1997, and 1998 seasons to find a Cup racer who'd logged double-digit victories. And four wins in a row? Nobody had accomplished that feat since Jeff did it in 1998.

The No. 48 team was simply over the moon after rallying to pull it off, but for Jeff there was a feeling of emptiness. "We were so close," he says. "You've got all that confidence and

TOP: Jeff and Ingrid at the 2007 Vanity Fair Oscar Party hosted by Graydon Carter at Mortons in West Hollywood, California.

you're feeling good, like nothing can bring us down, this is our year. And then all of a sudden somebody gives you a wakeup call . . . Jimmie and those guys, they just flat-out beat us. It was tough. That 2007 season, you know, it took the wind out of my sail."

At home, there was enough happening to keep him from ruminating too much in the off-season. On June 20, he and Ingrid welcomed their first child, Ella Sofia, and despite being in the midst of a championship hunt, Jeff was able to attend the birth in New York. "It was a great moment," Ingrid recalls. "He cried really hard. He was so happy."

The new baby meant a new routine. And for someone whose schedule was as rigid as Jeff's, it took some getting used to. There was no more late-to-bed, late-to-rise, as was his habit; he had to be on his daddy game when the sun rose.

"When Ella came, people asked me, 'Has it affected how you race?' And when they ask those questions, they're thinking that now that I'm a father, I have to be more cautious on the track, I have more at stake. And those things are true. But how it affected me is you have a child that's up every couple of hours, you're not getting good sleep. . . . So you get to the racetrack and you're just exhausted and it's harder to stay as focused doing your job without proper sleep."

However, if there was any question whether fatherhood might slow Jeff's roll, all fans had to do was recall the second half of 2007. He had taken on the field just as aggressively as he always had. Jeff was simply too competitive, father or not, to ease off the throttle. And coming into 2008, he was being pegged as a championship favorite. But by the time the Chase rolled, he was sloughing through what, by Jeff Gordon standards, was a ho-hum season, and he entered the playoffs, now called the Chase for the Sprint Cup, way down at tenth. He saved his best for last, posting seven top-tens down the stretch, but it wasn't nearly enough to catch the eventual champion, Jimmie Johnson, who won three times over the last eight races and walked away with his third straight title.

But what stung most wasn't finishing seventh or getting shown up again by his stable-mate, though that certainly cast a pallor over the No. 24. It was the fact that over thirty-six races, he'd registered zero wins. "We just weren't where we needed to be," Jeff says. "Sure it stung a little more because the 48 team was so good, but it was more so because our team wasn't where it could be." By the beginning of 2009, he came close to winning several times. Through the first six races, he had two fourth places, including one at Martinsville, where he won the pole, and finished second twice, at Fontana and Atlanta. He was perched at the top of the point standings, but with the premium the Chase format put on wins—awarding extra points for victories—he and Steve Letarte knew they'd have to get back to form to stay competitive.

On April 5, at Texas Motor Speedway, where Jeff hadn't had a win in sixteen attempts, they finally reeled it in. The team had a fast car that day, and some vintage driving from Jeff— along with great midrace adjustments by the crew and a final lightning-quick pit stop—put them ahead of Jimmie Johnson in the final laps. Jeff took the checkered for the first time in seventeen months, snapping his forty-seven-race winless streak. Their good form continued; Jeff was the runner-up in eight races that season, but there were no more wins. When all was said and done, he had racked up twenty-five top-tens, matching the third-highest total of his career, and had finished second in overall points. He performed well in the Chase, but again, it wasn't enough. Jimmie Johnson was crowned the champion for a record-setting fourth time in a row.

OPPOSITE: TOP: Ingrid and Jeff with newborn Ella, 2007. BOTTOM LEFT: Jeff and baby Ella at the track before the Dickies 500 race at Texas Motor Speedway, November 4, 2007. BOTTOM RIGHT: Jeff holds his daughter Ella with Ingrid in victory lane after his win at the Ford 500 at Talladega Superspeedway, October 7, 2007.

12

IT'S NOT WHERE YOU START, IT'S WHERE YOU FINISH THAT MATTERS

"I'D LIKE TO TAKE YOU ON A SUNDAY DRIVE," Jeff began as he stood at the podium in front of an audience of fellow superstar athletes and philanthropists as the evening's recipient of the 2012 Heisman Humanitarian Award. Jeff was the first motorsports athlete to receive the prestigious honor, bestowed in recognition of those from the sporting world who have given significantly of themselves for the betterment of others. "For me," he continued, "it's being strapped very tightly by a six-point harness into an 850-horsepower racecar, traveling down a long straightaway, accelerating at speeds of 200 miles per hour plus. Imagine what that's like with forty-two other cars, inches away from you. It might sound a little frightening to you. To me, that's a normal Sunday drive. But what I do find frightening," he said with a sudden slight quiver of emotion in his voice, "is the thought of a child being told that they have cancer. Or the thought of millions of older Americans not knowing where their next meal is coming from. That's frightening to me."

Fear can either paralyze us or motivate us. For Jeff, it motivated him to take action. But the inspiration for his philanthropic activism came long before he rose to the ranks of iconic NASCAR superstar. "I remember my parents' business as a child; I was around people in wheelchairs—paraplegics, quadriplegics," Jeff recalls. He remembers one man in particular, a quadriplegic who was able to drive although he had very little control of his hands and arms. "He did it with the hand controls that my parents built," Jeff says with pride. "So even though it was a *business*, it was to help people."

OPPOSITE: Leah Wasson and Jeff pose at a Jeff Gordon Children's Foundation bowling tournament fundraiser.

It was while driving for Bill Davis Racing in the Busch Grand National series that Jeff got his first glimpse of the positive impact *his* business as an emerging celebrity racecar driver could have on those in need. Bill Armour, Davis's PR man, suggested the idea of visiting children in hospitals. "Initially I remember thinking, 'Why do you want me to go?' And they're like, 'Well you know, these kids are sick.' 'Okay, I'll go, but why me?'" Armour took Jeff to Brenner Children's Hospital, located in Winston-Salem.

"That was eye-opening for me," Jeff remembers, "realizing I could go in there, talk about what I do, sign an autograph . . . and give them pause from all the other stuff going on in their life that probably wasn't too positive."

Jeff continued making hospital visits, but in July 1992 the need for his help hit close to home. No sooner had he and his crew chief Ray Evernham begun work on the career opportunity of their lifetime, a chance to build a Cup team from scratch for Hendrick Motorsports, than Ray received the terrifying news that his one-year-old son, Ray J, had been diagnosed with leukemia. For the next several months, Jeff watched powerlessly as Ray's little boy was subjected to chemotherapy, radiation, and long stays in the hospital.

"It was an education for Ray and his family and for all of us," Jeff recalls. "I got on board . . . and we basically generated more awareness and funding for leukemia and lymphoma."

Jeff started by making contributions to the Leukemia & Lymphoma Society, hoping that he would be able to impact outcomes for kids like Ray J.

By 1995, Jeff's new desire for philanthropic work led him to the Make-A-Wish Foundation, a nonprofit organization that arranges experiences or "wishes" for children with life-threatening medical conditions. He soon discovered that children battling cancer made the most wishes. For Jeff, this reality spoke to the emotional and physical toll the disease takes on kids and their families. It deepened his desire to educate himself about the science of cancers in children.

While Jeff continued his donations and fund-raising for numerous charities, he didn't feel like he was making a real impact. "We received an overwhelming amount of requests to help animals in need, hungry people, every disease you can imagine and think of," he says. So in 1999, Jeff decided to establish his own foundation.

TOP: Jeff with Ray Evernham's son, Ray J. RIGHT: Jeff doing a Make-A-Wish meet and greet.

He soon realized the ambitious undertaking meant partnering with hospitals and research-ers. In 2005, construction had begun on the campus of Carolinas Medical Center–NorthEast for a new children's hospital. This was the kind of opportunity Jeff had been looking for.

He began discussions with the medical center about how he could help support the hos-pital that would ultimately serve so many children, including those in the racing community. His vision was to create a family-friendly atmosphere for the hospital's pediatric patients. He wanted the design of the hospital to include an enhanced healing environment to reduce anxiety and stress for the children and their families. With an initial gift of $1.5 million and a promise of an ongoing partnership, the Jeff Gordon Children's Hospital opened its doors in December 2006, featuring a peaceful, serene setting with a sculpture garden, aquariums, and enlarged photographs throughout the facility, taken by Jeff and Ingrid, of African wildlife.

The hospital serves children regardless of their ability to pay. It offers intensive care and a range of subspecialty services.

Torn between his passion for the foundation's work and the demands of his racing career, Jeff decided he needed to bring on an experienced foundation director who could execute his vision. Jeff met Trish Kriger in 2006 through her sister-in-law, who worked with Jeff and knew his foundation was in need of an executive director. It seemed like a perfect fit for Kriger given her many years working with charities and nonprofits, her passion for children, and her own experience with childhood cancer as the sister of a leukemia survivor.

"When I met with Jeff, we didn't talk about NASCAR—we talked about Jeff's passion and what he wanted to do," Kriger says. "He wanted to give kids the same chance he had, which was to do something they loved without the impediment of child abuse, cancer, ill-ness, lack of education, hunger—but cancer was the one thing that really came out in our conversation." While the foundation supported various children's causes, ranging from abuse and illness to education and hunger, childhood cancer was always a priority.

TOP: Jeff cutting the ribbon during the opening ceremony for the Jeff Gordon Children's Hospital, December 2006.

In 2008, Jeff refined the mission of the foundation to solely support children battling cancer, by funding programs that improved their quality of life, treatments that increased survivorship, and pediatric medical research dedicated to finding a cure.

Jeff began looking to duplicate their efforts at the Jeff Gordon Children's Hospital with other pediatric centers around the country. His criteria included "who is doing really impactful work, who is geared towards our cause, primarily pediatric cancer, and, who makes the most sense." Riley Hospital for Children in Indianapolis, Indiana, with its family-centered pediatric care, met the criteria. "When we looked around the country at all the different children's hospitals, they rose to the top."

"He was very interested in understanding the details," says Dr. Wade Clapp, a pediatrician and scientist at the Indiana University School of Medicine at Indiana University–Purdue University Indianapolis and also the chairman of the school's Department of Pediatrics based at Riley. When he first met Jeff, Dr. Clapp was a cancer investigator. "The [Herman B.] Wells Center for Pediatric Research included forty-six basic science investigators, and about a dozen of us study pediatric malignancies," says Dr. Clapp. "[Jeff] was interested in understanding how what we were doing was going to improve care for kids." At the time, Jeff was starting to formalize his foundation's board of directors and asked Dr. Clapp to join.

Dr. Clapp was researching a slow growing cancer on the peripheral nervous system that had no treatments. They were helping a young girl from Los Angeles who was involved in a clinical trial. "I had been working for several years," Dr. Clapp recalls. "We'd done a series of studies that ultimately enabled us to take a drug that was developed by an adult oncologist for leukemia. We found that it actually hit a specific target that's critical for plexiform neurofibroma, a cancer that occurs in babies and young children." For the girl they were treating with the drug, the tumor shrank significantly.

"The drug doesn't actually attack the tumor cells; it attacks other cells that the tumor uses to enable it to grow," Dr. Clapp explains. "Jeff wanted to know how this worked and the process of how we got there, which was a series of genetic and biochemical studies." Since then, they have had clinical trials on a subset of tumors in younger kids. "Five years ago we had zero drugs, now we have three," says Dr. Clapp.

"Childhood cancer isn't just one disease—there are over a dozen types of childhood cancer and countless subtypes, each requiring specific research to develop the best treatment for every child," Jeff notes. "By working closely with leading pediatric oncologists, we deter-

TOP: Jeff helping out during a Jeff Gordon Children's Foundation bowling tournament fundraiser. RIGHT: Jeff with Dr. Mark Kelley outside of the Jeff Gordon Children's Foundation Research Lab at Riley Hospital for Children, Indianapolis, Indiana.

mine the most promising research to fund and create funding priorities that will generate the greatest impact for children with cancer."

One of many kids who has benefited from Jeff's work at Riley (known as a "Riley Kid") is Olivia Pierce. Olivia was diagnosed at three months old with retinoblastoma cancer in her left eye. Always in her signature red-rimmed glasses, Olivia's infectious energy, can-do attitude, and ever-present smile belie the thirty-five surgeries, eight rounds of chemotherapy, and the removal of her left eye when she was an infant.

"We always knew there was a connection between Riley Hospital and Jeff Gordon," recalls Shannon Pierce, Olivia's mother. "Growing up in Indiana I knew about NASCAR and I had an awareness of Jeff Gordon, but I really wasn't knowledgeable or aware of his commitment to Riley at that point. . . . For us it hits close to home to know within the four walls of Riley Hospital for Children, they're researching Olivia's type of cancer and looking for a cure—not only hers but many types of cancer," Shannon says. "Jeff is a big-name celebrity but he knows these kids. He knows Olivia's story. As a parent it's very humbling; it's a privilege to be associated with him.

"When Olivia was diagnosed with cancer at three months old, she wasn't expected to make it to her first birthday," Shannon adds. "Olivia beat the odds because of the great physicians and the best care ever at Riley. It's people like Jeff Gordon that are committed to this. A million thanks to Jeff wouldn't be enough."

"Jeff Gordon has a big heart," says Olivia, who turned nine years old in 2015. "He always tells me to be strong, never give up, and there will be a way to stop cancer one way or the other. . . . I told him fighting cancer is a lot like driving a race car—it's not where you start, it's where you finish that matters." Olivia has stayed in touch with Jeff, and some of her artwork adorns the walls of the foundation's headquarters in Charlotte.

While Jeff has met many children with cancer through his foundation, he had a special connection with Leah Wasson, who met him when she was three years old. Leah is from Pittsboro, Jeff's hometown in Indiana. "She and I did a photo shoot together and some different things around Riley," Jeff remembers. "She was a part of our whole campaign one year."

Leah and her family would come to Indianapolis to participate in the fundraising bowling tournament. One year, about a month before the annual tournament, when Leah was seven years old, she relapsed.

"I was driving when I got a call from the hospital telling me Leah passed," Kriger says. When she called Jeff to give him the news, there was complete silence on the other end of the phone. The next day Jeff asked that a picture of Leah be sent to him at the track. That weekend, as a personal and private tribute to his young friend, he drove with Leah's picture in his car.

"Knowing there's a child that you met, you spent time with them and their parents, and they're no longer with us," says Jeff, "nothing strikes home harder than that."

TOP LEFT: Olivia Pierce presenting her artwork to Jeff, which now hangs in the foundation's main office in Charlotte. TOP RIGHT: Jeff and David Corcelli draw together at Riley Hospital for Children.

*   *   *

Jeff's commitment to pediatric cancer research evolved into a global effort. He developed a relationship with the Clinton Global Initiative (CGI), founded in 2005 by former president Bill Clinton. The nonpartisan organization convenes global leaders to devise and implement solutions to the world's most pressing problems, including global cancer.

In 2011, through Jeff's involvement with CGI, his foundation granted Partners In Health and its sister organization, Inshuti Mu Buzima, $1.5 million over three years to bring treatment to children suffering from cancer in Rwanda. Prior to Jeff's funding, these patients had little or no access to cancer treatment, let alone high-quality cancer care.

"In the United States, there are statistics that tell you there's an eighty percent cure rate [for some pediatric cancers], so, definitely, strides have been made," Jeff says. "The flip side of that is Rwanda." When most think of this small southeastern African country, they think of the horrific genocide that took place there in 1994. But the country has stabilized and made huge strides in health care, with the exception of cancer treatment. "They weren't getting treatment at all," Jeff says. "Their doctors and hospitals didn't have the ability to do biopsies."

There was also no access to screening, diagnosis, chemotherapy, radiation therapy, or surgery. Rwandans had to travel great distances in search of treatment that was ineffective. "In some cases, people were walking miles to three different hospitals, and they were getting over-the-counter medications for pain when what they needed was the cancer treatments we could provide," Jeff says.

Preferring to experience things firsthand, Jeff decided to go to Rwanda with Dr. Lawrence Shulman, director of the Center for Global Cancer Medicine at the Abramson Cancer Center, to see the Butaro district hospital for himself. "Going to Rwanda is no picnic," Dr. Shulman emphasizes. "It is not a vacation spot. Just getting there is difficult. Getting to the hospital is more difficult. It's miles and miles of dirt roads in a remote volcanic mountain range of northern Rwanda, near the border with Uganda. It's not an easy trip, and it displays the level of his commitment to have gone multiple times.

"We walked through the hospital and saw child after child with cancer growing out of their heads, out of their stomachs, out of their chests," Dr. Shulman remembers of the experience. "They were lying there waiting to die. The death rate was essentially one hundred percent."

RIGHT: (left to right) Lawrence Shulman, MD and Director, Center for Global Cancer Medicine at the University of Pennsylvania/Senior Oncology Advisor at Partners in Health; Agnes Binagwaho, MD and Minister of Health of Rwanda; Chelsea Clinton; former president Bill Clinton; Jeff; Paul Farmer, MD and Chief Strategist and Cofounder of Partners in Health.

Jeff's foundation got involved, and helped create the Butaro Cancer Center of Excellence at Butaro district hospital. The Jeff Gordon Children's Foundation has donated almost $2 million so far, the largest single donor in the creation of the center. Jeff is more than just a donor. "He's a true partner in this work," Dr. Shulman adds. "This is more than just writing a check. He cares deeply about what we're doing. He cares deeply about the children we're able to treat in Rwanda."

The program is now viewed internationally as a model for how to develop high-quality cancer care in a very poor resource setting. "What's happened in Rwanda has established a precedent that this can be done in the poorest of settings," Dr. Shulman says. "Jeff Gordon and his foundation has helped make a difference in thousands of lives."

"Jeff knows a lot about his subject," Kriger says. "He gets the science behind this. Is he wearing a white lab coat? No. But he reads about it and he understands. He knows he can leverage his notoriety but he can't do that credibly if he doesn't get what he's talking about. So he really works at it."

Jeff believes his commitment to the foundation has a lot to do with who he aspires to be as a person. "I'm a man of my word. So if I give my word, I'm gonna do my best to stand by it—and if I'm gonna stand by something, I want it to be something that I can truly be proud of," Jeff says. "I think that relates to driving . . . being a dad, a husband, a philanthropist, a representative of a company . . . that's just the way I like to do things."

From the start, Jeff wanted to know how to continue the foundation's growth after he finished racing. "That's pretty forward thinking. He's very humble, concerned and wants to solve problems," Dr. Clapp says.

"Most of us are lucky if we find one thing in life we are passionate about," Jeff said in his closing remarks at the 2012 Heisman Humanitarian Award ceremony. "I found that, in racing, at an early age. But I've also been very fortunate to have found another passion and that's helping others in need. This award inspires me to continue putting as much effort as I can into the things I know are the right things to do, and I hope it will also inspire others."

TOP: Jeff and Ingrid visit with children in a village near the Butaro Cancer Center of Excellence in Rwanda, 2011.

13

A RENEWED COMMITMENT

BY 2010, JEFF HAD BEEN RACING competitively for more than three decades and was coming up on his eighteenth season in the Cup Series. The years of wear and tear were beginning to take a toll on his thirty-eight-year-old body. Despite injections and therapies and regular sessions with a specialist, he often found himself racing in pain. The fact that he hadn't won a championship since 2001 and that he'd won just once in seventy-seven races only made it worse.

He raced to win, not to finish sixth or seventh or have a "pretty good" season, or even for the money. The previous year, he had become the first NASCAR driver in history to surpass $100 million in career race winnings, a figure that paled in comparison to what he'd earned in sponsorship dollars, endorsement deals, and other business arrangements. "I've gotten paid a lot of money for doing this—far more than I ever thought I would—but at no time was I ever doing it for the money," he says. "I've never searched for that. What I have searched for is the opportunity to race and be competitive and win."

He couldn't help but harken back to his years with Evernham, when everything had seemed to serve itself up. "I wasn't doing anything special other than what I had always done," he muses, "but with more confidence, resources, and the right people. We just clicked as an organization. It wasn't that we weren't working hard, but it just seemed to come so much easier."

Winning had always sustained and motivated him, but now he was working that much harder for diminishing returns. "If your teammate is kicking your butt every weekend and winning championships, you ought to be as well," he says. "So I asked myself, 'What am I doing wrong? Maybe I need to change my approach. Maybe it's time.' But then I realized rather than 'change,' I needed to recommit to the things that have always worked for me, believe in myself and go to the track and, if anything, work even harder at it—at the physical fitness side, what I was eating, and through time spent with the team trying to analyze what the cars were doing. I just tried to do my job even better, something that honestly I never had to focus on but now the game was changing and I had to change along with it."

The problem was, things weren't improving. If anything, they got a bit worse in 2010. The team would be highly competitive one race, then barely register the next, and they still weren't mustering any wins. At one point, at Letarte's suggestion, and with Rick Hendrick's full support, the crew chief and Jeff booked a weekend fishing trip with a sports psychologist

OPPOSITE: Jeff Gordon talks with crew chief Alan Gustafson in the garage at Indianapolis Motor Speedway, 2011.

to see if they could get to the bottom of what was holding them back.

Jeff did have a nice run of five straight top-fives in the summer and still made the Chase, but his fall was probably most memorable for the scuffle with Jeff Burton after being wrecked under caution at Texas. And for the second time in three seasons, there had been no wins.

"In my opinion," Jeff says, "2010 was one of the worst seasons I've ever had. And I was not motivated anymore. I'd always had enough confidence that I felt like if we got down a little bit, I could get us back up, that we would find a way to get back. That year, I wasn't so sure. I felt like we pretty much exhausted every option."

There was no bitterness or recrimination among the team. Everyone had put their back into it, particularly Letarte, who felt he'd tried every trick in the book to get the No. 24 out of its straitjacket. There was simply something intangible missing.

"If I really look back on it," Letarte explains, "Jeff and I never really recovered from not winning the championship in 2007. We put together a record year, just phenomenal. We did everything we could do, and we got beat. Truly giving everything you have in sports is kind of like being in love. When you're really in love, you let your guard down and you let it all happen. . . . And when it doesn't work out, you become heartbroken. Sports are the same way. I call it the 'sports hangover.' And that was a sports hangover that I don't know if we were ever going to get over together."

Jeff wouldn't argue that the disappointment of 2007 had played a crucial role. But his issues now ran deeper. Taking stock of his life and his career, he came face-to-face with the reality of the situation and for the first time seriously considered hanging it up.

"I always said that if I'm not enjoying it, I'm not healthy, and I'm not competitive—I don't want to be doing this," he recalls. "And 2010 was that kind of year—all three were lining up. I just thought, 'Okay, maybe it's me. Why am I doing this? How much longer do I want to be doing this? My back hurts. I'm not having fun.' How do you climb out of that?"

He called Rick Hendrick. "I'm not feeling it anymore," Jeff remembers telling the boss. "And I'm not doing the team justice because we're not getting the results." Hendrick wasn't quite ready to have his four-time champion, a racer who had brought Hendrick Motorsports its first championship and helped make them the premier organization, bail on his storied career with less than two months before the next season, especially with a new primary sponsor coming on board in AARP–Drive to End Hunger and no replacement driver.

If they were going to do it, they needed to do it right. They needed time to notify the media and the fans; they needed to organize a send-off season. But not *this*. This was not the way to go out. "I talked him into one more year because I just hated to see him stop," Hendrick says.

But what really woke Jeff up was Ingrid. She didn't want him moping, and she didn't want to hear any talk about retirement. "We had a lot of conversations about it," Jeff says. "She

TOP RIGHT: Steve Letarte and Jeff decided to part ways in 2010.

was as frustrated as I was that the results weren't coming. But seeing her want more for me, more for the team, and our family, motivated me. She knew I could still do it."

As he began pulling himself out of the pit of self-doubt, he realized there was perhaps an even more important reason to continue: Ella, who was now three years old, and her brother, Leo Benjamin, who had been born in August. "I wanted them to experience seeing their dad racing," Jeff says. "It was important to me that they get old enough to have some sort of understanding of what I did."

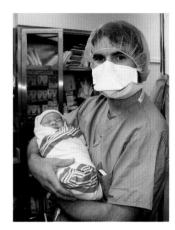

So just before Christmas, Marshall Carlson, Hendrick Motorsports's general manager at the time, came to Jeff and said they were thinking about doing some reshuffling, and, since he had once shown interest in Alan Gustafson, would he be interested in having Gustafson crew chief for the 24 team? "Absolutely, one hundred percent I'm interested," Jeff told him. "Alan was Kyle Busch's crew chief when Kyle was a rookie, and there were a lot of times when Alan came to me, and we would talk about setups and things they were doing with the cars. I was really impressed with him then as well as when he was Mark Martin's crew chief almost winning the championship together in 2009," Jeff says. "I wasn't unhappy with Steve. I liked him as a person and as a crew chief, but I didn't see us getting to the level I was hoping for. I also thought that Dale Jr. and Steve would be a good fit. Steve has a big personality and is good at bringing that out in others. It ended up being a great fit." So Dale Earnhardt Jr. and Steve Letarte were now in the 48/88 shop, and Jeff was paired with Alan Gustafson in the 5/24 shop. Back pain be damned, Jeff would give it one more shot.

But if they were going to approach the season the way Jeff and Ingrid had discussed it—putting everything he had into a run for a championship—there were a few things he needed to make clear. He was going to eat, sleep, and dream racing. He wasn't going to have time to be the super-indulgent daddy or the attentive husband. His biggest priority was going to be the race car, the track, and the team. He wanted to make sure they all knew what they were getting into. "I'm on board," Ingrid assured him. "Let's do it."

"So 2011 was an opportunity not only to make the change with Alan and the team but also to recommit myself to racing," Jeff says.

It wasn't the only relationship that changed. For five years, Jeff had watched Jimmie Johnson—the closest friend he'd ever had in racing—completely take over the sport, capturing title after title. In 2010, Johnson had won his fifth straight title, surpassing Jeff's championship record, and their friendship was challenged. "I think it's natural when friends are also competitors. When you see someone else accomplishing what you want to accomplish, it's difficult," Jeff admits. Now Jeff was leaving the building they'd shared since 2002 to join a new crew.

"We'd spoken about how competition was putting a strain on our relationship," Johnson says. "Being so close to someone off the track, and having my hero be my mentor, and then watching the emotional side, the friendship side, kind of fracture, and him not be there to have cool experiences with in life, and to not be with him as a friend to share it—there's a pain and a sting that goes with that.

"He has said a few times that when the competition is gone, we'll hash this out and it'll all make sense. At some point, I have a feeling we'll be on rocking chairs having a beer and sorting it out."

But in the meantime, Johnson was just another guy in another car trying to keep Jeff from winning. As the old-timers might say: that's racing.

TOP: Jeff holding his newborn son, Leo, 2010. BOTTOM: Ella and Leo.

The following few years with Gustafson were a period of personal rejuvenation for Jeff. In the second race of 2011, he snapped his sixty-six-race winless drought and then went on to win twice more, claiming third place on the career victories list. He would win three more times over the next two seasons and make the Chase each time. He showed some spark in 2013 but ultimately finished sixth behind Jimmie Johnson in his sixth championship season. It wasn't spectacular, but Jeff was pouring every ounce of sweat and passion he could into it, and the team was learning, building, and progressing. Ultimately, the pieces came together, and 2014 would rival anything he had accomplished in six years.

The first ten races of that season saw Jeff reel off seven top-tens and four top-fives. He was already leading in points when he grabbed his first win of the season at Kansas and was still holding the top spot when they rolled into Indianapolis for the twentieth race of the season. By then, he already knew that the following season, 2015, would be his last. In the spring, he had made his decision and secretly informed Rick Hendrick, who understood it was pointless to try to squeeze any more out of his golden boy.

The Brickyard had always been a special place for Jeff, ever since his first monumental victory there in 1994. He'd won the iconic race a total of four times. There was no telling what his 2015 season would look like; he realized this might be his last shot. Rick Hendrick felt the same. "This is your day," he told Jeff that morning. At a ceremony preceding the race, the mayor of Indianapolis proclaimed July 27, 2014 to be Jeff Gordon Day. In receiving his plaque, Jeff joked, "I just hope my competitors are respectful of this."

They didn't have to be. The No. 24 team came with one of the strongest cars that afternoon, and Jeff helped them prove it, running up front most of the day before pulling away from his Hendrick Motorsports teammate Kasey Kahne on a restart with seventeen laps to go. "A great restart on my part, which I can't say I'm known for, was crucial," Jeff recalls. "He really had the preferred line, and I had to be super aggressive. So it was intense. It was everything," he says. When he crossed the finish line to roars from the appreciative hometown crowd, he crossed the threshold into history, becoming the only NASCAR driver to capture five Brickyard 400s and tying Forumla 1 racer Michael Schumacher for the most career wins at the track.

The kissing-the-bricks ceremony after the race provided a clear picture of how much Jeff's life had changed, when Ingrid, Ella, and Leo joined him for the photo op. "That moment right there, where you're able to achieve something so great and you're able to see the look in their eyes—you know, they're there, they're experiencing it. Certainly for Ella, she'll never forget those moments. And I know I won't. It can be hard to make your kids proud of what you do as a parent, and that was one of those moments."

⋆ ⋆ ⋆

On the track, he continued to delight everyone, going on to win at Michigan three races after the Brickyard and finishing second at Richmond to enter the Chase in second position, just three points behind Brad Keselowski.

The Chase had been restructured again that season, with sixteen racers qualifying and the four lowest-performing drivers being dropped after each three-race period. At

OPPOSITE: TOP LEFT: Jeff smoking up the finish line by doing a few celebratory doughnuts in front of the pagoda at the finish line following his historic Brickyard 400 win, July 27, 2014. TOP RIGHT: Jeff celebrating his record setting fifth win at the Brickyard 400, 2014. MIDDLE ROW: Jeff proudly watches as Leo and Ella kiss the bricks at Indianapolis Motor Speedway, 2014. BOTTOM: Jeff and his family kiss the bricks in honor of his historic win, 2014. THIS PAGE: TOP: Ella and Leo give their Papa a high-five after his Brickyard 400 win, 2014.

the tenth and final race in Miami, the final four teams would compete against each other for the championship.

Jeff came out swinging in the first three-race series, notching a dominating win at Dover over Keselowski and a runner-up finish at Chicago. That was more than enough to overcome a disappointing twenty-sixth-place showing at Loudon, and he easily advanced to the Chase's next round. Another runner-up finish at Charlotte helped him move on again, and heading into Martinsville, he was one of eight drivers left. The team's performance over the next three races would decide whether Jeff would race for a championship at Homestead.

The No. 24 clearly had a strong car at Martinsville, and Jeff ran well all day. But a penalty for speeding on pit road cost him the lead, and he finished second behind teammate Dale Earnhardt Jr. Still, it was enough to push him to the top, and he went to Texas the following week leading the field. A good show there would likely punch his ticket to the finale at Homestead. A win there would seal it.

And it looked like that was where things were headed in Fort Worth. After a restart with seventeen laps to go, Jeff moved up from third to second, behind Jimmie Johnson. Four laps later, Kasey Kahne crashed on the backstretch, so the yellow came out one more time. On that restart, with eight laps left, Jeff got the jump on Johnson in Turn 2, took the lead, and began pulling away. With four laps to go, it was clear no one could catch him. He was going to Homestead to race for a championship. And then, the unthinkable. Far back in the pack, Clint Bowyer got loose and slid into the wall. The caution came out. It was the only thing that could have reeled Jeff in. Now he'd have to line up again for a last-lap shootout.

"We had it won so many times, and the caution kept coming out," he says. "Then you have to rerack, do another restart. I knew 2015 was going to be my final year at the time, and so I knew how crucial and important that race was."

He chose to line up on the outside of the front row, with second-running Jimmie Johnson beside him on the inside. Just behind them were Kevin Harvick on the outside and Brad Keselowski on the inside. And then the flag dropped. Jeff spun his tires slightly but still had a decent start. Shooting into the first turn, Jeff came down from the outside to get side-by-side with Johnson, leaving just enough of a gap for the hard-driving Keselowski to try and squeeze into the opening between Jeff and Jimmie. Keselowski and Jeff made contact. As Keselowski and Johnson took off, the No. 24 dropped like a dead bird, finally spinning out, a casualty of a flat tire from the contact. Jeff would finish the day twenty-ninth. It had taken just a split second for his dream of a fifth championship to receive a serious stomping.

As the race winner, Jimmie Johnson, turned celebratory donuts on the front straightaway, Jeff pulled up next to Keselowski's car on pit road. By the time he climbed out, there was already some pushing and shoving among the crews of the No. 24 and Keselowski's No. 2. Jeff made his way around Keselowski's car, where he had some strong words for the young 2012 champion. Keselowski answered back, then turned away.

"What he did on the track was not that terrible," Jeff admits. "It was a risky move. But it was the way he handled it afterwards that was unacceptable in my opinion—to just sit there and brush it off, kind of smug. And for his team to stand there and try to protect him. I thought that was ridiculous. And that's why it escalated."

When Kevin Harvick came around the other side and nudged Keselowski toward Jeff, Jeff lunged and grabbed the driver's collar. And then all hell broke loose. Fists started flying,

TOP: Jeff signing autographs at Las Vegas Motor Speedway, May 9, 2014. BOTTOM: Jeff celebrates winning the 5 Hour Energy 400 at Kansas Speedway, May 10, 2014.

with a good dozen folks shoving each other, wrestling, punching, and kicking. By the time NASCAR officials broke it up, Keselowski had abrasions on his face and mouth, and Jeff was bleeding from the lip.

"Looking back on it, I probably overreacted a little bit," Jeff says. "But at the moment, I didn't care about that. I cared that my race was done, and potentially our championship hopes. . . . It was not only a huge emotional letdown but a huge hit in the points. There was a lot going on, a lot of pressure, emotion, adrenaline, a lot of things had built up. And when it goes bad, it just sends you over the top.

"So I was mad at him, but I was just as mad at myself for allowing somebody to put me in that position and kind of give me a cheap shot. It's my job to prevent that from happening. And in the clutch, I didn't get it done. I allowed Brad to get in that position."

The fracas at Texas was all over the news, but it certainly wasn't the first time Jeff had gotten physical at the track. Since 2006, there had been wrecks and retribution, arguments and hands-on confrontations with Matt Kenseth, Jeff Burton, and Clint Bowyer. It was a noticeable change from the quieter, more controlled Jeff Gordon the public had come to know earlier in his career.

While Texas may have been a huge setback, Jeff still had a chance of moving on to the final round at Homestead. It would all depend on how he performed—and how the seven other remaining Chase hopefuls performed—at Phoenix. In the end, the only way he could have done better was to win. He finished second after running in that spot nearly the entire day behind the eventual victor, Kevin Harvick. And when he crossed the finish line, he was going to the finals. But just behind him, Ryan Newman bumped Kyle Larson into the wall and passed him in the final turn to secure an eleventh-place finish. That put Newman through and dropped Jeff just a single point below the cutoff.

With an understandably frustrated tone in his voice, Jeff addressed his team on the radio. "Let's just go win at Homestead, that's all we can do. You guys did everything great this year." In the post-race interview, he was composed but still smarting about what had gone down in Texas. "This makes last week hurt that much more," he said. "I'm not happy about it, but at the same time, I'm really proud of what we've done this year."

The boss wasn't happy either. No Hendrick driver made the final four, dashing their chances for a twelfth team championship. "He should have won the championship," Hendrick says. "He got screwed by Brad taking him out in Texas. I think we would have beaten Harvick at Homestead."

"It was an amazing, very competitive year, winning races and all that," Jeff remembers. "And even though we didn't go to Homestead as one of the final four, I felt like we were a championship-caliber team." In that final race, Jeff dominated the competition and finished in the top ten. He may not have been racing as a contender, but that finish did help him secure at least one point of pride—for the third time since NASCAR had introduced the Chase format, Jeff led all other racers in the overall point standings for the season.

It had been a spectacular climb, both for the team and for Jeff personally, since that moment four years earlier when he had teetered on the edge of putting his helmet away for good. He had wanted to contend for a title, and all that could really be said was that fate had intervened.

★　　　★　　　★

TOP: Jeff focusing on the race at Las Vegas Motor Speedway, March 8, 2014. BOTTOM: Leo raises his arms in celebration of Jeff's win at Dover International Speedway, September 28, 2014.

Rick Hendrick knew. Alan Gustafson knew. Ingrid and Carol and John knew. And that was really it. Jeff had kept a tight lid on his decision to retire after the 2015 season while Hendrick set the wheels in motion, notifying the current sponsors and courting new ones, Hendrick signed nineteen-year-old Chase Elliott, the 2014 Xfinity Series champion, to take over the No. 24 in 2016, and handled the myriad of other issues related to winding down Jeff's driving career at Hendrick Motorsports.

Now, as they came upon the new year, the only thing left to do was tell the rest of the world. The only question was when. Jeff, hoping to make an announcement just before the new season began in Daytona in mid-February, had assured Ingrid there was no need to cancel her scheduled January trip to Belgium. And while she had hesitated, she ultimately packed her bags and boarded the plane.

And then word came down. NAPA Auto Parts, who had just signed on as the new primary sponsor of the No. 24 for 2016, was eager to make the news of their deal public. But they couldn't go ahead until Jeff had disclosed his pending retirement. Everyone agreed that Thursday, January 22, would be the day.

"I was fine with it," Jeff recalls. "I was already prepared for it to happen. . . . But what I underestimated was that day. When I woke up, it hit me."

"He called me when he was driving up to Hendrick to make the announcement," Carol remembers. "And I knew it was coming, but I didn't know it was going to be that day. He was very emotional. We both were."

When he reached his office, he began making a series of tough phone calls. He first contacted each of his sponsors, most of whom already knew the news was coming. Then he called his teammates: Jimmie Johnson, Kasey Kahne, and Dale Earnhardt Jr.

"[Dale] was the most shocked," Jeff remembers. "He's like, 'No, man, that cannot be happening. You're messing with me. That can't be true.'" Jeff assured him it was. "And he said, 'I'm having a hard time. I hear you, but I don't hear you. I'm having a hard time letting these words sink in.' And he told me how appreciative he was that I thought to call him."

Meanwhile, downstairs, all the No. 24 team members were gathering in the shop for what they had been told was an important announcement. When Jeff came in and informed them, he struggled to keep it together. "Telling them definitely impacted me in a big way because of how hard they work, how supportive they had been, how much I had enjoyed working with these guys," he says. "The coolest thing was that every single one of them came up and shook my hand and thanked me for all that I'd done for the team and for them. . . . It's still hard for me to hold back my emotions about that experience."

Once the media had been notified, Jeff headed out to do a video press conference and a series of interviews for newspapers and television. The reaction from the public and other drivers came quickly. There was shock. Disbelief. A tremendous outpouring of love and respect. There was plenty of sorrow to go around, too, especially among the fans.

At one point, while he was preparing for a television interview, Jeff decided to check his text messages. There was one from his mom.

"I knew it was going to be on the sports news," Carol remembers, "so I was watching, and it came across on the ticker thing: 'Jeff Gordon Announces Retirement.' I had tears in my eyes. So I texted Jeff and said that I never would have thought that watching *Sports Center* would make me cry."

"I remember her texting me and me thinking, 'Oh, I shouldn't have read that.' When I got it, it made me tear up again," he laughs.

It was a day full of bittersweet experiences, but perhaps the most heartrending moment was one that occurred before he'd even left the house that morning.

"I was shaving when Ella walked in," Jeff remembers. "She was curious to know why I was shaving. And I said, 'You know, I'm going to be telling people that I'm no longer driving.' And she said, 'What? What do you mean you're not driving anymore?' And I said, 'This year, it will be my final year, so I'm letting everyone know.'

"'No,' she said. 'You can't do that today, Papa!' And I told her I was sorry but I'd already made that decision. She said, 'What am I going to tell my friends? What are they going to say? If you're not driving, they're going to think different of me.' She was basically saying that because I was famous, she was sort of famous and that because I was no longer going to be driving, I wasn't going to be famous and neither was she. I said, 'Let me finish up here, Princess, and you go back to your room and get dressed for school and we'll discuss it some more.'"

"She left and I just lost it. I started crying out loud. Well, she comes walking back in and says, 'What's wrong, Papa, what's wrong?' I said, 'I'm sorry. I'm happy. I just can't believe this day has come, and I'm proud and everything, but I'm just really emotional.' . . . I thought of how far I had come from just being a kid, getting started, looking up to people like A.J. Foyt and Rick Mears and then to be thought of by other kids the same way.

"And I just thought, oh my gosh, what an amazing career, what an amazing thing for me to actually be able to say, on my own terms, that I'm walking away from something that has been the most incredible experience and changed my life forever."

TOP: Jeff surveying the track, Auto Club Speedway, March 23, 2014.

14
THE FINAL CHECKERED

FROM THE TIME PREPARATIONS BEGAN for 2015, Jeff knew his final season was going to be a balancing act. There had been enough forewarning that NASCAR, the fans, the sponsors, the press, the tracks, and pretty much the rest of the world were ready to send off the champ in style. On one hand, Jeff wanted to be present enough to savor that flattering farewell tour to the fullest and soak up the accolades in the company of his family and friends. On the other, he worried about limping through the final checkered like some worn-out warrior.

After his great run in 2014, NASCAR's new changes to the cars' horsepower gave Jeff some concern going into the season. "It was a pretty significant reduction," Jeff says. "I always like cars with more horsepower and not less."

Naturally, he and the team would have to work hard, as they always had. A championship? Challenging, he thought to himself. A win? Sure, that would be great—even expected—but he wasn't going to heap any extra pressure on himself if it didn't happen right away. "I went into the season thinking I was going to enjoy this final year and just take it all in, and no matter what happens on the track I'm just going to enjoy myself," he recalls. "I'm not going to let a bad finish ruin my final year for me."

That uncharacteristically light-hearted approach seemed to pay dividends immediately. After a thousand and one interviews and other demands in the week leading up to the Daytona 500, he went out and won the pole. Before the race, he was lauded with a series of video tributes from other racers, most of them far younger, many who had grown up idolizing the man they'd now be competing against for the final time. FOX race broadcaster and three-time Winston Cup Series champion Darrell Waltrip, who in 1993 had pointedly asserted Jeff could never cut it in the Cup Series, now professed him one of the greatest drivers of all time.

By the time the race was halfway run, it looked like Jeff might have a fourth Daytona 500 victory to add to that book. He had a strong car and led all but twenty-three of the first 110 laps. "At the time we were leading, I was enjoying it—my final year, my final Daytona. And the thought did go through my mind of how great it would be to win," he admits. But on the restart after a caution flag, he gradually slipped into the lower portion of the top ten, where he hung around for the second half of the race. With ten laps to go, he'd worked his way up and

OPPOSITE: Jeff anticipating the final Cup Series race of his career, Homestead-Miami Speedway, November 22, 2015.

was battling for third before getting knocked back again, falling victim to Daytona's wreck roulette on the final lap. His promising season debut devolved into a thirty-third-place finish.

After the race he was philosophical. "I'm still smiling and enjoying every moment of it," he told a FOX reporter. "I'm just in this place that's so foreign to me but so incredible, to just be taking it all in and enjoying every moment."

It was a bit harder to keep smiling the following week, when he got caught up in a late-race wreck in Atlanta, bidding an unceremonious good-bye to the track where he'd first grabbed Rick Hendrick's attention, and where he'd run his now mythical Cup race No. 1 against a retiring Richard Petty back in 1992. It was tougher still when, a week later, after capturing the pole in Las Vegas—the seventy-ninth of his career—he was crunched in practice by a spinning Danica Patrick and had to start dead last in a backup car. To add insult to injury, after working his way into contention, he rammed the back of Jeb Burton, who had slowed up when Jimmie Johnson blew a tire, and, with reams of duct tape holding his Chevrolet's busted nose together for the last eighty laps, he hobbled over the finish line in eighteenth place.

With three disastrous races kicking off Jeff's swan song, one reporter called him the "poster child for the unlucky." It certainly seemed apt. "I just can't believe the way these races have been going," he said at the time. But then the pendulum slowly began swinging the other direction. He finished ninth at Phoenix, seventh at Fontana, and ninth at Martinsville in a race he felt he could have won if he hadn't been penalized late in the race for speeding on pit road again.

After an Easter break that included a visit to the White House with Ingrid and the kids for the president's annual holiday celebration, Jeff returned to Texas for the first time since his run-in with Brad Keselowski. But the only battle he had this time was with the car. Fortunately, a call by Alan Gustafson to go with just two tires instead of four during a late pit stop helped Jeff secure a seventh-place finish. At Bristol the next Sunday, where Ella and Leo were named grand marshals of the Food City 500, he had an excellent shot to win, starting second in a two-lap overtime restart, but ultimately finished third behind Jimmie Johnson and race winner Matt Kenseth. That first top-five may have boosted him to ninth in the

TOP LEFT: Jeff gives his mom a hug just before the Daytona 500, February 22, 2015. BOTTOM LEFT: Jeff gets "good luck" kisses from Leo and Ella at Texas Motor Speedway, November 8, 2015. RIGHT: Jeff races past Joey Logano and a "Thank you Jeff" tribute banner at Las Vegas Motor Speedway, March 8, 2015.

standings, but he wasn't blowing anybody's doors off and felt like the No. 24's performance was middling at best.

"We ran so well in 2014," he says, "and we got into 2015 and we just weren't there. We weren't as competitive as we had been. It wasn't from lack of effort. The effort was there, but the speed just wasn't there."

It was just a quarter of the way through the season, but the circumstances were beginning to hammer away at his "let's enjoy this" attitude. He didn't want to emotionally sequester himself from all the hoopla on and off the track, but he found himself growing edgy. "It's a fine balance between making sure the team understands you're committed to driving the car the best you can with as few distractions as possible and the reality of there being more demands on your time," he says. "And I think during the first part of the season, the demands definitely were a distraction, more than I anticipated."

But the biggest squeeze on his time and attention wasn't the fans, the press, or the sponsors—it was his own self-imposed effort to make his final season as memorable for everybody else as it was for him. He had invited scores of old friends, race colleagues, and acquaintances, including some he hadn't seen for twenty years, to join him at upcoming races in Charlotte and Indianapolis. But perhaps most pressing was the post-Homestead party in Miami he and Ingrid were planning for two hundred guests.

"He decided to have a party to celebrate his career, and that was, I think, a great decision," Ingrid recalls. "Instead of just going home . . . we're going to celebrate it." But getting it set up meant phone calls and discussions, venues, dancers, and DJs to hire, menus to work out—a million tiny details that all needed attention.

"The way John taught me was that if we're going to do something, we're going to do it right," Jeff says. "This was sort of my way of giving back to all those people and friends who supported me. And there's a lot of time and effort that has to go into making it right. If we're inviting people to come, I want them to have the right experience."

"Making experiences," whether it was for his kids and wife, his friends, his teammates, his fans, children with cancer, or anybody else, was something Jeff had always prided himself on. "I remember when we would win," recalls his former crew chief Robbie Loomis, "he would go to the new guys on the crew and just love seeing the looks on their faces and the

TOP LEFT: Jeff chasing down teammate Dale Earnhardt Jr. at Texas Motor Speedway, April 10, 2015. TOP RIGHT: "The Last Lap" party invitation hosted by Jeff and Ingrid, November 22, 2015.

excitement. . . . Jeff loves surprising people and seeing their excitement and joy at experiencing something they could only experience because he gave it to them."

And while Jeff kept all those responsibilities secret from Gustafson and the crew, he found that he increasingly had to remove himself from the organizing process. "I started getting really frustrated because things weren't going well on the track and I was really busy off the track planning these things," he remembers. "It became a bit overwhelming."

On April 27, a day after Jeff logged an eighth-place finish at Richmond to keep himself in the top ten, the No. 24 team began a two-day tire test at Indianapolis Motor Speedway. Organized by Goodyear to help the company gauge what type of tire was best for the season's new aero and horsepower package, the test also gave a select group of Cup teams the opportunity to gain some valuable insight into their cars' handling characteristics.

By that time, Jeff was noticing Gustafson's growing frustration. "Things weren't going well," Jeff says. "He was frustrated with me, I was frustrated with him. The car wasn't where it needed to be." At the same point in the previous season, they'd already had four top-five finishes; now they had one. At Indy, they were fast the first day, but not fast enough to put a grin on either of their faces. "What can I do to help this situation," Jeff remembers thinking. "Can I be giving the team better information and details about what the car is doing?"

He figured it might be a good idea to take the team out for dinner, do a little bonding, and enjoy some of the last moments he was going to have with his teammates. Almost everyone came along. Gustafson didn't. "Typically Alan was the first to join in and be a part of team get-togethers like this. I think he was totally focused on Indianapolis, he really wanted to win that race," Jeff says. "So I'm hanging out with the team, taking them out to dinner, drinking wine. And that led to probably too many drinks. . . . One thing led to another, and the next thing you know, the next day we're all not feeling too good. . . . And Alan was pissed. He was super-pissed. He just said, 'We're not fast, and I've got nobody here to work on the car because these guys are so hungover they want to either throw up or go to bed.' I felt terrible."

That night, Jeff and Gustafson exchanged text messages. Jeff assured him that everything he'd said had been spot-on. "You were right, I was wrong," he recalls telling Gustafson. "From this moment forward, you're going to have nothing but the best from me."

"It's a delicate situation," Gustafson admits. "He's the only guy at the track competing with these circumstances, all these other events going on. And it changes your perspective

TOP LEFT: Displayed in a commemorative case, the steering wheel from the Corvette Z06 pace car Jeff drove to kick off the 99th running of the Indianapolis 500, May 24, 2015. MIDDLE LEFT: A selfie Jeff took in the Chevrolet Corvette pace car at the Indianapolis 500, May 2015. BOTTOM LEFT: Ingrid, Leo, Ella, and Jeff pose at the Indianapolis 500, May 2015. RIGHT: Jeff pacing the field at the Indianapolis 500, May 2015.

a little bit. So we vowed to each other that we weren't going to phone it in and just make it through."

Jeff's happy-go-lucky approach just wasn't working. "That impulsive thought process is not really me at the racetrack," he admits. "I had said I was going to go into this relaxed, calm, cool, that no matter what happens, it happens . . . Well that's not possible.

"We could very easily just sit and hang around and ride off into the sunset, but that's not who I am, that's not who Alan is and that's not who this team is."

On May 3rd, Jeff came into Talladega with more career wins at the track than any active driver, and a racecar that crushed the competition in qualifying. Starting from the pole for the eightieth time in his career, he led forty-seven of the race's 188 laps but was again robbed of a potential opportunity for victory when he was nabbed for speeding on pit road. "The setting on the front splitter was too low," Jeff explains. "When coming to pit road, the hard braking caused the nose to go down. Once the splitter hit the hard surface, I could no longer slow the car, there was no grip." He rebounded from that unfortunate thirty-first-place finish with a fourth place at Kansas, which kept him ninth in the points.

The non-points invitational All-Star race at Charlotte started with a special treat when Jeff was surprised on stage during driver introductions by John, Carol, Ingrid, the kids, and Ray Evernham in front of a sea of fans holding signs reading, "Thank You, Jeff #24," but he wasn't particularly thrilled with his fourth-place finish. At the very least, he said after the race, he could take some of what he'd learned into the following week's Coca-Cola 600, where twenty-two years earlier he'd won his first Cup race and wept in Victory Lane. But handling issues and a late race pit stop for fuel left him finishing in fifteenth place. "That was a lot of darn work for us to finish fifteenth," he remarked afterward.

There was one bright spot on the track for him that day, but it didn't come at Charlotte. Earlier in the afternoon, he'd boarded a flight from North Carolina to Indianapolis, where he was honored as the pace-car driver for the ninety-ninth running of the Indy 500. "That was amazing. Definitely one of the highlights," he says. "It was surreal. I couldn't believe they thought of me to do it. And for me, it was probably more significant than people realize." Indeed, for a kid who grew up idolizing A.J. Foyt, Al Unser, Rick Mears, Johnny Rutherford, and Mario Andretti, it was the next best thing to competing in the storied race. "To be able to go and pace that race in my final year as a racecar driver was huge. It was a once in a lifetime event."

TOP: (left to right): Jeff's wife Ingrid; son Leo; his mother Carol; daughter Ella; stepfather John; and Jeff on stage for the special ceremony honoring Jeff before the All-Star race at Charlotte Motor Speedway, May 16, 2015. LEFT: Jeff and Ray Evernham in front of hundreds of cheering fans holding "Thank You Jeff" signs, Charlotte Motor Speedway, May 16, 2015.

And if all the extracurricular activities and planning weren't enough, Jeff had also found time to work as a broadcaster for FOX Sports, calling Xfinity Series races at Texas, Bristol, and Talladega. On May 21, he had ended any speculation about what he'd be doing after he hung up his helmet, announcing his plan to join Darrell Waltrip and Mike Joy in the booth as a FOX race analyst, beginning with the 2016 Sprint Cup season.

While a number of his peers, among them Ray Evernham and sprint-car racer Jack Hewitt, had warned that he would never find anything that would bring him the same satisfaction as sitting behind the wheel of a race car, Jeff was more than satisfied with his decision, and talking about Cup cars was perhaps as close as he could come to the thrill of racing.

It was a decision that pleased NASCAR's Brian France and also Rick Hendrick, who, although he still had Jeff signed to a lifetime contract, saw it as an opportunity for Jeff to continue to serve as one of the sport's—and one of Hendrick Motorsports'—great ambassadors. "He's earned the right to do whatever he wants to do in the morning when he wakes up," Hendrick said, "and not have to satisfy me, the fans, or the sponsors. It's going to be such a relief to him. I know him well enough to know he doesn't need the fame, but he's going to be more popular on TV, you watch. He's not going to be beating anybody, so all of his fans and then the rest of the fans are going to love to see him."

The chips were falling into place for the post-Cup phase of Jeff's career, but on the track, despite their best effort, the team seemed to be dragging along. Things came to a head two weeks after Charlotte, at Pocono, when toward the end of a race in which Jeff started fourth and then ping-ponged from the front of the pack to the back several times, eventually finishing fourteenth, he and Gustafson got into an expletive-laced feud on the radio. The press picked up on it, and within hours the fight was all over the Internet.

"We had a horrendous day," Jeff recalls. "Nothing went right. In my opinion, we needed more track position, but Alan pitted us. I was questioning the call. He was questioning me. But there were things that led up to that. Maybe they weren't clear-cut moments, but it was just a building up of his frustration, my frustration, the team's frustration."

The two got things sorted out, but the exchange was indicative of the pressure both of them were starting to feel to make something good happen. "It's my job to make sure I'm giving everything, the best I possibly can," Gustafson said. "It's his job to make it go. There are times, obviously, that it gets difficult and you have to disagree. I never in my life want to disrespect Jeff, and I never will. But at the same time, I'm passionate about what I do, and I'm going to fight for success, and the success of this team.

"There's pressure, a ton of pressure. I want him to be the champion. I want him to quit at the top. I want him to do that—for the person he is more than for the driver."

★   ★   ★

The race in Sonoma presented more than just the opportunity to add to his Sprint Cup–record five victories at the road course. It was a chance to journey back to the beginning, to the little bull ring–sized quarter-midget track in Rio Linda, about an hour from the Sonoma Raceway, where in the 1970s, as a five-year-old, Jeff, and John, had first discovered he possessed something special behind the wheel. "It's the whole thing coming full circle," Jeff says.

Jeff arrived with his own young children—and a small entourage—to show them that patch of his history, a bona fide piece of racing Americana that, in fact, he had helped save

TOP: Jeff having a frustrating day at Pocono Raceway, June 7, 2015.

from insolvency some eight years earlier. With races raging and a couple hundred people in attendance, he put his hand to the track and felt its hard-packed dirt. Then he toured the grounds, signing autographs, and chatting with children and well-wishers—some of whom had known him back in the day and hadn't seen him in years, and some to whom he was quite simply a superhero.

"The only thing I could compare it to is when I got Rick Mears's autograph at Indianapolis, or one time in Indiana when I got the Kinsers' autographs," he says. "To me, that was the only time I could think of, looking at a driver and looking up to them as somebody I wanted to be like or that I thought of as a hero or role model." But that was him now. As much as his life had been transformed, being back at that Rio Linda track was as close as he could come to stepping into a time machine.

"What I loved was that very little had changed. And it started bringing back a lot of memories of racing there and the great times I had. That truly is where it all began," he says. And as he stood watching the little three-horsepower engines howl and buzz, soaking in the sights, sounds, and smells of the tiny track, he was gripped by a certain nostalgia. "I was wishing I could go back to those days and just watch from afar," he remembers. "I wish I could see what I was doing, what my thought process was, what my personality was like—and what might have been there to show I might go on to become a NASCAR champion one day."

At Sonoma Raceway on June 28, he picked up a sixteenth-place finish. A month later, he continued his trip down memory lane when he was honored with a parade and celebration in his adopted hometown of Pittsboro, Indiana. "If you want to look at the steps of how I got to where I am today," he says, "Pittsboro played a huge role in that, and so did a lot of people that were there that day." A thousand locals and folks from surrounding areas lined the ten-block stretch of downtown to cheer Jeff on as he rode by in a white convertible flanked by a couple high school buddies.

"What was cool," says his old friend Bruce Pfeifer, "was we'd point people out, and he knew everybody. He was like, 'Are you kidding me? That's so-and-so?'"

Even his mom got in on the act. "I got to wave at my son in a parade," Carol gleefully told one reporter. "I love that."

At a ceremony in the local park, with news helicopters hovering above and children bouncing on trampolines, he received nearly every distinction a small-town-boy-made-good could warrant, with the governor proclaiming July 23, 2015, Jeff Gordon Day in Indiana and presenting him with the Sagamore of the Wabash award, the state's highest civilian honor. The local police chief made him an honorary officer and outfitted him with a badge. Even his old high school gave him a plaque featuring a replica of his diploma. "This is one of the best

days of my life, and I say that sincerely," he told the crowd.

"When you talk to him, Jeff's just the same," says his friend Chris Cooper. "I laughed because he's the same kid from high school. We sat and told stories and joked and clowned around. When you get him alone, it's just us again. We can laugh and be the goofballs we used to be. He was like a kid again. It was great."

TOP RIGHT: Jeff and Ella wave the checkered flag at Jeff's first track, Capitol Quarter Midget Track, Rio Linda, California, June 20, 2015. BOTTOM RIGHT: Indiana Governor Mike Pence proclaiming July 23, 2015, Jeff Gordon Day and presenting Jeff with the Sagamore of the Wabash award, the state's highest civilian honor. Pittsboro, Indiana. LEFT: Jeff riding in a special No. 24 emblazoned Chevrolet Camaro convertible from Indianapolis Motor Speedway, waving to his fans during the "Jeff Gordon Day" parade in Pittsboro, July 2015.

TOP: Jeff posing with some of his heroes, competitors, and friends from his sprint and midget career next to his No. 24 3M Chevrolet prior to the 2015 Brickyard 400. (left to right) Steve Kinser, Randy Kinser, Rick Ferkel, Kelly Kinser, Jeff Gordon, Gary Stanton, Jimmy Sills, Jack Hewitt, Kenny Jacobs, and Rodney Duncan.

Some admitted they had a tough time explaining to their children and wives and coworkers that they weren't awed by his presence; they were just glad to see the Jeff Gordon they'd always known. "To my son, he's an icon," Greg Waters says with a smile. "I guess he kind of is. We know he is. But he ain't."

Three days later, in a suite at Indianapolis Motor Speedway just before his final Brickyard 400, Jeff gathered a veritable who's-who of his sprint and midget career, from owner Rollie Helmling and car builder Bob East to legendary racers like Jack Hewitt and Steve Kinser; there were his heroes and competitors and friends, each of them instrumental in their support of his career. He'd spent a lot of time organizing the get-together. "It was so special to me that they came," he says. "They had all played unique roles in my career, whether they knew it or not."

It would have been icing on that week's cake if he could have gone out and done something special in front of that crowd, but he nailed the wall in the first third of the race while attempting to avoid a sideways-spinning Clint Bowyer. The crew tried to make some quick repairs on pit road and send him back out, but he soon pulled off again. The car was garaged for more extensive work. He would ultimately join the race one last time completing only 110 of the race's 164 laps and settling for forty-second in the forty-three-car field. It was the worst Brickyard finish of his career and one of the greatest disappointments of his final season.

★   ★   ★

In the time between Sonoma and Indianapolis, the No. 24 picked up four top-tens, and following the Brickyard debacle, they logged a third-place finish at Pocono. The next four races were uninspired, with finishes of forty-first, seventeenth, twentieth, and sixteenth. Twenty-five races into the season, Jeff had only three top-five performances and still didn't have a win. The idea that he might not get a win, or worse yet, might not qualify for the Chase, had been hanging over the team.

"Once we got past the summer and we hadn't won, then the pressure was on," Jeff says. "I didn't want to go through my final year without winning. All I had hoped for was to be competitive, and we weren't even that. Heck, we were just trying to get top-fives and make the Chase first and foremost. It was touch and go for a long time before Richmond whether we were going to do that or not. When there's sixteen cars that make it to the Chase and you can't be one of them, and you're at Hendrick Motorsports driving the No. 24 car, you've had a really rotten year."

It galled him that the story of his twenty-third and final season had gone from celebration and expectation to one of raised eyebrows at the mediocrity of his performance. "It started to turn into 'Well, is he even going to win a race?' and 'Boy, they're not very good.' And that bothered me more than anything, for the team, for me, for Ingrid and the kids. I didn't want that. Plus, Ingrid and I had invited quite a few people down to Homestead and for the after-party. We knew it would be a much different experience for all of us if we didn't even make the Chase."

From the first third of the season on, he had been struggling with finding his edge, enough to have purchased a book a friend had recommended to him, on confidence and winning streaks and handed out copies to Gustafson and several others. John Bickford asked what the team needed. Rick Hendrick asked what they needed. Even Ingrid had discussed with Jeff the possibilities of approaching things differently. Nothing had seemed to work. Maybe it was just unluckiness. The only thing Jeff could do was to keep doing what he'd always done.

Jeff told himself, "Don't stop doing what you know how to do, what you do best as far as the driving techniques. Don't try to reinvent the wheel. Don't try to change yourself. Just do what's worked for you in the past, but do it with confidence and kind of let that spread to others."

It didn't work magic, but it at least kept them right on the Chase bubble. Heading into Richmond, the final race before the Chase, Jeff held the fifteenth spot of sixteen qualifying positions. All he had to do was hold on. Surprisingly, even competitors, who in NASCAR are notorious for almost never offering words of encouragement to fellow drivers, wanted to see him make it.

"They were extremely supportive, even more than I anticipated, especially as it started winding down," Jeff recalls. "Rarely does a competitor ever say, 'Hey, man, I'm pulling for you'

TOP: Jeff and the No. 24 team grabbing a third-place finish at Pocono Raceway, August 2, 2015.

or 'Man, I think it'd be really cool for you to win here, or win the championship,' but I had competitors say that to me. It was kind of overwhelming, but really gratifying at the same time."

And when the checkered flag fell at Richmond's Federated Auto Parts 400 on September 12, Jeff and his team breathed a huge sigh of relief. Their seventh-place finish, after starting twenty-third, secured them a spot, one of just five winless teams to make it to the Chase. When he stepped out of the car, Rick Hendrick hugged him from behind, wiping the proverbial sweat from his brow, and waggishly proclaimed to the press that Jeff would be driving for one more season in 2016. "Don't listen to him," Jeff replied.

★   ★   ★

"The one thing we had done pretty well all year long, as bad as we performed, was be consistent," Jeff remembers thinking before entering the Challenger round of the Chase. "The one positive was that we were slightly improving—we might have been fourteenth, but we were doing it on a consistent basis. And my opinion was that if we could pick up our performance slightly, we were going to advance past round two. And then we've got Martinsville. You never know what's going to happen, but we've got a great record there."

In the Chase's first race, at Chicago, Jeff had a strong performance. He was running in the lead on the final restart when he took a risk and decided to stay out on older tires. Denny Hamlin, who ended up in Victory Lane, made an aggressive move on the restart and got inside of Jeff, who lost momentum and started fading because others had fresher tires. He finished fourteenth. The result might not have been great, and a win would have automatically put him through to the next round, but his confidence was bolstered by the performance. "At Chicago, we were on fire," he says. "Really, I thought we were going to finish first or second in that race. On that last restart, if I hadn't screwed it up, I think we probably would have won. I was very encouraged by that."

His seventh-place finish at Loudon in the next race bumped him up to tenth in Chase points, and with a so-so performance and twelfth-place finish at Dover, he captured the seventh position among the championship hopefuls, sending him, along with eleven other drivers,

TOP LEFT: Jeff and Leo share a moment together pre-race at Martinsville Speedway, October 26, 2014. BOTTOM LEFT: Jeff and crew chief Alan Gustafson talk during practice for the Daytona 500 at Daytona International Speedway, February 13, 2015. RIGHT: The No. 24 3M Chevrolet races past a "Thanks Jeff!" sign at Dover International Speedway, May 31, 2015.

into the Contender round. For a team that had sweated bullets about actually getting there, things were starting to look up.

And Jeff now had one more accomplishment in his final season to be proud of. By starting the Loudon race, he surpassed Ricky Rudd as NASCAR's "Iron Man," with 789 consecutive career starts in the Cup Series—more than any driver in history. Not since his first run in Atlanta on November 15, 1992, twenty-three years earlier, had Jeff ever missed a race. Baseball's Iron Man, Cal Ripken, offered his new racing counterpart a public tribute, highlighting Jeff's "passion and skill" and "his ability to compete at the highest level of such a demanding sport for so long."

"That was very cool. I know Cal, and it meant a lot to me," Jeff says. "That was big. It takes a lot of effort, no matter who you are. If you're a racecar driver and you race long enough to get those kinds of numbers and stats, you have to have done a lot of things right and be pretty fortunate."

He was hoping his good fortune would carry into the second round of the Chase, and he was beginning to feel the weight of a grueling season lift. "We did exactly what I felt we could do," he recalls. "We were putting consistent finishes together, showing a little more speed. And we were building on that, which was nice. We had momentum—the first time we'd had it all year."

He qualified poorly for the Charlotte race, but transformed a day of struggling to find the balance of the car into an eighth-place finish. Kansas the following week was not kind. In a race that was most memorable for Joey Logano spinning out Matt Kenseth, Jeff struggled mightily and felt like he was on the verge of wrecking in every corner. He figured maybe he wasn't getting the proper information to the team to make adjustments. He ultimately got tenth place—"one of the hardest top-tens I've ever had to go through," he said at the time—but his confidence, and the team's, had taken a major hit.

Still, he went into the next race at Talladega with an uncharacteristically good attitude, given his general "white-knuckle" dread of the place. "It was certainly the first time in many years where I went to a restrictor-plate track, especially Talladega, very positive," he recalls. Even though he'd suffered through problems on those tracks, he also felt like he'd had some of his strongest moments that season at Talladega and Daytona.

"I felt like we had a slight advantage. But I was sort of like, screw it, whatever happens, happens," he remembers. "I was going to do everything I possibly could throughout the whole weekend to stay positive. It's about an eighty percent chance that you're going to wreck in the race, typically. And part of me was like, gosh, maybe the twenty percent is on my side today, because the last eight races I wrecked."

The bet paid off. He started from the pole and posted a third-place finish, becoming the only Hendrick driver—Jimmie Johnson and Dale Earnhardt Jr. having been eliminated—to make it to the penultimate round of the Chase.

TOP: Jeff, accompanied by his daughter, Ella, greets enthusiastic fans during driver introductions at New Hampshire Motor Speedway, Loudon, New Hampshire, September 27, 2015.

*　　*　　*

Just days before his first Eliminator round race at Martinsville, Jeff was sick as a dog, laid up with a sinus infection. "I remember feeling really, really horrible," he recalls. His doctor had prescribed a combination of medications to knock it out, but even the drugs made him woozy and discombobulated.

"I took it, but I had such a bad reaction to it. It was really making me feel strange," he recalls. "And I was concerned whether I was going to be able to give my best." By race day, he found that the worst of the bug had passed, "but the medication was messing with me more than the illness at that point."

It wasn't how he wanted to approach Martinsville, where his eight career wins were more than he had at any other track. He wanted to be firing on all circuits. But he knew feeling under the weather or not, once he strapped into that race car, he was going to be able to bring something to the game. "I went into the race with confidence, and we qualified pretty good," he says. "But once I was in the race, I wasn't feeling great about our chances. We were burning tires off the car faster than we should have, so I had to hold back the whole time. I felt like I had a faster race car, but I could never show it. I couldn't get everything out of it because as soon as I tried, the rear tires would completely wear out and we'd start dropping. It was like holding back a racehorse."

Jeff had led for a short time in the first half of the race, but by the midpoint, it was the No. 22 of Joey Logano and the No. 2 of Brad Keselowski swapping the lead.

Then everything began to change, slowly at first, with sixty-six laps to go. On a restart after a caution, Keselowski, who started on the front row, inside, slowed up to allow his team-mate, Logano, to drop down into the lead, creating a bottleneck. Kurt Busch, who was behind Keselowski, wasn't too happy about having his progress slowed, and got into the crawling No. 2's back bumper, which sent Keselowski up the track into Matt Kenseth, who was trying to drive by on the outside. The resulting wreck took out Kenseth, Keselowski, and Busch. Jeff, who had been sixth on the restart, avoided any damage.

But there was more to the wreck than sheet metal now. There was a personal battle brewing. Kenseth's championship hopes had been quashed two races earlier at Kansas when he was spun by Logano. To make matters worse, Logano had gone on to win all three races in the Chase's Contender round. Kenseth was on the verge of blowing his top. "He was mad," Jeff remembers. "But I didn't think he was mad at Logano at the time, because the No. 22 didn't have anything to do with that crash. But of course I knew of the incident in Kansas."

Logano remained the leader. After some patchwork on pit road, Kenseth's team managed to get his car back on the track, but by that time, he was slow and several laps down. "So now I'm running second," Jeff recalls, "and I've got Jamie McMurray just beating on my bumper. I'm holding him up because my car hadn't quite kicked in yet." With less than fifty laps to go, Logano pulled ahead of Jeff by five or six car lengths. Jeff was followed closely by McMurray and Kyle Busch. Up ahead, Jeff saw Kenseth's hobbled No. 20. "I'm not thinking they're going to have an incident," he says, "but when we got on the front straightaway and I saw Matt come up, I was like, 'Uh-oh, this is really happening.' And sure enough, boom!"

Kenseth got into Logano's left-rear quarter panel and drove him hard into the wall on Turn 1, totaling both cars. "I just said, 'Oh boy, this is going to get big,' because I figured there would be a brawl. I mean, this guy just took out the leader of the race. He had his reasons for doing what he did, but I just thought, wow, that was huge—one, because of what happened, but it was also huge because I felt like Joey was my toughest competition at that time, and he'd just been eliminated."

After a long red-flag interval to clean up the track, the yellow flag came out, and Jeff and Gustafson decided to pit for new tires, along with most of the field. A.J. Allmendinger and Denny Hamlin stayed out, and Jeff started behind them, in third, on the restart. "I felt like we were going to blow right by these guys and we're going to be sitting in a perfect position. I felt like it was ours to lose at that point," he says. But the No. 24 didn't have the getup to overtake them, and he was still running third when another caution flag fell. With twenty-eight laps left, Jeff's car began to come back to him, and he knew he had to make his move. He muscled up on the inside of Hamlin. "He wasn't happy about it," Jeff remembers. "He was blocking me and trying to prevent me from getting position on him to make the pass, because he knew if I got by, it was over for him. We had some contact, but I made the pass."

Then he zeroed in on Allmendinger in the lead. Jeff could sense it wouldn't be much of a hunt. Allmendinger was still on old tires. "I felt like there was a pretty good chance he'd fade." With twenty-two laps to go, Jeff was riding right up on his back bumper, and Allmendinger relented. "I was thinking, 'He can't put up too much of a fight on those old tires,' but we are talking about A.J.," Jeff says. "He can be very aggressive, but luckily I was able to get by without much of a fight.

"But then Jamie McMurray came up through there and got into second, and he was pretty darn fast. He was running hard." There were seven laps to go. "Just don't make any mistakes," Jeff told himself. "Run your line." And then another caution—Sam Hornish Jr. spun out. "I was like, 'Ahh, man! Are you kidding me? You've got to be kidding me. This is not happening right now!'" They restarted again with just three laps remaining, Jeff on the front row, inside, and McMurray just outside of him.

LEFT: Jeff out in front of Jamie McMurray at Martinsville Speedway, November 1, 2015.

165

TOP LEFT: Jeff stands on the No. 24 AARP Member Advantages Chevrolet window at the finish line after winning the Goody's Headache Relief Shot 500 at Martinsville, November 1, 2015. BOTTOM LEFT: Jeff celebrates in front of the flag stand at Martinsville Speedway, 2015. OPPOSITE: TOP LEFT: Jimmie Johnson gives Jeff a congratulatory hug after his Martinsville win, 2015. TOP RIGHT: Jeff and Ella celebrate in a shower of glittering confetti in Victory Lane. MIDDLE RIGHT; Jeff and his family proudly apply NASCAR's "Winner" sticker to the No. 24 AARP Member Advantages Chevrolet in Victory Lane at Martinsville Speedway. BOTTOM: Jeff, Ingrid, Ella, Leo, and the entire No. 24 team poses in celebration of the Martinsville victory, 2015.

They took off side-by-side, McMurray battling hard. But Jeff got a good jump coming out of Turn 4 and put a little bit of a gap between them. They took the white flag—one lap to go. "I got through turns one and two pretty good. And then I drove down in three, and my whole thought was, all right, Jamie drives in really deep, so I can't let him get to me. I overdrove it a little bit, and I remember him kind of getting close to me, but as I got the car turned and back on the gas, I knew we had it won."

Jeff took the checkered flag for the ninety-third win of his career, the first win of the season, and an automatic berth to the championship race at Homestead. If there was someone at Martinsville Speedway that evening who wasn't screaming their lungs out for Jeff Gordon, they must have been hiding beneath the grandstands. "All of that emotion, it was like a volcano eruption," Jeff recalls. "It was just intense and crazy and wild."

After his victory lap, he parked his car on the start-finish line, balanced himself on his side door, and jubilantly raised his arms to the crowd. The noise reached a whole new crescendo. "I could see there was no one filing out," he says. "They were standing up in their seats, cheering."

He hopped down off the car, grabbed the checkered flag, and saluted the crowd once more. "Jeff Gordon might be celebrating as much as we've ever seen," the broadcasters remarked. Then, helmet still on, he ran and jumped into the arms of his waiting team, who mobbed him. "You see the look in their eyes, the excitement, the joy," he says. "You see how they're running at you. You don't have to say anything to them. You feel it, you know how significant this was for them, they know how significant it was to me."

The cheering went on and on, and so did Jeff's excitement—with his crew, with his teammates, with his family, and with the media. It was as if somebody had lit him on fire and he just kept burning, illuminating everyone around him. "It was a huge win, a huge win. And it went back to all the expectations and pressure and hopes of the season, all those things. That's why I was so excited," he says. "And the way that I celebrated was because I knew how huge that moment was for the season, for my career, for our championship hopes, for Ingrid and the kids and for all our friends and family that were coming to Homestead. The significance was massive.

"For me, the best part of that win was seeing Ingrid and the kids there," Jeff continued. "The kids were feeding off of Ingrid's energy and excitement as they watched from the bus. They realized the significance of it. So to see them all happy and excited and understanding the moment was incredible for me and that was the moment that I will remember the most."

Later that night, when the applause died down, he spoke with Carol, who had watched the race on TV. "Jeff called me after that race . . . I was so, so happy for Jeff and so, so happy for the team. It was just too good to be true. I mean, what a fairy tale that was. And then he told me, 'I'm afraid to go to bed because I'm afraid I'm going to wake up tomorrow and this will all really be a dream.'"

★   ★   ★

"The win at Martinsville lifted a tremendous amount of pressure off," Jeff says, "but at the same time, now we had an opportunity to win the championship." It had been a long, painful grind of a final season, and no one, especially after those dog days of summer, had truly expected Jeff Gordon to be there at the end racing for a title. So in many ways, just getting

to Homestead was the pinnacle, and everything after Martinsville was mere gravy. But the championship was a delicious possibility.

The press went into overdrive. They wrote more than just the nostalgic paeans to the extraordinary racecar driver winding down a brilliant career. Now the storyline was about the greatest career finishes in sports history, about that select group of athletes who walked away at the top of the game and about what it would mean for racing if Jeff Gordon could actually pull this thing out of a hat.

"Those next three weeks were some of the most enjoyable ones of my life. It was rewarding on so many levels," he recalls. "We didn't have to worry about Texas. We didn't have to worry about Phoenix. All we had to do was focus on how to win at Homestead. I was going to the racetrack and smiling, watching all these other guys stressing out. I felt like I was the only happy driver in the garage. Me and my team were the only ones enjoying it. The guys were whistling, they're all happy."

Jeff had never asked for gifts or honors in his final season, but they had come in droves. From the tracks alone, he'd received a Bandolero race car with Ella and Leo's names inscribed on the doors, a blackjack table, a helmet, an eighteen-liter bottle of wine plus one of his favorite bottles, ninety-six bottles of whiskey, a check for the Jeff Gordon Children's Foundation, a weekend at Michigan's Mackinac Island, a Bristol Motor Speedway terrace named in his honor, and a model train set, to name a few. That was in addition to all the tributes that had taken place at races throughout the season. But the most eye-catching gift was certainly the present he received at the AAA Texas 500 the week after Martinsville, when track president Eddie Gossage, done up in full cowboy regalia, approached him leading two Shetland ponies—one for Ella and one for Leo.

"What the hell am I going to do with two ponies," Jeff remembers thinking at the time. "I don't want two ponies." He had no place to keep them, no place to board them, no idea of how to take care of them. He immediately texted Carol, "I really hope you like ponies." Carol replied: "The ponies are not coming here, so don't even suggest that." John chimed in, texting Carol: "Yeah, they're coming here. Where else are they going to go?"

Ultimately, they found stables in Charlotte so the kids could visit. "I was not too thrilled with it at the beginning," Jeff admits. "But since then, they're probably one of the best things I got all year."

★   ★   ★

Homestead was still the sole target, and the team focused their efforts on prepping the car for that final race, but they also showed surprising grit in their two free-pass contests in the Eliminator round, notching a ninth-place finish in Texas and a sixth in Arizona.

And once the cars were all loaded back in their haulers at Phoenix, the final field was set. Jeff would battle it out in Florida one week later against the defending Cup champion, Kevin Harvick, as well as Martin Truex Jr. and his former Hendrick Motorsports teammate Kyle Busch. Jeff couldn't have been more excited. "You feel very special to be a part of that final four. Knowing this is my final race, my final year . . . it's like somebody scripted it and made it happen for you. It was almost too good to be true."

As for pressure, even that felt like a positive burden, coming into it as the dark horse. "There's way more pressure when they expect you to win or you're the favorite to win.

Jeff,

My main goal before you made your last lap around a racetrack, was to meet you. If you are reading this letter, then mission accomplished!! First and foremost, I want to thank you for all the wonderful memories of **watching you race. I have enjoyed you taking the checkered flag and joined you** in the agony of defeat. I have been the faithful fan who has supported, defended and cheered you on week in and week out. I want to congratulate you, not on retirement, but for successfully closing this chapter of your life and opening the next. What an emotional time this is for you and your fans, but an exciting time as well. I look forward to seeing what God has in store for you next. Now you will have more time to pursue the other loves in your life: your beautiful wife, adorable kids, the Jeff Gordon Foundation, and countless other projects you have lined up. I know you will approach these new endeavors with the same poise and tenacity as you have racing.

I also want to thank you for always being a man of character. It has been such a pleasure following you throughout your career. I have been asked many times over the years, why am I a Jeff Gordon fan? I say, "sure, he can race…the best out there, but I am a Jeff Gordon fan not only for the race car driver he is, but for the person he is, on and off the track".

I have had the great opportunity to watch you race at Daytona, Texas, Martinsville, Darlington, Talladega, Atlanta and Charlotte. Because of your willingness to be open and engaging with your fans, by posting of family pictures, sharing personal stories and allowing yourself to be human yet humble, you have allowed fans like me to feel like you are family. Whether I make it in person to Homestead or not, I will watch that race with tears in my eyes and pride in my heart. Not just because my favorite racecar driver is making his final lap, but because someone I have considered a part of my life for over 20 years is moving on to bigger and better things!! Good luck my friend, I wish you success and happiness.

I just want to say one last time…….**THANK YOU FOR THE MEMORIES**!!

Blessings,

Theresa

We weren't. We were the one that survived and did a great job and executed. We weren't expected to be there, but we won Martinsville and we were there. And that's the story of my final race, my final season. So it was all positive and good. Oh, and by the way, we might surprise some people."

The night before Homestead, Jeff met Ingrid and a group of about ten friends at one of his favorite restaurants in Miami. But as the evening wore on he found himself checking his watch. Bucking tradition on the advice of Jimmie Johnson, he had decided not to stay at a hotel with his family and helicopter to the track in the morning, but to spend the night on his own, in his motorhome at the speedway. Bidding his guests good night, he made the hour-long trek out to Homestead in the rain. In his bus, he watched a little television, surfed the web, and relaxed before turning in for the night.

In the morning, he rose before his alarm, at eight o'clock, and started to let it all sink in. "All the way up to Homestead, I had been saying to myself that the day is slowly coming. It hasn't hit me and sunk in just yet, but it's coming. And that day, I woke up and it was, 'Wow, this is it. This is it.'" The culmination of twenty-three years of Cup racing—the very last chapter in a racing story that had begun nearly forty years earlier. He could feel it welling up inside him.

TOP: One of the thousands of letters and "well wishes" Jeff received once word of his retirement was made public.

TOP: Jeff suiting up for his final Cup race, Homestead-Miami Speedway, November 2015. BOTTOM: The commemorative ring box Jeff gave each driver competing at Homestead, 2015. OPPOSITE: ROW ONE LEFT: A specially made helmet featuring images from throughout Jeff's career. Jeff wore the helmet for his final Cup race, and then presented it to Rick Hendrick. ROW ONE RIGHT: Jeff doing a pre-race interview with NBC. ROW TWO LEFT: The No. 24 Axalta Chevrolet prepped and ready for Jeff's final ride. ROW TWO RIGHT: Jeff with racing legend Mario Andretti (left) and British Formula One champion Lewis Hamilton (right). ROW THREE LEFT: Jeff and Ella walk out during driver introductions. ROW THREE RIGHT: Ella hides behind a podium while Jeff poses with the three other championship contenders. BOTTOM: Jeff and family posing with Rick and Linda Hendrick and the entire No. 24 team prior to the race.

Still in his sweats and T-shirt, he made himself some coffee, raised the blinds, and then he saw Carol coming toward the bus. He opened the door and invited her in. "As soon as my eyes met hers, I immediately grabbed her and started crying," he recalls.

"I was crying pretty good," Carol says. "It was just one of those moments that happened. It was awesome. I'll cherish it forever."

They sat and talked about Vallejo and Pittsboro, about the Busch Series and the Cup and what an amazing and crazy journey it had been, about how neither of them, or John, or anybody for that matter, could have anticipated these past four decades with all their twists and turns. He told her about the appreciation he'd received from the press and other drivers, the handshakes and heartfelt words in the garage area, about the congratulatory tweets and the mob of fans that had spontaneously broken into chants of "Jeff, Jeff, Jeff" as he walked to the garage the previous day. And then they hugged again. "Don't read the papers," she warned him before she left. The tributes would get him all choked up again.

"It was like I'd already won, you know," he says of that moment. "I get to have this conversation with my mom on this day. There was nobody I would have rather had that moment with than her. She's my mom, but she had been there and helped make this happen. Making the choices she made. Leaving my dad, finding John, supporting the racing in all its aspects. Going along for this ride the whole way. And so there was nobody more significant to have that moment with. Even as significant a role as John has played, to me, that moment with my mom was the most special."

Everything that day seemed like a scrapbook moment, from the whole family being there to share the experience with him, even his sister, Kimberly, and his father, Billy, to his friends and Formula 1 champion Lewis Hamilton and racing legend Mario Andretti, who toured around the track with him, lending their support. Even former president Bill Clinton tried to call him to wish him well. Everywhere he went, there were mob scenes, there was cheering, there were fans thanking him, just looking for a final glimpse of their hero. Not even the periodic rain showers could dampen the mood. "There was just a great vibe and a great feeling to the day," he says. "I really was on this high-on-life kind of energy right from the start."

In one of the day's more touching moments, Richard Petty thanked him for everything he'd done for the sport—for helping build it and transform it, for shepherding it into a new era, and for bringing millions of fans so much enjoyment and so many memories—and handed him ninety-three dollar bills, for his ninety-three wins, to stuff into the custom-made money clip he'd presented to Jeff and all his other competitors at his final race back in 1992.

It was the money clip he'd received from Richard Petty that inspired Jeff to present a commemorative gift to each of the drivers competing in his final race. Jeff gave each driver a black carbon-fiber ring box, engraved with the driver's starting position on a small plaque that read, "Thanks for the Memories.—Jeff Gordon."

"I wanted the day to be remembered not just by the fans, but by the drivers as well. I think everybody really appreciated it. I got a lot of texts from drivers saying, 'You're a class act, man.' 'Thank you very much.' It was the younger drivers that seemed to appreciate it the most. The fact that I'd thought of them, that meant the world to them," he says.

At the drivers' meeting, where there were more than a few No. 24 hats on the heads of his rivals, they showed a video celebrating Jeff's career. After the meeting, he went back to his trailer to do his stretching regimen, ride a few minutes on the exercise bike, and get ready for the race.

TOP LEFT: Jeff gives Ella a kiss on the cheek pre-race, Homestead-Miami Speedway, November 22, 2015. MIDDLE LEFT: Jeff reminiscing with racing legend Mario Andretti, Miami, 2015. BOTTOM LEFT: Jeff visiting pre-race with British Formula One champion Lewis Hamilton, Miami, 2015. TOP RIGHT: Jeff competing in his final championship race, Miami, 2015.

When the announcer trumpeted out his name, the crowd erupted and rose as Jeff made his way down the stage, holding his daughter's hand. Whether they had loved him or hated him over the years, for that moment, win or lose, he was everybody's hero, everybody's champion. It wasn't just his career coming to an end. It was an era. It was the last link to Petty and Earnhardt and all the other erstwhile greats who bumped and rubbed back when stock-car racing was still largely a regional deal and Jeff was a wide-eyed pup.

And then, after a few delays due to a passing rainstorm, Jeff walked off toward his car, followed by scores of friends, family, supporters, photographers, and journalists. On any other day, he would have grown anxious and impatient by all the distraction and mayhem just moments before climbing into his car to compete for a championship. But he insists, "There was nothing that was going to upset me at that point on that day. It was the opposite of the norm, where I'm so tuned in to getting into the car and I can't wait to get rid of all the people and get in and do my job," he says. "I think I would have been disappointed had I not just taken it as it came."

Thirty minutes later, following all the kisses and embraces and well wishes, track officials managed to clear everyone off, and Jeff climbed in and buckled up. At one point, his interior technician Jordan Allen, after handing Jeff his helmet and steering wheel, got a little glassy-eyed, and Jeff good-naturedly lambasted him. "Really? Right now, Jordan? I'm getting ready to freaking drive off and you're doing this now," he said. "He had all weekend to do that, and he did it right then. I was joking around, just enjoying the moment, having fun with it all and being pretty loose. I wasn't nervous. I wasn't emotional or anything at that point. I was just going through the motions, but in a fun way." And then he was off.

As soon as the green flag dropped, Jeff realized the car had a bit more pace than he had anticipated. "I knew we had a decent car going into the race but not the best car. So it was a pleasant surprise when we got the green and it felt as good as it did," says Jeff. After an early caution and restart, he worked his way up from sixth place to third place, where he battled door to door with Kevin Harvick for several laps before Harvick was able to knock him back. After a second restart, on lap thirty-six, with all four championship contenders running in the top six, Jeff jumped out to the lead. He couldn't hear the roar of the crowd, but he could sense it. "I was excited," he says, "and I felt like others were excited. And I was like, all right, maybe we actually have something for them today."

But the cautions were falling like rain, and within four laps, they had to do it all again. This time, although he started up front, it didn't work out so well. Kevin Harvick quickly blew by him, followed by Kyle Busch. "I could tell they were a little better than we were," he admits. He soon dropped back to eighth, then to ninth, with Martin Truex Jr. eventually passing him, and he languished back there. "I was like, yeah, we're not good enough. I hoped that we could adjust and that maybe when the sun went down, it might change. Maybe we'd get good track position on a pit stop or a restart or whatever. But we just never recovered after that. We had a car that could maintain track position, but we didn't have a car that could drive up through there."

With six laps left, he did manage to move up from tenth to sixth, ahead of Truex, but the other contenders, Busch and Harvick, crossed the finish line in that order, the win giving Busch his first Sprint Cup championship.

"I would say it was the most amazing race we, and I, ever had, up until the green flag dropped," Jeff says. "And there's no doubt that's true. Everything leading into it couldn't have been better. But it just wasn't the Cinderella story; it wasn't the perfect ending. And it wasn't from lack of effort. I've never seen the team work so hard. They were so excited because they felt like they built a car that could go down there and win. And I believe they did, but we missed something—some detail in the setup—and we just didn't have the speed of Harvick and Busch."

Climbing out of the car, he couldn't help but be disappointed, for himself, for the team, and particularly for Gustafson, whom he would have loved to celebrate a title with. "I'd won four championships, and I didn't have to have this championship, although it would have been icing on the cake and amazing to go out of the sport like that," he says. "But for someone like Alan, he's sitting there thinking, 'I don't know when my next opportunity is coming to be in this position again.' So I wanted to make the most of it."

He hugged Rick Hendrick and gave him his helmet, while members of the team began to gather round. Always the competitor, he was having trouble letting go of the race enough to really let the significance of the end of his career seep in. As he gave a quick interview to a FOX broadcaster, Ella came up and nuzzled him, followed by Ingrid and Leo. "It's a happy, good day," he said. "I wanted that win, but we're still going to celebrate."

By the time Jeff had congratulated Kyle Busch, finished his post-race interviews and given one last wave to the fans, he and Ingrid were running late for the big party and had

TOP RIGHT: Ingrid, Ella, and Leo congratulate Jeff after the race, Miami, 2015. BOTTOM RIGHT: Jeff ready for his post-race bash in Miami, 2015. LEFT: Over 200 family, friends, and colleagues celebrating the conclusion of Jeff's incredible Cup Series career. It was the hottest ticket in town, November 22, 2015.

to hightail it back to Miami to get ready. Eventually they made it. "It was great," Jeff says. "It was good getting to see and interact with a lot of people who have been friends throughout many years, and family and all that. . . . We had a great time."

The great time went on and on, with people jumping into the pool and one of Jeff's teammates dumping an ice bucket on his head like a football Gatorade shower. But nothing was going to ruin his night. When they shuffled back to the hotel, it was five o'clock in the morning.

★　　★　　★

At the NASCAR year-end banquet in Las Vegas on December 4, they venerated Jeff like a motorsports saint. It was hard enough for him to accept the adoration of his peers and fans without getting emotional, but then, as third place finisher among the season's top 10 drivers, he was expected to get up and say a few words. He'd never enjoyed giving banquet speeches—"There's nothing else I do all year that I get as nervous about," he confessed—and he knew this one would be particularly tough, it being his last. Having Ingrid and the kids in attendance made it that much more challenging to hold back the floodgates of emotion.

Before his scheduled introduction by host Drew Carey, they played a video of his fellow drivers saluting and congratulating him on his illustrious career. "It was hard for me not to get caught up in that moment. So I didn't want to hear it," he admits. "In the back of my mind, I'm sitting there going, 'oh man, this is going to be an absolute disaster. I'm going to go up there and I'm going to be babbling, tears running down. I'm not going to be able to get through any of this.' My heart was racing, sweaty palms, the whole thing."

When the video ended, it wasn't Drew Carey who came to the podium to offer the prologue to Jeff's speech. It was Tom Cruise. The actor had been a big supporter of Jeff's since the two met at the post–Academy Awards party in 1997. "That they got somebody of his significance to come do that and that they surprised me, that hit me hard," Jeff recalls. "I just looked at Rick Hendrick and said, 'Oh shit, I'm screwed.'"

As Cruise spoke about his life and achievements, his charitable works at home and around the world, the four-time champion sat with Ella on his lap, his chin quivering, dabbing his

TOP: Jeff and Ingrid at the Last Lap party in Miami, November 22, 2015. BOTTOM: Jeff and Tom Cruise share a laugh on-stage at the NASCAR Sprint Cup Awards banquet at the Wynn Las Vegas, December 4, 2015.

tearing eyes with a napkin. Coming to a close, Cruise said, "Transcendence—few reach it. He did. And although many of us want to say, 'We'll miss you,' what we really mean is, 'We thank you.'"

"When he said that, I'll never forget it," Jeff says. "It just, man, it really got to me. That was very, very cool. And I was just trying to figure out how I was going to get through it. I was trying to take some deep breaths and get prepared."

As he came to the stage to a standing ovation, he was surprised again, this time by NASCAR's chairman and CEO Brian France, who presented him with the prestigious Bill France Award of Excellence.

And then he gathered himself and spoke. When he talked about stepping away from racing, he was briefly overcome and had to pause. He said he thought his retirement wouldn't truly sink in until he got to Daytona in 2016 and stepped into the broadcast booth instead of the No. 24, but it was clear that it was starting to hit home. He struggled against getting overly sentimental, but the crowd cheered in appreciation. He choked up again when he came to thanking Rick Hendrick and his parents.

Jeff's passion, his emotion, the warmth, the love—it was all on display. But what he felt most keenly, and what he most poignantly expressed, was a deep sense of gratefulness—gratefulness for the people, the circumstances, and the opportunities that had allowed a young boy from California to turn his childhood dream into something far more immense and far more meaningful than he ever could have imagined.

"I think, wow, I grew up as a kid wanting to be a professional racecar driver, and I got to have a lot of success as a young kid and all these cool experiences, traveling all over the place. And I got to go race against some of my heroes and race sprint cars, and that was something I always wanted to do. I got to win some big races, graduate from high school, and go on and become a professional racecar driver and do it at a level I never thought was possible. And for that, I'm forever grateful and amazed at the same time.

"But there's also a lot of talented racecar drivers out there that never got that chance, never got that opportunity, who could have excelled as much or more than I did. But for whatever reason, the stars aligned. I met this person and that person, and I got to drive this car and get this sponsor and have fans and win races. And that's cool. That's just extremely cool.

"But I think that even with all the accolades, what I'm most proud about is how I did it, how I went about it. Because whether you like me or not, you have to see the effort that I put into it—into what I did on the racetrack and what I did off the racetrack."

That night at the banquet, Brian France summed it up best. He told Jeff that his award would "always be a reminder that you gave everything you could to the sport you loved so much."

TOP LEFT: Jeff delivering an emotional farewell speech at the NASCAR Sprint Cup Awards banquet at the Wynn Las Vegas, December 4, 2015. TOP RIGHT: Ingrid, Ella, Leo, and Jeff pose in formal attire for the media prior to the NASCAR Sprint Cup Awards banquet at the Wynn Las Vegas, December 4, 2015.

JEFF'S TEN FAVORITE TRACKS

IN HIS TWENTY-THREE FULL-TIME NASCAR Cup Series seasons, Jeff competed on some of the most challenging racetracks in all of motor sports. In his own words, Jeff reflects on the significance of his ten favorite tracks and shares some of his most memorable moments.

ATLANTA MOTOR SPEEDWAY

LOCATION: Hampton, Georgia; 20 miles south of Atlanta.
MILE AND SHAPE: 1.54-mile quad-oval track
TRACK FACT: It opened in 1960 as a 1.5-mile standard oval.

I LIKED ATLANTA FROM THE FIRST TIME I raced there in the Busch Grand National car for Bill Davis. I won the pole and the race. It's superfast with great transitions and big, long sweeping corners. You have to push the limits of the car to get on the edge and stay on the edge. I liked that aspect of it, especially in my earlier years. I was able to utilize some of my dirt-track skills.

The track has changed tremendously since then. They've completely reconfigured how the corners are laid out. It took a little while for it to age and develop a more abrasive surface, and that's what everybody loves about it now. It wears the tires out. There's a groove on the bottom, in the middle and at the top, which is how it used to be. It's just a fun, exciting, and fast racetrack.

ATLANTA 300—MARCH 14, 1992

You're always a little bit intimidated by the unknown, and in 1992 the track was an unknown for me. We showed a lot of speed and I had the car to win. I just had to make sure I didn't screw it up.

It was a Busch race and we dominated that weekend. Harry Gant was second, Hut Stricklin was third, Davey Allison fourth, and Mark Martin came in eighth. I even had a couple of great battles with Earnhardt but eventually he had head gasket issues and came in thirty-first. These were all Cup guys. So to win the race from the pole against those competitors my first time on the track was amazing. Rick Hendrick happened to be there watching me that day. As he's said, "I was just waiting for the wreck and the wreck never happened." I ended up winning the race and Rick was like, "Wow, who's *this* guy?" That was my introduction to Hendrick Motorsports.

CRACKER BARREL OLD COUNTRY STORE 500—MARCH 11, 2001

This was one of my favorite finishes . . . even though I didn't win. The shock of Dale Earnhardt's death at the Daytona 500 the month before carried into the next several races. Dale had won the Atlanta race the previous year, so it was another reminder he was gone. Then here comes this guy, Kevin Harvick, who Richard Childress put in Dale's place. The rest of Dale's team was the same and they were fired up. Determined to honor Dale in every way they could, and even though it was only Kevin's third race in the Cup Series, he kept the car in contention. Dale Jarrett and Jerry Nadeau were battling for the lead, Harvick was in third, and Dale Earnhardt Jr. and I were right there in fourth and fifth.

Harvick made his move on the bottom to take them three-wide and make the pass for the lead with five to go. It was awesome. Jarrett got loose and Dale Jr. cut down a tire, then I passed Nadeau. I made my move on Harvick. We were side-by-side, but it was too late. He crossed the finish line about half a bumper ahead of me. Richard Childress and the whole team were crying. The crowd in the stands was going crazy, especially when Kevin drove around giving the three-fingered salute out his window in honor of Dale. Watching the replay sends chills up my spine to this day.

ADVOCARE 500—SEPTEMBER 7, 2011

At that point in my career, Jimmie Johnson was the dominant driver. He almost passed me a couple of times but couldn't quite complete them. We were both driving all out and sliding the cars to the limit. Jimmie made one final run for it on the last lap, but he had to back off to keep from putting his car in the wall and I won. So to battle him and get my eighty-fifth win—which moved me up to third all-time—was a huge moment for me personally and for us as a team. I was pretty excited about that one, and it definitely adds to the significance of Atlanta in my career.

BRISTOL MOTOR SPEEDWAY

LOCATION: Bristol, Tennessee

MILE AND SHAPE: 0.533-mile oval track with 36-degrees of banking in the corners

TRACK FACT: Bristol Motor Speedway was formerly known as Bristol International Raceway and Bristol Raceway.

I LOVE WALKING THE TRACK AT BRISTOL. Most tracks don't allow you to walk them without permission and going through security. But that's not the case at Bristol. It's even more special at night when the lights are on. It's almost like a Zen thing for me. I'll probably continue to do it when I visit even though I won't be driving it. This is one of those tracks that brings out the fan in all of us.

They've reconfigured the track so it's totally different from when I first raced on it. It was still concrete then, but the way the banking worked, you wanted to be nailed right down to the bottom of the racetrack. And because there was only one groove, your job was to force your opponents to make a mistake, get them off the bottom, and get your nose in there. That's how you made your passes. But when you worked out the setup, it was like magic.

Today, Bristol is even more special to me. For years, I'd go to different tracks and see a driver's name on the grandstand, and I hoped that one day I'd do something significant enough to earn that. At my final race there in August 2015, they honored me by dedicating a terrace at Bristol as the Jeff Gordon Terrace. I'll get to enjoy that honor for years to come.

FOOD CITY 500—APRIL 13, 1997

It was the perfect storm: Bristol, Rusty Wallace, and our *silent* rivalry. I say silent because it really wasn't well-known. In fact, *I* didn't even know about it until Dale Earnhardt told me.

It started with my first Cup win at the 1994 Coca-Cola 600. Rusty dominated that race. He led the most laps, and in his mind, he thought he should have won it. But I ended up winning and he came in second, so I think he kind of felt like we stole his thunder there. He hated me, literally hated me. Rusty and Earnhardt were pretty good buddies, and he had a lot of respect for Dale. Rusty felt like, "Hey, *I'm* Earnhardt's rival. *I'm* the guy who's supposed to battle Earnhardt. I have my fans and sell my merchandise and I get my sponsors because of that,

and I'm going to win my share of races and championships up against Earnhardt." Then I came along and he didn't like it. So he brought that attitude to Bristol.

In the day race of 1997, Rusty dominated. But on the long runs, I was actually better, and that's what happened. We finally had a long run, and he wore out his tires. I was running second and getting heat from Terry Labonte behind me in third. I got close to Rusty, but he blocked me. I thought, man if he blocks me again, I'm not going to check up. So in the closing laps, I could see Rusty's car was getting loose. He was freaking out. He had to be thinking, "Man, I had this race won, what is going on here?" Then he started putting some decent laps together. I couldn't get close enough to get underneath. Then he hit lap traffic and the gap closed in the first turn, and I was ready to make my move. Coming out of turn two, my front bumper was right on him, so entering turn three, I went for it. I just got my nose under him and *bump* he's out of the way. I didn't wreck him, I moved him just enough to swing under for the win. To me that's acceptable racing. Apparently Rusty didn't agree. A year later, in 1998, I was racing him at Richmond and he just flat out wrecked me. For years after, I'd say "I know you wrecked me at Richmond" and he'd deny it, saying it wasn't intentional.

SHARPIE 500—AUGUST 24, 2002

Four years later, I used the bump 'n' run again on Rusty, this time under the lights. Just like back in 1997, I felt Rusty had that race won. I was being young and aggressive and kind of not giving a crap. I stalked him and really put pressure on him. I had a run with ten laps to go, and he cut me off. So I thought, okay, if I get another shot at him, I'm going for it. In typical Rusty fashion, his cars always turned the middle really well at Bristol, which made him fast. But his car was always loose on the exit. I focused on getting my car to drive off the corner really well and straight. Again, he hit lap traffic at the worst possible time, so I decided to take him right then. I didn't hit him hard—but I hit him hard enough.

He never said anything to me. It's hard to get too pissed off at the guy behind you if he's actually faster than you and you're at a one-groove racetrack like Bristol. But just a few years ago, Rusty finally admitted, "Yeah, I deliberately wrecked you at Richmond back in '98." So now when I watch the 2002 Bristol replay, it was worth it.

FOOD CITY 500—APRIL 19, 2015

As a dad, this moment is definitely a highlight: my kids giving the "start your engines" command. One of the reasons I continued to race as long as I did was so Ella and Leo would get to see what I love doing. In this case, they got the chance to be a part of it.

It had been raining that day and we were waiting for the track to dry. So Ingrid and the kids stayed in the bus until it was time to come over. We asked for an estimate on the time and NASCAR said they'd have the track dry by 3:00 p.m. Well, it was 1:45 and all of a sudden they were calling drivers to the cars. So we were scrambling, trying to call Ingrid and get the kids to the track. I was freaking out because at that point NASCAR was on a schedule: "National anthem at this time, command to start the engines at that time." So they started the national anthem and the kids weren't there. I had to get in the car. I climbed in and then *boom*, Ella and Leo were there.

As their dad, I was nervous because I wanted it to go well for them. I wanted them to enjoy the experience and just have a great time with it. They stepped up to the microphone and got the cue, and they just nailed it. I mean the whole thing, from the timing, how they did it, and then Leo ad-libbed "Vroom!" at the end. I'll never forget the smiles on their faces. You couldn't see my reaction because of my helmet, but I was so excited. I was clapping and giving them a thumbs-up. I just absolutely love that moment.

CHARLOTTE MOTOR SPEEDWAY

LOCATION: Concord, North Carolina, 13 miles northeast of Charlotte

MILE AND SHAPE: 1.5-mile quad-oval track

TRACK FACT: This is a motorsports complex with a spectator capacity of 94,000.

CHARLOTTE WILL ALWAYS BE A SPECIAL PLACE FOR ME. It's one of the racetracks that launched my career. I first drove by it in 1990 when I was headed to the Buck Baker Racing School at Rockingham Speedway, and I was blown away. I thought it was spectacular then and it hasn't changed much over the years. It's more modern and impressive than most tracks. I like the way they covered the back of the grandstands and built a whole section of condominiums. It's probably one of the most challenging and physically demanding courses, considering the g-forces you pull through the corners. It's one of those tracks that I put in the category of nearly perfect from the standpoint of transitions—the challenges in the banking in turns one and two versus the multiple grooves that run on turns three and four.

COCA-COLA 600—MAY 29, 1994

Charlotte's been my home track for over twenty years. I have a career full of memories at that track, including five Cup wins and three All-Star victories. But my very first victory, the Coca-Cola 600, stands at the top. You never know what you are capable of until you accomplish it. It's one of the toughest races to win, especially because of its length. It's the only 600-mile event on NASCAR's schedule.

In that race, I remember Ray Evernham called for a two-tire pit stop late in the race. A lot of people thought it was a gamble. But we actually had tested it in practice. Ray knew exactly how far two tires would take me, which, that day, was all the way to Victory Lane and one of the greatest days of my life.

NASCAR ALL-STAR INVITATIONAL—MAY 16, 2015

At my final All-Star Race, NASCAR and Charlotte Motor Speedway had a surprise waiting for me during the driver introductions. They brought me out last. It was so cool. As I took the stage, my first surprise was seeing Ray Evernham there to greet me against a backdrop of fans holding up "24" signs. Then out came Ingrid and the kids, and my mom and my stepdad. I was overwhelmed. It was funny because I saw my parents earlier and I asked them, "Why are you guys here? I never see you at driver introductions." I'm so glad we got to experience that as a family. It was something I'll never forget.

SONOMA RACEWAY

LOCATION: Wine country about 50 miles north of San Francisco
MILE AND SHAPE: Includes a drag strip and a 2.52-mile road course
TRACK FACT: Sonoma Raceway was formerly Sears Point Raceway and Infineon Raceway.

IN A WAY, SONOMA IS ALSO A HOME TRACK, yet I never laid eyes on it until I was a Cup driver. I'd heard of it when it was called Sears Point, and I had driven by it once or twice. But I never gave it much thought because it was a road course and a drag strip. It wasn't anything I raced on at that time.

Yet it's significant to me not only because of how close it is to Vallejo, my childhood hometown, but also because of the success I've experienced there. It went from being one of the most challenging places in the beginning of my Cup career to one of my best tracks.

Racing at Sonoma is all about finesse. It's about being aggressive but not too aggressive, finding grip in the tires and trying to maintain that grip. So you have to be mindful of tire management and just remain smooth and consistent. Unlike the other big tracks, where aerodynamics play a huge role and the way a car is set up changes so much, the setup for Sonoma has stayed very constant.

SAVE MART/KRAGEN 350—JUNE 25, 2000

I started fifth and stayed in the top ten most of the race. I knew we had a faster car that day, but that doesn't always mean you're going to win. There were about twenty-five laps to go when I passed Kenny Wallace and got back into the lead. It was right then when Robbie Loomis got on the radio and told me I was going to have to be really careful to manage the fuel. He said, "You probably have enough to make it to the finish line but not enough to get back around, so save me some." I did ... and we won. This race gave me my third straight win at that track and my sixth consecutive road-course win—a streak that began at Watkins Glen back in 1997.

DARLINGTON RACEWAY

LOCATION: Near Darlington, South Carolina
MILE AND SHAPE: 1.366-mile oval track
TRACK FACT: Darlington Raceway has a spectator capacity of 75,000.

IT'S BEEN CALLED "TOO TOUGH TO TAME," and while tracks will adopt nicknames for marketing purposes, this one lives up to its reputation. It was always tough for me, a challenging track with a very narrow groove right up against the wall. It reminds me of Winchester Speedway, a fast and dangerous track in Indiana where I raced midget cars and sprint cars. The reputation of both tracks intimidates you before you ever get there. Drivers say, "Oh man, have you been to Darlington yet? You're going to get a Darlington stripe, good luck there." Well, it's hard not to get so close to the wall that you get that stripe when you're racing for 500 miles. The place is crazy fast. The same thing happens to drivers at Winchester, but I won my first race I ever ran there. The same thing happened at Darlington. I was thinking, okay, I'll go see what this is like. Then I strapped on the helmet and started driving and thought, this is cool, this place is awesome. Yeah, it was difficult and lived up to a lot of the hype, but I can't say it intimidated me. It challenged me, but I liked it.

MOUNTAIN DEW SOUTHERN 500—SEPTEMBER 3, 1995
SOUTHERN 500—SEPTEMBER 1, 1996
SOUTHERN 500—AUGUST 31, 1997
PEPSI SOUTHERN 500—SEPTEMBER 6, 1998

The year 1995 was a very special one. It was a year of being strong, building confidence, and winning big races. We had gone from being a team that won a couple of races and showed some glimmers of hope to becoming the team to beat. It was also the year we got the first of four consecutive Darlington Southern 500 victories, which pretty much underlined the dominance of the No. 24 team. Capturing what would be the last Winston Million prize after the 1997 Southern 500 was icing on the cake.

THE DODGE AVENGER 500— MAY 13, 2007

We really shouldn't have won this race. We were a third-place car that day and had to overcome a lot of obstacles. We struggled with the handling, and the car started to overheat with sixty laps to go. Plus, we were at Darlington, a track that eats up tires. On top of all that, I was questioning Steve Letarte's strategy. Steve's a great poker player, and I think one of his strongest suits is not being afraid to gamble. But that's exactly what we did on pit stops that day. Everybody else came in to get fresh tires, and he decided we should stay out. The rest of the team was thinking, "Are you crazy?" We also didn't think we were going to make it because the engine was overheating. That was partly because I was behind other cars so there was less air getting to the radiator. If I came down pit road and stopped, the temperature would go higher. But this is Steve's genius. His strategy that day was to stay out so the car would be in front. His strategy worked, and we won the race. Then, of course, once we stopped in Victory Lane, the engine over-heated and the radiator just exploded and water shot out everywhere. Meanwhile, my stepfather, John, decided, "Oh, Jeff's engine isn't going to make it. Let's beat the traffic and go home." My sister, Kimberly, had never seen me win a Cup race, but they left before the race was over. They were listening to it on the radio and my sister was yelling, "I can't believe it. I've never seen Jeff win a race and now you decide to leave and he wins!" John felt terrible.

DAYTONA INTERNATIONAL SPEEDWAY

LOCATION: Daytona Beach, Florida

MILE AND SHAPE: 2.5-mile high-speed tri-oval

TRACK FACT: This track was built by NASCAR's founder, William "Bill" France Sr.

THIS IS AN IMPRESSIVE TRACK, both for its size and its place in the history of the sport. It's the home of NASCAR's Super Bowl, the Daytona 500, and if you could ever choose a track and a race, this is the one you want to win. Without winning the Daytona 500, your career will have an unchecked box. I'm very proud that I won three times. Watching from the grandstands or on TV, you almost can't believe forty-three cars are racing three wide, inches apart at 190 to 200 miles per hour. I always thought the big, long grandstands on the front straightaway were impressive. My first time on the track was to test with Bill Davis. I remember being so excited just driving through the tunnel. I was familiar with Daytona from watching the races on TV, and I'd driven by it heading to sprint-car races in Florida. So to finally get to drive on the track was very cool. I'd never been on a track that size and didn't know what to expect. Mark Martin, who used to drive for Bill Davis, told me to just "hold it wide open." What? It made no sense. "Yeah," he said, "you just keep it floored." I couldn't comprehend that. I laugh about it now because going wide open at Daytona is the easiest thing you do all year. Driving the track doesn't take the same skillset as it takes to drive at Charlotte or Bristol or a road course. Those tracks are "driver tracks" and this is more of a "car track." I went from being excited to race there at the beginning of my career to dreading it the last few years. Being competitive at Daytona is really more about the performance of the car, drafting, and a little bit of luck to not get caught up in the wrecks.

DAYTONA 500—FEBRUARY 16, 1997

We didn't have the fastest car, but we made the best of it with some great teammates. With twelve laps to go, I dropped below Dale Earnhardt and passed him to be in second. He got a little loose and slid down with Dale Jarrett, which flipped Earnhardt on top and over Ernie Irvin. After the track was cleared, there were seven laps to go. I was behind Bill Elliott, but my teammates, Terry Labonte and Ricky Craven, were behind me in third and fourth. It took about two laps for them to push me past Elliott, and then they both passed him. The Hendrick Motorsports team was in first, second, and third. Then there was another big wreck, so the race ended under the caution flag but I had my first Daytona 500 win. When I got to Victory Lane, someone handed me a cell phone so I could call Rick Hendrick, who was too ill at the time to attend. "This one's for you," I told him. It was great that we could include him in the celebration.

DAYTONA 500—FEBRUARY 14, 1999

By the second half of the race, my car was decorated with big black doughnuts on the sides, indicators of how rough it got during that race. I was soaked in sweat, and my hands were beginning to cramp from correcting the car after taking so many shots. I remember we got into the late stages of that race, and Ray Evernham just laughed. Everyone in the race was doing all they could to make sure that I wasn't going to win, but here I was, running up in the top five the hard way. With eleven laps to go, I was second behind Rusty Wallace, who really wanted to win his first 500. Dale Earnhardt and his teammate Mike Skinner were moving into position to draft by me, but I split them apart and used that to stay behind Rusty. I had a run on him and tried to get to his inside to make the pass. Rusty was protecting the inside lane like he should have and forced me down to the apron. I could see that Ricky Rudd was running very slowly down there and my brain was doing a lot of math real quick. There are races where things happen almost in slow motion. You can remember every little bump, move, and thought you had. What happened on that lap happened so fast, I look back and figure that it was just pure instinct.

At the last possible instant, Ricky eased a few feet to the left. I forced my way to the right and Rusty hesitated just long enough for me to slip by, up the banking and into the lead. It was an awesome finish.

DAYTONA 500—FEBRUARY 20, 2005

Tony Stewart led more than half the laps that day and was the car to beat. So except for the fact it was the first Daytona 500 with a green-white-checkered, it was a pretty typical race. On the last restart, my future teammate Dale Earnhardt Jr. got behind me for a lap. But then Kurt Busch had a run and went to the high side. I had to move up in front of him and was able to hold him off to the finish. Besides becoming only the fifth driver to win at least three Harley J. Earl trophies, the win was my first since the Hendrick Motorsports plane crash just a few months before. It was an emotional Victory Lane ceremony, and I dedicated the win to the memories of those we lost and their families.

MARTINSVILLE SPEEDWAY

LOCATION: Ridgeway, Virginia, just south of Martinsville
MILE AND SHAPE: 0.526-mile oval track
TRACK FACT: It is the shortest track located in Henry County.

THERE'S NOTHING NATURAL ABOUT MARTINSVILLE. It's one of the oldest, shortest, and trickiest tracks in the series. A stock car doesn't do anything you want it to on that track. Our cars have a lot of power, very small tires, and not a lot of down force. At Martinsville, we try to accelerate, brake, and turn the sharpest turns, and experience the most wheel spin. It goes against all physics. But because of the success I've had there, it's grown on me as a track. I love the place.

ADVANCE AUTO PARTS 500—APRIL 10, 2005

Coming back and winning the spring race the season after the tragic plane crash was one of the hardest-earned and most satisfying victories of my career. Five laps into the race, I was three laps behind in fortieth place. I wasn't thinking about brakes, tires, nothing—just going as hard as I could. I bumped, finessed, pushed, shoved, and picked off positions one at a time to make up the laps. I even got into two fender-banging duels with Kurt Busch late in the race. I wasn't happy that a sixteenth caution flag came out with less than ten laps to go, but I stayed focused. Eventually, I pulled away from Kasey Kahne with three laps to go and won by a couple car lengths. I'll never forget seeing Rick Hendrick there to greet me as I pulled into Victory Lane. He poked his head in the window and just said, "Thank you, thank you, thank you." It hit me like a ton of bricks. Winning never felt better. It wasn't going to erase the memory of the tragedy. But symbolically the victory became a tribute to our ten team members and friends who were killed. It was a reminder that life goes on, and Martinsville could once again be a place we looked forward to race.

MICHIGAN INTERNATIONAL SPEEDWAY

LOCATION: Brooklyn, Michigan
MILE AND SHAPE: 2-mile moderate-banked D-shaped speedway
TRACK FACT: This facility has a seating capacity of 71,000.

MICHIGAN'S ALWAYS BEEN A FAVORITE TRACK. It's not always the best racing. It's not always at the top of many people's list. It often has long green flag runs which sometimes isn't thought of as the most exciting racing. But as a racecar driver—and purely from a driver's standpoint—I just loved racing that track because it's big and fast with wide, sweeping corners, long straightaways, and multiple grooves. Any track that you can search for a groove is a track most drivers enjoy. It's like Atlanta and Charlotte in that respect. It's a track where you can change your arc into the corner. You can go in on the top and come off the bottom, or you can go into the middle and come off the top.

KMART 400—JUNE 12, 2001

When you win a race, it gives you momentum going into the next week. We dominated at Dover and so we were very excited about our chances at Michigan. We won the pole and I knew we had a good car, but Ricky Rudd sure didn't make it easy. He started second, and we pretty much stayed that way for most of the day until we both got messed up on a late pit stop. I had to go back in for a loose lug nut, and Ricky had a tire issue. We came out tenth and eleventh with twenty-five laps to go. We were able to race back through traffic and catch the leader, Sterling Marlin, when there was a caution flag with ten laps to go. I was able to get back into the lead, and got away from Ricky a little bit, but five laps later there was another caution. I got a good restart, and Ricky stayed with me. But he drove it in a bit too hard when he tried to make a pass going into turn one on the final lap. Not only was it a great race, it was also the one hundredth win for Hendrick Motorsports, which I was very proud to get for Rick.

PURE MICHIGAN 400—AUGUST 17, 2014

The weekend started off very fast. I won the pole, set a new track record of 205.558 mph for the qualifying lap and led for sixty-eight laps. But it came down to a final restart. Joey Logano, who led for more laps than we did and had been strong on restarts all day, was next to me with seventeen laps to go. I thought he had a good start, but I had one, too. Restarts are not only crucial, but they are intense because of the speed we're carrying there. I won the race, earning my third trip to Victory Lane that year and my ninety-first career victory. Jimmie Johnson won at Michigan in the June race that year giving Hendrick Motorsports a clean sweep and bragging rights for Chevrolet in the backyard of Motor City.

ACKNOWLEDGMENTS

THIS BOOK WOULD NOT HAVE BEEN POSSIBLE without the dedicated, enthusiastic, and generous cooperation of Jeff Gordon. I am enormously grateful and honored for his confidence in me to tell the story of his life and career. The person I got to know is purposeful, humble, fiercely competitive, naturally curious, perceptive, compassionate, and passionate. Over the course of eight months in 2015 and 2016, interviews took place whenever and wherever his schedule permitted; in cars, planes, and his motor coach at the tracks as well as at his homes in New York and Charlotte. I logged well over 35,000 miles in the process but it would not have been possible without Jeff's continued involvement and commitment to make himself available and offer input at every step of this project. I am also greatly appreciative of his wife, Ingrid Vandebosch-Gordon, for contributing her story and for her creative contributions to the design of the cover and interior of the book. It's my sincerest hope that this book justifies both Jeff's and Ingrid's trust in me.

I am extremely grateful to John and Carol Bickford. They welcomed me from the outset. It's just their nature. They both graciously sat through hours of interviews sharing details of their incredible journey. It was John who introduced the idea of this book to me and made sure all doors were open during its researching. I'm certain I would not have been able to tell as thorough a story without his direction and encyclopedic memory. Although John occasionally reminded me, "there was only one seat in that race car," there's no doubt a measurable percentage of Jeff's success is due directly to John and Carol's unfaltering love and dedication.

I am also grateful to the other members of Jeff's family for sharing their personal recollections and insights with me, especially his father, Billy Gordon, his sister Kimberly (Gordon) Combs, his nephew Brandon Perry, and his stepbrother, John Bickford, Jr.

I am greatly appreciative for the support and cooperation of Hendrick Motorsports, especially Rick Hendrick, Jimmie Johnson, and Dale Earnhardt Jr. for generously sharing their stories and perspectives.

I am truly grateful to Tom Cruise for generously consenting to provide the foreword. His passion for the sport and admiration for Jeff are genuine and he could not have been more gracious.

I am appreciative of the team at Jeff Gordon, Inc. for their support and cooperation, including Michael Holland, Ryan Hutcheson, Dan Guffey, Jon Edwards, Patience Compton, Jennifer Jones, Eddie Millsaps, and Archie Kennedy.

Thank you to the Jeff Gordon Children's Foundation, particularly Trish Kriger, Executive Director, and D. Wade Clapp, M.D., a member of the Board of Directors, for agreeing to be interviewed about the work of the Foundation. I would also like to thank Allison & Quinn Clarke, Jayson & Tatum Parker, and Shannon & Olivia Pierce for sharing their courageous stories of battling cancer, the ways in which they've benefitted from JGCF, and how they're helping other children and families with their fight against childhood cancer.

I am profoundly appreciative of the time and access provided by Ray Evernham. Ray graciously sat for a lengthy, insightful, and candid interview which was essential to this project, in addition to granting me access to his substantial photo and clipping collection. Thank you to Ann Eaton at Ray Evernham Enterprises, LLC for her kind hospitality during my visit and for providing content in this book.

My sincerest thanks to Brian Whitesell, Robbie Loomis, Steve Letarte, and Alan Gustafson for willingly sharing their knowledge, recollections, and perspectives. This book is better because of it.

The sprint/midget/Silver Crown and initial Busch Grand National era of Jeff's career has not been as well documented as his Cup career. For that reason, I am all the more grateful to the following individuals who each offered their time and recollections to add to the richness of that era in the story: Rollie Helmling, Terry Winterbotham, Fred Ede, Jr., Jack Hewitt, Cary Agajanian, Dave Heitmeyer and Hugh Connerty.

I am particularly grateful to Bill and Gail Davis. For many reasons, they could have refused to participate. Instead, they could not have been more gracious and willing to share their perspective, further insuring the integrity of the story. Visiting with them was one of the highlights of this experience.

There are several people I had the honor of meeting and interviewing who played very important roles at various points in Jeff's career. Among them: Bill Armour; Ron Miller; Lee Morse; Mike Helton; Howard "Humpy" Wheeler; and Bobby Labonte. Each provided a unique perspective that enhanced the authenticity of the story.

Dave Despain and Terry Lingner each had a hand in helping Jeff's star rise and I am grateful for their contributions to this book.

Motorsports journalist Bill Holder offered not only his time but after his interview, he forwarded his entire Jeff Gordon folder stuffed with clippings, photos, and artifacts. Bill was an invaluable resource and I am extremely grateful to him.

Bob Brannan, who oversaw Jeff Gordon, Inc. for over nine years, provided his perspective on several pivotal moments in Jeff's life and career. Ron Faust and Hal Price, who helped facilitate Pepsi's sponsorship of Jeff's career. Their firsthand accounts, along with Hal's handwritten notes, were invaluable.

I appreciate having had the opportunity of speaking with Greg DeCaires and Rod Sherry, Jeff's longtime friends. Both were able to provide insights into Jeff's life on and off the track when he lived in Vallejo, California.

To Jeff's close-knit friends in Pittsboro, Indiana—Bruce Pfeifer, Chris Cooper, Jim Bear, Greg Waters, Jason Love, and Jeff Broshears. Their interview was one of my more memorable experiences. Jeff's friend Andy Graves picked up Jeff's story after he left Pittsboro. I am grateful to each of them for being so welcoming and candid.

Last, but certainly not least, I am indebted to my intrepid team. Todd Schindler, for his incredible writing and editing talent; Lynnsey Guerrero, for his invaluable editorial contributions and his irreplaceable role as a sounding board for ideas and research; and the team at becker&mayer, for their perseverance and support in making this book a physical reality. And of course, my son James and daughter Jillian for their unwavering love and support throughout.

OPPOSITE: Jeff Gordon, four-time NASCAR Cup Series Champion, walking the track at Watkins Glen, August 8, 2015.

Produced by becker&mayer!, LLC.
11120 NE 33rd Place, Suite 101
Bellevue, WA 98004
www.beckermayer.com

If you have questions or comments about this product, please visit www.beckermayer.com/customerservice.html and click on the Customer Service Request Form.

Written by Joe Garner
Design by Rosanna Brockley
Editorial by Delia Greve
Production coordination by Tom Miller
Production design by Sarah Plein

Printed, manufactured, and assembled in Shenzhen, China, August, 2016.

10 9 8 7 6 5 4 3 2 1
ISBN: 978-1-60380-396-0

Special thanks to all who provided images, in particular Nigel Kinrade Photography, Phil Cavali Photography, Saturday Night Live/Mary Ellen Matthews/ NBC Universal – Digital Media Distribution Group Ann Eaton, Ray Evernham Enterprises, LLC, Mrs. Susan Baker, Rob Quillen, Kevin P. Schlesier and Buz McKim, NASCAR Hall of Fame and the NASCAR Hall of Fame Collection, Gift of R.J. Reynolds Tobacco Company, Steve Barkdoll, Dale Fischlein, Don Smyle Media, and Kellogg Company.